NOTES AND RESOURCES
FOR TEACHING

THE
BEDFORD
READER

NOTES AND RESOURCES FOR TEACHING

THE BEDFORD READER

TWELFTH EDITION

X. J. Kennedy • Dorothy M. Kennedy

Jane E. Aaron • Ellen Kuhl Repetto

Bedford/St. Martin's   Boston • New York

Manufactured in the United States of America.

8   7   6   5   4   3
f   e   d   c   b   a

For information, write: Bedford/St. Martin's, 75 Arlington Street, Boston, MA 02116   (617-399-4000)

ISBN 978-1-4576-4888-5

PREFACE

In finding your way to this preface, you may already have discovered the innovations in the twelfth edition of *The Bedford Reader*. (If not, they are summed up in the text's own preface.) Here we describe the various resources for teachers provided in this manual.

"Teaching with Journals and Collaboration" (p. 1). *The Bedford Reader* includes quite a bit on journal writing and many opportunities for small-group collaboration, and here we support the text with background on these popular techniques — benefits, pitfalls, suggestions.

"Teaching Visual and Multimodal Literacy" (p. 4). We suggest ways to use an exciting feature of *The Bedford Reader*: the introductory material on critical reading of visuals and the many images and multimedia selections appearing throughout the book and in the integrated e-Pages.

"Reading, Writing, and Research" (p. 7). This section gives an overview of the text's crucial chapters on critical reading, the writing process, and academic writing in Part One, as well as the Appendix on documenting sources in APA style.

Chapter introductions. For each rhetorical chapter we preview the method, predicting difficulties that students may have with it and suggesting various uses for the selections that illustrate the method.

Selection introductions. For each selection we highlight what students may like (or dislike) about the piece, suggest topics for discussion and collaboration, and mark connections to other selections.

Answers to questions. For each selection we also give answers to the questions on meaning, writing strategy, and language that follow the selection in the text.

Comments on the "Writers on Writing." For each comment by a selection author on his or her process, we suggest how the author's reported experience may be instructive for students. Note that the index at the end of the text lists each of these comments under the topic it addresses, such as choosing a subject or outlining or revising.

As always, these resources are intended not as a pedagogic *CliffsNotes* but as the notes of colleagues with whom you might care to hold a dialog. The answers to questions, especially, are necessarily brief, and undoubtedly you and your students will find much to disagree with. We hope you will also find views to test and enlarge your own questions to prompt better answers.

CONTENTS

TEACHING WITH JOURNALS AND COLLABORATION

Our users report that they often employ journal writing and small-group collaboration in their writing classes. *The Bedford Reader* and this instructor's manual support these techniques in several ways.

JOURNALS

The Bedford Reader includes a discussion of journal writing in Chapter 2 (see p. 30) and a journal-writing assignment just after every selection in the printed book (for example, pp. 107 and 111).

More and more instructors use the journal as a teaching tool because it offers students a place to experiment with their ideas without the pressure of producing a crafted, polished essay. This opportunity for creative thinking can also lead to more provocative classroom discussions and formal essays.

One advantage of journals from the teacher's perspective is that they encourage students to share the responsibility of preparing for discussion. You can require a journal entry as part of every assignment, as the first step of writing a paper, or as an integrated part of class discussion. You can allow students to keep their entries on loose pages for easy submission or ask them to keep a paper or electronic notebook so they (and you) have all their entries in one place. You can use the structured journal prompts at the end of each selection, or you can allow students to write anything at all, in any direction, as long as they write something. Most instructors find that journal writing, like any other teaching technique, requires trial and error in the classroom. One teacher's pleasure is another's pain, after all; and some classes will sit slack-jawed before the same assignment that fires others into animated participation. Following are some general guidelines for those who do or want to use journals.

However often or seldom you require journal entries, try to present them in the context of other writing and discussion in the course; the danger of using journals in an unstructured way is that they can become busywork. Explain to students that it's in their best interest to use their journals as idea books: safe places to record notes and impressions, grapple with difficult issues, respond to the essays in *The Bedford Reader*, and generate ideas for more formal writing assignments. They'll find that papers, discussions, and tests are easier because of the time they spend responding to what they read. Your promise not to grade the entries will guarantee more experimentation. However, you may need scheduled or surprise checks to ensure that writing is actually being committed to paper, and of course some students will be disappointed if you don't personally respond to their personal entries. One productive system is to schedule one or two submissions — emphasizing that they're just for a check in the gradebook toward a discussion grade — while encouraging unscheduled submissions for your comments on a particular entry whenever a student wants them. A student who is worried about a paper can get your early feedback, or a student who prefers writing to speaking can have a conversation with you.

Many students will be unfamiliar, even uncomfortable, with required writing that is informal and ungraded, so you may want to coax and guide them into writing. For those who are anxious about your expectations, emphasize that a journal provides a free space where there are no right answers and where organization and sentence structure may simply reflect the student's train of thought. For everyone, make use of the open-ended journal assignment after every selection in the printed book: It asks students for personal recollections or gut responses to the selection, in an effort to help them recognize their own connection to it. Farther on, a "From Journal to Essay" writing topic asks students to hone their personal responses into structured essays, sometimes personal, often critical. You can use the journal prompt by itself to get students writing and talking. Even if you don't build journals into your course, you might find some of the prompts useful as in-class freewriting prompts or as remedies for dull discussions. Try assigning a journal entry for a particular selection and then asking volunteers to read theirs aloud and lead a discussion for five minutes or so. Try asking pairs of students to trade journals, read each other's entries on a given topic, and write responses. Try giving the journal assignments as starting points for small-group discussions.

Some students will have strong responses to the essays in *The Bedford Reader* and will not need any prompting to come up with "something to write about." Definitely encourage students to stray from our suggested avenues of response if they have another idea to explore. The main purpose of journals, after all, is to challenge students to articulate their own ideas more fully.

COLLABORATION

Working in small groups creates unique opportunities for students to examine the concepts of a course and the process of writing. Like journals, small groups are a useful testing ground for ideas and a means for exploring the nuances of issues. Often less intimidating than a whole-class discussion, a small group can provide students with a more collaborative forum for voicing their opinions. In fact, many teachers find that a major benefit of small groups is that they require all students to participate actively both as talkers and as listeners.

Small groups can augment learning in a variety of ways. Discussions might center on an opinion presented in a selection on writing style or rhetorical strategy or on solving a problem raised by an author. (This manual's introductions to the selections often suggest possible directions.) The result could be a collaborative written response that you collect or a series of brief presentations in which groups explain their responses to the rest of the class. Or, keeping it more informal, you may choose simply to roam and eavesdrop throughout the group sessions to see that groups stay focused and to discover what kinds of conclusions they are reaching.

Groups can also enhance whole-class discussions. Try having small groups spend the first fifteen minutes of class brainstorming answers to difficult questions as a precursor to a whole-class discussion. Have groups do outside research related to upcoming essays and report their findings to the class as a whole. Toward the end of the semester, you may feel confident enough in your groups to allow them to take turns planning and running class discussions.

Small groups can also be invaluable as writing workshops, to help students learn to become better readers and revisers of their own essays. Once students get to know members of their group well, they will begin to trust the feedback they receive. From brainstorming on an essay topic to providing suggestions on drafts, peer readers are often uniquely able to point out what works in an essay, what is confusing, what needs expanding, and so on.

You may have to teach students how to give this kind of feedback. Toward that end, Chapter 2 sets the stage with ideas about what problems to look for in a draft and suggestions for revising effectively. With the general checklists for revision and editing in hand (see pp. 39 and 41), try modeling a workshop process for the class, beginning with a conversation about what *constructive criticism* means. Ask a volunteer to bring copies of a draft paper to class, or copy a paper from a previous term, or even copy something of your own. Distribute copies to the class. Have the author read the paper aloud, as would occur in the small group. (If the author isn't present, ask a volunteer to read.) Ask the author to explain his or her main concerns about the essay (introduction doesn't seem to fit rest of paper, organization feels choppy, transitions awkward, and so on) — or if there is no author, take this role yourself. Then lead the whole class in a discussion of the essay, starting with what works particularly well and moving to what doesn't work. (Often students will shy away from criticizing a peer, and you may need to get the discussion going.) Give the author (you, if you're role-playing) plenty of opportunities to respond to people's comments. During the discussion, point out what works in workshopping and what doesn't. The most useful feedback will reflect the reader's understanding of the essay ("I got confused when you . . ." or "I wish you would give more details so I could see this place better" or "I don't follow your logic in paragraph 3"). *Discussion* of how to solve such problems will be more fruitful than blunt suggestions like "This passage should be cut" or "You should just rewrite this sentence like this."

Of course, negotiating personality conflicts and overcoming shyness and other qualities that can silence a small group can sometimes be tricky. To minimize these problems, have students compose a "personals" ad on an index card at the beginning of the term, explaining that they're searching for their workshop soul mates. Write a few questions on the board, such as what their strengths and weaknesses are as writers, readers, and talkers or how they respond to constructive criticism. Such self-portraits may not be entirely accurate, but they can help you group students according to complementary abilities and attitudes: You can group some who like to do research with others who like to talk in front of a large group; some who struggle to organize essays with others who feel that organizing is their biggest strength; some who are experienced in collaboration with others who aren't.

Small groups give students a chance to practice the ideas and strategies gleaned from lectures and reading. And such collaborative learning eases some of the burden on you, too: Students will not only gain a great sense of authority over their learning but also share the hot seat at the front of the room.

TEACHING VISUAL
AND MULTIMODAL LITERACY

Throughout *The Bedford Reader* we provide many opportunities to incorporate visuals and multimedia into writing classes: A section in Chapter 1 extends critical thinking from texts to illustrations; every rhetorical chapter opens with an image or related images, along with a caption that prompts students' critical responses; a few of the written selections center on illustrations that we also reprint; and in the integrated e-Pages (*bedfordstmartins .com/thebedfordreader*), at least one multimedia selection — video, audio, visual, or textual — enhances the possibilities for engaging students with each rhetorical method.

THINKING CRITICALLY ABOUT VISUAL IMAGES

In Chapter 1 on reading we offer a detailed approach to thinking critically about visuals (pp. 22–26). Paralleling the method for evaluating written texts, the approach involves five steps: getting the big picture, analyzing, inferring, synthesizing, and evaluating. A photograph provides a rich opportunity to apply the method.

Students generally like looking at images, and they often form immediate, almost visceral responses to what they see. The challenge, then, may be to guide their responses along critical pathways. For instance, they may need coaching to perceive the value of information about artists or advertisers or historical and cultural contexts — and they may need help gathering such information. In analyzing an image, they often benefit from small-group discussions in which they hear several points of view. Similarly, in the inference phase they can listen to the meanings attributed by others with different backgrounds and outlooks. Finally, as they evaluate images, they may need encouragement to step back from their natural emotional responses and judge the worthiness of the image's purpose and its success in fulfilling that purpose.

CHAPTER-OPENING IMAGES

Each rhetorical chapter in Part Two opens with a visual representation of the chapter's method at work, accompanied by background information and questions about the image(s).

- A drawing tells a story of romantic disappointment (narration, Chap. 4)
- A photograph depicts a riverside shanty (description, Chap. 5)

- A cartoon proposes "low-energy drinks" that could counteract today's trendy jolters (example, Chap. 6)
- A well-known painting and a contemporaneous photograph play off each other (comparison and contrast, Chap. 7)
- A photograph makes a telling comment on a doll-making factory (process analysis, Chap. 8)
- A cartoon deconstructs a kid's bologna sandwich (division or analysis, Chap. 9)
- A table categorizes typical household budgets by income status (classification, Chap. 10)
- A cartoon examines the effects of texting while driving (cause and effect, Chap. 11)
- A US Army advertisement probes the meaning of *strong* (definition, Chap. 12)
- An alternative version of the Stars and Stripes makes a strong argument about the United States (argument and persuasion, Chap. 13)

We anticipate that these images will inspire you and your students in several possible ways:

- Because each chapter opener shows a rhetorical method at work, it provides an additional way to introduce the method. The images may especially help students who resist or struggle with reading.
- The caption accompanying each chapter opener provides background on the image so that students have essential information for a critical response. The questions in each caption encourage reflection and discourage a snap judgment such as "I like it" or "I don't like it" or "I don't get it," and they can serve as journal or discussion prompts. Using the caption questions or your own assignments, you can devise various class or small-group projects centered on the chapter openers. For instance, the Grant Wood painting and the Ben Shahn photograph in Chapter 7 open up worlds to investigate — the backgrounds and interests of the artists, the effects of the Great Depression on farmers, the effect of medium on perception (note that the sample textbook passage in Chapter 5 offers an art historian's take on the painting; see p. 153). For another example, the cartoon in Chapter 11 practically begs for a more detailed and substantiated examination of the problem of distracted driving and presents an opportunity to discuss the advantages of simplifying causes and effects.

ILLUSTRATIONS ACCOMPANYING TEXT SELECTIONS

Five of *The Bedford Reader*'s text selections include illustrations. In each case, the juxtaposition deepens the meaning of both the written text and the illustration.

- Joyce Carol Oates's poem "Edward Hopper's *Nighthawks*, 1942" (p. 186) describes and interprets Hopper's famous urban scene, which we show in full view and in a detail. "Joyce Carol Oates on Writing" (p. 191) comments on the making of the poem and further interprets the painting.
- Student Laila Ayad's "The Capricious Camera" (p. 361) models the close analysis of a photograph. Examining an arresting image from World War II, Ayad makes a point about the Nazis' agenda of racial purification and about the ambiguities of photography.

- "Why We Lie" (p. 440) reproduces a sample math puzzle to help explain Dan Ariely's unusual research project and includes an infographic that visually summarizes his cause-and-effect analysis.
- Christopher Beam's "Blood Loss" (p. 449), about changing trends in murder and mayhem, includes a bar graph interpreted by the author.
- In "The Rise and Fall of the Hit" (p. 455), Chris Anderson uses three line graphs to reinforce his point about the effects of niche media on the entertainment industry.

MULTIMEDIA SELECTIONS

The Bedford Reader now has integrated e-Pages — videos, audio selections, comics, graphics, and essays accessible online (*bedfordstmartins .com/thebedfordreader*). Chosen for their value as models of the rhetorical methods in everyday life, each of these selections demonstrates the richness and complexity that be achieved when words are combined with visuals or sounds. Each is also accompanied by a streamlined set of editorial apparatus: full introductions to the creator and the piece, three or four questions on meaning and strategy, and two suggestions for writing, one of them pointing out connections between the e-Pages selection and a traditional essay in the printed book.

In most cases you might wish to share these pieces in class, viewing or listening with your students as a group; or you could assign them just as you would the traditional essays in the book. They are all the work of quality writers or artists and will reward close examination; each of them is not only entertaining but also thought-provoking.

- Native Americans on a South Dakota reservation use an online tool that combines photography, audio, and text to share stories about their lives (narration, Chap. 4).
- "The Santa Ana," a classic by beloved essayist Joan Didion, is read by a popular actress for a recently released audiobook (description, Chap. 5).
- A prizewinning Mexican American writer with a growing fan base reads his own essay about the transformative powers of fiction (example, Chap. 6).
- A video sketch by a popular comedy team examines behaviors of our pets that we might not endure from our friends (comparison and contrast, Chap. 7).
- A viral marketing video criticizes manipulative advertising tactics (process analysis, Chap. 8).
- Caribbean novelist Jamaica Kincaid performs her always enjoyable and always provocative short story "Girl" (division or analysis, Chap. 9).
- The US Census Bureau charts historical immigration trends in a series of interrelated graphics (classification, Chap. 10).
- A reporter and a graphic artist use interactive Web technology to explain the physics of roller coasters (cause-and-effect analysis, Chap. 11).
- A digital cartoon explains a misunderstood personality type and offers suggestions to help people get along with each other (definition, Chap. 12).
- A lengthy (and controversial) magazine article, accompanied by several snippets of readers' online reactions and one self-contained response, presents an opportunity to examine both a complex argument and critical reading in action (argument, Chap. 13).

PART ONE

READING, WRITING, AND RESEARCH

The first three chapters of *The Bedford Reader* provide a substantial and well-illustrated discussion of critical reading, the writing process, and academic writing (including research and documentation in MLA style), and an Appendix offers guidelines for citing sources using APA style. The outline of this material (below) is followed by a description of the contents.

Chapter 1 gives step-by-step instructions on attentive, critical reading, including examples of annotating a text, summarizing, and using analysis, interpretation, synthesis, and evaluation. A sample essay by Nancy Mairs and a student's marginal notes along with our commentary illustrate the steps. Then a section shows students, again by example, how to apply their faculties for critical thinking to visual images. (For more on this topic, see p. 4 of this manual.)

Chapter 2 then details the stages of the writing process, including aids to discovery (journals, freewriting, and the rhetorical methods themselves); a stress on the thesis and thesis statement; suggestions for drafting the introduction, body, and conclusion of an essay; and detailed advice on and examples of revising and editing. This section also includes the stages of a student's response to Mairs's essay, from first journal entry through annotated final draft. This paper also serves the next chapter as an example of response writing.

Chapter 3, "Academic Writing," aims to help students surmount one of their biggest hurdles: learning to write critically about what they have read. The chapter focuses on response writing and research writing, emphasizing synthesis in both cases. The writing and research help includes extensive sections on synthesizing ideas; avoiding plagiarism while integrating summaries, paraphrases, and quotations; evaluating both print and online sources; and documenting sources in MLA style. Concluding the chapter is an annotated research paper by the same student who wrote the response paper in Chapter 2. She writes on a similar subject, modeling the way reading can expand and refine ideas, and reflects on the process in a writers-on-writing commentary.

We provide the Appendix, "APA Documentation," as a resource for students who are writing in the social sciences or who might be asked to use the American Psychological Association's documentation system for any of their papers. Designed as a reference tool, this section includes an overview of APA style, models of parenthetical citations, and guidelines and sample entries for a list of references. The Appendix concludes with excerpts from the research paper in Chapter 3 adapted to APA style, showing how the documentation system works in practice.

You can use Part One and the Appendix in various ways, depending on your students' needs and, of course, your own inclinations. Many instructors teach directly from this material, especially when students are unfamiliar with the processes of critical reading and writing, have little experience with academic writing or with research, or have no other text to rely on. Other instructors ask their students to read the material on their own — it does not assume previous knowledge and so can be self-teaching. Still others select for classwork the parts they wish to stress (summary, say, or the thesis statement) and ask students to cover the remaining sections on their own.

PART TWO

THE METHODS

4
NARRATION
Telling a Story

To write a short account of a personal experience is, for many students, a first assignment that looks reassuring and possible to fulfill. Instructors who wish to begin in this way may assign for reading one or more of this chapter's essays by Angelou, Tan, Smith, and Dillard: These writers give students a sense of what a good writer can do with material perhaps much like their own: recollections and observations of ordinary experience from childhood and high school days. (The student writer, Smith, also draws on information gathered from informal research to weight and broaden his understanding of some unusual pets.) Díaz takes a different approach and shares a story told to him by his mother, expressing with awe what another person experienced in another time.

The e-Pages for narration present intriguing multimodal oral histories, a collection of first-person accounts of life on an Indian reservation along with a "true" ghost story. By juxtaposing Jackson's "The Lottery" with the fictional and nonfictional narratives of the other selections, this chapter gives you a chance to ask, "How does fiction differ from nonfiction?"

Not all freshmen feel comfortable writing in the first person. Some may writhe under a burden of self-consciousness. Some may feel guilty about not following the doctrine of a high-school teacher who once urged them to avoid *I*. A few members of the composition staff at Chapel Hill reported encountering this problem, and because of it, some preferred to begin their courses with *The Bedford Reader*'s chapter on description. Writing in the third person seems to give some students greater assurance about constructing that crucial first paper in which they're trying hard to please.

MAYA ANGELOU
Champion of the World

A story within a story, Maya Angelou's suspenseful narrative invites attention to both its method and its matter. Inside the story of what happens in the general store (told in the first person, as Angelou looks back to her childhood), we follow the story of the Louis-Carnera fight. Suspense builds from the beginning, in the introductory glimpse of the people crowding in eagerly, in the "apprehensive mood" compared to a sky "streaked with lightning" (par. 2), and in the scraps of conversation. Larger events of the history of civil rights form a background to this narrative—for example, the fact that African Americans were not safe at night, although we learn this only at the end of the story.

You might begin by asking students what they know of the career of Joe Louis. (In some classes no one may know of him.) You could break the class into groups of three or four and have them research what it meant in the 1930s for an African American to become a prominent and universally admired athlete. Come up with a few contextual categories: Louis's career overall; other firsthand reminiscences of boxing in the 1930s; African American life in the 1930s. Each group could then present its findings for five to ten minutes, ending with a whole-class discussion of Angelou's memoir. (Note: If this sort of background research is something you'd like to have students do fairly regularly, you might consider rotating the responsibility so that just one group works and reports on any given essay.)

Audio aids: Angelou reads excerpts from *I Know Why the Caged Bird Sings* on a set of CDs with the same title, produced by Random House Audiobooks. The recordings may be ordered or downloaded from *Amazon.com*.

Angelou's essay is paired with Amy Tan's narrative "Fish Cheeks" (p. 110) for discussion and writing. Both writers recall experiences as "outsider" children in a predominantly white culture.

QUESTIONS ON MEANING

1. Like the rest of the autobiography from which this selection is taken, "Champion of the World" seems written for a dual purpose: to recall vivid and significant moments of the author's life and to reveal the ironic situation of African Americans in the United States in the 1930s—able to become world champions but not able to walk a country road at night. This irony is given great weight by being placed at the end of the story.

2–3. As Angelou indicates in much of her story, and especially in paragraphs 16 and 17, the pride of the race depends on the fight. Not only pride but a whole future rides on the outcome: "If Joe lost we were back in slavery. . . ." Everyone in the store believes this, but the author's view is not so simple. Obviously she doesn't share the notion that if Joe Louis lost it would be clear that "God Himself hated us"; she is exaggerating the assumptions of the people in the store to emphasize the ideological importance of the fight.

4. The error makes untrue a small corner of the story (and might distract people who recognize it), but the fact that Angelou mixed up Louis's fights does not discredit what she reports experiencing.

QUESTIONS ON WRITING STRATEGY

1. Every sentence in the first paragraph contributes to our sense of the importance of the coming events. Note that, with space inside the store at such a premium, children (except infants and toddlers who could fit on a lap) are banished to the porch outside.
2. From paragraph 1 we feel anticipation and a tension that mounts to a crisis in paragraph 15, when the contender rains blows on Louis and staggers him. Short, punchy sentences add speed and force to Angelou's account: "We didn't breathe. We didn't hope. We waited" (par. 18—and, incidentally, a good example of parallelism). The whole device of telling the story of the fight through a radio announcer's spiel is particularly effective because, as Angelou makes clear, the listeners in the store hang on the announcer's every word. Using radio as a medium in story-telling can increase suspense by leaving much to the imagination.
   Anyone familiar with the history of boxing will predict the winner as soon as the name of Joe Louis emerges; others may not be sure until Louis rallies in paragraph 20.
3. Students who sense the irony will probably express it in any of several ways. Some will say that despite all the hopes and dreams bound up in the fight, Louis's victory hasn't delivered his people. Maybe Louis is the strongest man in the ring, but African Americans in rural Arkansas are still vulnerable. Angelou's irony in the final line is so strong that it is practically sarcasm. Isn't there a suggestion, too, that on this particular night some whites, resenting the Louis victory, will be out to punish any African Americans they can find alone or in small numbers?
4. Here, as everywhere, direct quotation lends immediacy to any scene an author creates.
5. The descriptive details in paragraph 27—drinking Coke "like ambrosia," eating candy "like Christmas," boys "blowing their breath in front of themselves like proud smokers"—move the story ahead and recreate the special joy and pride of the occasion.

QUESTIONS ON LANGUAGE

1. Singing commercials for razor blades; sales pitches designed to "string" the listener along. It is possible that Angelou finds irony in the sponsor's product, too, since a racist, stereotypical view of poor African Americans might have them fighting with razors or razor blades.
2. Examples of strong verbs include "perched" (par. 1); "grunted" (6); "poured" (10); "pushed" (12); "groaned," "ambushed," "raped," "whipped," "maimed," "slapping" (16); "clutched" (17); "slid" (21); and "shouted" (23).
3. Nonstandard English here makes the people gathered in the store come alive for us. (This story offers a great opportunity to point out the occasional high value of nonstandard English. The comments in pars. 4 and 8 are so well put that they're hard to forget.)
4. The definition of *white lightning* is hard to find in standard dictionaries. *The Dictionary of American Slang* defines it as "cheap, inferior, homemade, or bootleg whisky, usually uncolored corn whisky."

MAYA ANGELOU ON WRITING

Here are some responses to the questions for discussion.

1. What Angelou means by rhythm won't be easily defined, but for her, finding the rhythm of a subject is that early stage all writers go through when first preparing to write. It means (we'd guess) getting a sense of the size and shape of a subject—or perhaps working up some feeling for it.
2. Writing twelve or fourteen pages of longhand notes, setting down all she knows about the subject, may seem to some students an excessive amount of toil. But Angelou invites the observation that the more work you do before you write, the easier it is to write.

AMY TAN

Fish Cheeks

Amy Tan remains one of the best-known Chinese American writers on the current scene. This brief, amusing piece about a shock between two cultures is a good example of how much can be accomplished in very little space. Every detail contributes to the contrast between the two families and their cultures.

We have paired "Fish Cheeks" with Maya Angelou's "Champion of the World." Both essays illuminate the experience of being an outsider in America and the ways family can ameliorate or exacerbate a child's grappling with social identity. Tan, by the way, discussed the influences of such childhood experiences on her work as a writer with Roger Rosenblatt as part of the 2008 Chautauqua Institution morning lecture series; a video of their conversation, "Finding Meaning through Writing," is available on *YouTube*.

Some students may take offense at Tan's use of stereotypes for humor, while others may see her Asian Americanness as exempting her from criticism on those grounds. If this issue is controversial in your class, consider setting up small-group debates on the "political correctness" of the essay. Students who enjoy Tan's story should be encouraged to look further into Tan's works—such as *The Joy Luck Club* (1989), *The Kitchen God's Wife* (1991), *The Hundred Secret Senses* (1995), *The Bonesetter's Daughter* (2001), *The Opposite of Fate* (2003), and *The Valley of Amazement* (2013). Another valuable look at the Chinese American experience is Maxine Hong Kingston's *The Woman Warrior* (1976), a portion of which is reprinted on page 605.

QUESTIONS ON MEANING

1. Tan believes that her family will embarrass her.
2. Tan's mother wants to teach her not to be ashamed of her Chineseness, not to become completely Americanized. "Your only shame is to have shame" (par. 7).

3. Tan is ashamed of her background, referring to her family's "shabby Chinese Christmas" and "noisy Chinese relatives who lacked proper American manners" (par. 2). She resents her mother at the time, but eventually learns to appreciate the lesson she has taught her.
4. Tan's purpose is to amuse and entertain, yes, but possibly also to thank her mother and to impart her lesson to the reader.

QUESTIONS ON WRITING STRATEGY

1. Tan sets us up for a story right away. We know immediately that we're going to hear an anecdote about the minister's cute son—and an ethnic conflict.
2. The narrative progression is straightforward; each paragraph starts with a transition that places us in time: "the winter I turned fourteen" (par. 1); "When I found out" (2); "On Christmas Eve" (3); "And then" (4); "Dinner" (5); "At the end of the meal" (6); "After everyone had gone" (7); "And even though I didn't agree with her then" (8). This gives a sense of constant forward momentum to the story.
3. The irony lies in the narrator's inability to acknowledge or realize that the dishes she has described with such disgust in paragraph 3 are in fact her favorites. The Chinese Tan and the American Tan conflict with each other.
4. The descriptive paragraph is meant to be humorous and entertaining, and it will probably have the desired effect on non-Chinese readers: to make clear the culture shock the narrator thinks the minister's family will experience. (Some readers, though, may relish the description.)

QUESTIONS ON LANGUAGE

1. The comparison is amusing because the minister's son is compared to a chaste female figure even though it's a first crush and the narrator is "in love"; it also underscores both the cultural and nonsexual nature of her love.
2. Tan's language is typical of a young adolescent girl: "my mother had outdone herself" (par. 3); "Robert grunted hello, and I pretended he was not worthy of existence" (4); "Dinner threw me deeper into despair," "I wanted to disappear" (5).
3. Students' opinions may differ, but Tan's use of verbs in paragraph 5 is especially strong.
4. Tofu (a curd of soybean milk) comes from the Chinese *dòu*, "bean," and *fu*, "curdled." Once exotic in the United States, tofu is now a staple of many American diets.

AARON SMITH

Rat Pack

In the introduction to "Rat Pack" for *Patterns,* St. Clair County Community College's anthology of student writing, teacher Jaimy Gordon explains why Aaron Smith won a prize for this essay:

> I like everything about this witty, instructive and poignant essay. First, this writer can write: I mean, he has a lot to offer on stylistic grounds alone, with his savvy choice of word and phrase and the way he puts sentences together. The description of rat after rat is detailed, vivid and amazingly distinct. Second, the writer teaches me far more about rats than I thought I wanted to know, but always as an aside, in the course of the action, never by frontally explaining things to me. Third, he keeps me hanging, but also smiling, with deftly deployed ironic suspense throughout the essay . . . to hook me in. The rats, especially Norbert and the Brain, become fully developed characters I won't soon forget. And finally the writer quietly becomes an interesting character in his own essay too, because of the quality of the observation he bestows on his rats and the feeling he develops for them, to our surprise and his own.

What more can we say? We chose "Rat Pack" for *The Bedford Reader* for the same reasons. We suspect students will enjoy the essay as much as we do; we also hope they'll take inspiration from Smith's model. A student himself, he shows how much entertainment and insight a writer can eke from what might at first seem like a mundane, even trivial, experience.

QUESTIONS ON MEANING

1. He brought the initial four rats home, Smith says, because the experiment involving them was over and he "decided [the] rats deserved a better fate than whatever disposal method [his teacher] had in mind" (par. 1)— presumably euthanasia. A major theme of his essay is that he was not at all prepared for the responsibility of caring for them, and he was repeatedly surprised by the animals: They reproduced unexpectedly, they fought and developed friendships, they escaped their cages many times, they stole his heart, and eventually, of course, they died.

2. Although he clearly means to entertain, Smith also sneaks in a good bit of scientific information about rats and their behavior, gleaned from his experience and from Internet research conducted in response to crises. (The essay is not documented because all of the paraphrased and summarized information is common knowledge in the scientific community.) Readers learn, for instance, about the importance of the "milk band" (pars. 2, 7), about rats' reproductive behaviors and parts (3, 5, 9), and about their diet (6, 8, 10), as Smith explains their distinctive personalities and their general intelligence.

3. The point of "Rat Pack" seems to be that rats are highly intelligent—more so than people (or at least more so than the author claims to be). Smith comes close to stating his thesis in paragraph 10—"I think she

[Norberta] just wanted me to know that she knew I was stupid and she was smart"—but he stresses all of the rats' intelligence and his own bumblings throughout.

4. Smith seems to assume that readers will understand his allusions, although he does offer just enough context in most cases to grasp their general meaning: *Pinky and the Brain* and the *Angry Beavers* (par. 2) are both TV cartoons from the 1990s; Remy is the rat featured in the 2007 animated film *Ratatouille* (8); Hooded Justice (8) is a character from the DC comic *The Watchmen*; *Buffy*, *Wonder Woman*, *Superman*, and *X-Men* are well-known TV programs centered around superheroes. The one out-of-character allusion that might elude some readers is Ophelia (8), a reference to the doomed heroine in *Hamlet*. But even if none of the allusions connect for readers, they can still appreciate Smith's affection for the rats and enjoy his irreverent tone.

QUESTIONS ON WRITING STRATEGY

1. Smith's point of view as narrator is that of a subjective participant-observer. He writes with strong feeling, using a mix of first- and third-person pronouns depending on whether he's describing his own actions and thoughts or those of the rats that he observes and imagines.

2. "Rat Pack" is especially impressive for its use of detail. Smith leaves nothing to readers' imaginations: In every paragraph he describes the rats and their actions so clearly that each takes on a distinctive appearance and personality. At the same time, Smith chooses events carefully. Rather than try to summarize everything that happened over the year or so he had the rats, he picks out those scenes that are most telling. Readers should notice that the births (pars. 4–7) and the escapes (8, 10–11) get the most attention, whereas Smith dispenses with most of the deaths (13) quickly, dwelling only on the horror of Funky's "crippling disease."

3. Smith uses transitions both to switch focus between individual rats and to provide time-markers. Examples of the former include "And then there was Norbert" (par. 2), "I blearily peered in and saw Pinky" (4), and "Sure enough, there was Brain" (11); time-markers include "One morning around 6 a.m." (4), "When I awoke the next morning" (5), "About a week later" (6), "From then on" (8), and "One night" (8).

4. Smith names only ten of the seventeen rats he cared for, and focuses mostly on six: Pinky, Brain, Ginger, Hooded Justice, Ophelia, and most of all, Norbert/Norberta—"the group's unholy terror" (par. 3) yet clearly his favorite. By limiting his examples, Smith can provide enough detail to ensure that readers will develop an understanding that each rat was unique and, perhaps, come to share his affection for them all.

QUESTIONS ON LANGUAGE

1. Students may be interested to know that the word *subtle* can mean elusive, obscure, perceptive, expert, artful, or crafty. Smith uses it more in the last sense, suggesting an insidious element.

2. "Rat Pack" abounds in vivid and creative figures of speech. Metaphors such as "all the subtlety of a heat-seeking missile" and similes such as "like a wicked flash of white lightning" (both in par. 3) lend the author a engaging voice and hint at both the rats' and his own personalities. But the many personifications Smith uses to describe the rats give them hu-

man qualities and make them into fully fleshed-out characters that even rodent-wary readers would find difficult to resist. Just a few examples: "he'd be the old man telling you how much better things used to be back in his day" (2); "he was glaring at you and plotting" (3); "gave me a look that said, in volumes, how inappropriate she thought it was that she had to raise three kids with two adult roommates" (5); "she considered the whole fiasco to be my fault" (7); "self-elected empress of the horde" (10); "made sure to cover for each other's escapes" (11).

3. We'd call Smith's tone irreverent and nostalgic. He presents himself as not very serious and more than a little cheeky, yet his essay is infused with obvious affection for the rats and a wistful sense of loss.

4. Smith uses irony strategically. Beginning with "how difficult could four rodents be?" in paragraph 1, he consistently reveals his own inability to predict results, each time clueing readers in to what will happen next. Two ironic statements in particular move the story along: "As long as there were no more, it wasn't a big deal" (par. 6), and "I was confident they were unable to escape" (9).

AARON SMITH ON WRITING

Smith makes a good point that success of a story is in its telling. Students who insist that they don't have anything to write about might be reminded that many of the best narratives revolve around small moments (like accidental breeding), not major events. Whether they realize it or not, readers—and listeners—can be captivated by voice and style more than by subject matter.

ANNIE DILLARD
The Chase

This portrait of childhood beautifully captures the energy and idealism of youth. It originally appeared as a chapter in *An American Childhood* (1987), which one reviewer described as being "less about a coming-to-age than about a coming-to-consciousness, a consciousness so heightened by what appears to be an overactive autonomic nervous system that one sometimes fears her nerves will burst through her skin."

The narration of the chase itself (pars. 10–15) is an excellent model for students' own narrative writing. Point out the rhetorical devices Dillard uses to vary the narration and to make the chase seem endless (such as asyndeton, repetition, use of the plural in par. 13).

The story is also a good example of how narration can be used in the service of a larger theme, with implications that go beyond the events recounted. Dillard does more than simply tell a story; she makes an interesting observation about the death of enthusiasm.

Students might want to share in small groups their reactions to Dillard's contrast between a child's and an adult's point of view. Some may find Dillard's

description of adulthood overly cynical and her portrait of childhood roman-
ticized. Others may recall a time when they themselves expected more from
life, when their own senses of joy were greater. (Or they may have experienced moments when they suddenly caught themselves thinking or speaking like their parents.) Encourage students to discuss their reactions to this
theme and to come up with other examples of it from literature and movies.

QUESTIONS ON MEANING

1. Dillard wants to show how a harmless chase can take on epic propor-
   tions in the mind of a child. She wants to point out valuable qualities of
   childhood lost in adulthood: energy and wholeheartedness.
2. No. This driver is exceptional, the only one who has ever left his car
   (par. 9).
3. The pursuer is the only adult the narrator has encountered who "knew
   what I thought only children who trained at football knew: that you have
   to fling yourself at what you're doing, you have to point yourself, forget
   yourself, aim, dive" (par. 13). At the end of the chase he comes "down
   to earth" (19), addressing the children in the banal, perfunctory tones
   of an ordinary adult. Dillard is disillusioned because of the gap between
   her ideals and reality.
4. Nothing can live up to the glorious moment that was the chase. The
   pursuer has resumed the role of just another adult, parroting the words
   all adults are required to say at such moments.

QUESTIONS ON WRITING STRATEGY

1. Football serves as a metaphor for life in the story: Everything you do,
   you have to tackle, giving 100% of yourself.
2. From football to baseball, from baseball to snowball throwing: These
   transitions contribute to the essay's coherence. Baseball is a logical
   link between football (another boys' sport) and snowball throwing, in
   which the throwing arm is all-important. The lesson Dillard has learned
   from playing sports is carried over to a more general lesson about life.
3. Far from weakening the narrative, this is the story's epiphany, where
   Dillard explains the larger meaning the chase was to take on.
4. Dillard's narration seamlessly combines the articulateness and sophis-
   tication of an adult interpreter with a child's view of the events taking
   place.
5. Adults are lazy and take shortcuts. ("Any normal adult would have quit,
   having sprung us into flight and made his point," par. 10.) Unlike children playing football, adults are unwilling to fling themselves "wholeheartedly" (1) into things. With their "normal righteous anger" and
   "usual common sense" (20), they are victims of habit and routine. Children are willing to go all out; they know that life is "all or nothing" (1).
   (See also the second writing suggestion.)

QUESTIONS ON LANGUAGE

1. Dillard uses language with religious connotations to describe her pursuer. Besides "exalting" and "righteous," she also uses "glory" (par. 19)
   and "sainted" (21).

2. The children, though playing together, exhibit a "natural solitude" (par. 5). While being chased they are at once "exhilarated" and "dismayed" (14). The man chasing them is referred to as "our pursuer, our captor" and "our hero" (16). Dillard portrays childhood as a time of confusion and contradiction.
3. Dillard is imagining what the pursuer might have done if he had "trapped" her and her companion in crime: "fried" them in boiling oil, "dismembered" them, "staked" them to anthills; but his only option, disappointingly to her, is to "chew [them] out."
4. The sentence indicates how long and complicated the chase was and helps to bring the pursuer back down to earth. It is also anticlimactic after the imaginative digression about the Panama Canal and the lyrical tribute to the pursuer that precede it. It is a typically banal, "adult" question.

ANNIE DILLARD ON WRITING

Any student who has ever become tangled in a long, complicated sentence and gone around in circles, losing track of an idea, will find sense in Dillard's remark that short sentences "can get you out of big trouble." If we teach sentence combining, we sometimes risk creating monsters; some students — often the best ones — may try to make a sentence carry too much weight. But Dillard's advice shouldn't be construed as urging us to write in nothing but short, simple sentences, sounding like a first-grade reader as a result. A good point to suggest: Mix up your sentences; vary them in length. And don't worry at all about your sentences while you write a draft; deal with them when you edit.

JUNOT DÍAZ

The Dreamer

In this brief, personal story, the author captures the desperation of a young girl in a developing country while expressing the influence she had on him as a writer. For students accustomed to taking their own education for granted, the lengths to which Díaz's mother went to secure her schooling is likely to come as a shock.

Some discussion should certainly focus on Díaz's unique voice as a writer (see the questions on language and the critical-writing prompt). He is known for his loose, conversational style and a predilection for sentence fragments; this is the only work of his we have encountered that isn't also riddled with profanity. Although his style is unusual, it has won Díaz legions of admirers, not to mention a MacArthur grant and multiple literary prizes.

Students can be expected to know little or nothing about Dominican history, and so they may tend to gloss over the essay's hints at the brutalities inflicted by Trujillo. You may want to encourage them to do some research on the subject, but at least have them focus on those details in the story that suggest what it was like to live in the Dominican Republic under a harsh dictatorship (see the last question on meaning). Díaz tells readers just enough for them to understand why a girl would court sickness and abuse for a dream of a better life.

QUESTIONS ON MEANING

1. It seems that Díaz admires his mother for her defiance and determination in the face of impossible odds. That she would, as a young child, make herself physically ill and risk violence for an education is impressive. And as he explains in his conclusion, she represents desire and "courage" (par. 11)—a source of inspiration for his work and life. (We see evidence of his own determination and stubbornness in his comments on writing, p. 132.)
2. Díaz states his main idea in his conclusion: "I do believe that who I am as an artist, everything that I've ever written, was possible because a seven-year-old girl up in the hills of Azua knelt before a puddle, found courage in herself and drank" (par. 11).
3. Díaz writes to inspire his readers and to encourage them to take risks. He also wants to explain his sense of who he is as a writer.
4. The line suggests that Trujillo and his government inflicted great harm on the people of the Dominican Republic. Much can be inferred from the writer's casual remarks. We can tell, for instance, that rural Dominicans were desperately poor and generally uneducated (to the point of resisting education for their children). We know that they were "brutalized" (par. 1)—not only by the demands of field labor, but also by the police (2)—and that they feared Trujillo (3). We can guess that political dissenters were jailed and also that prison conditions were extremely bad. We see that some "idealistic educators" did what they could and that even the police were afraid of Trujillo (8). All told, Díaz paints a portrait of a nation suffering extreme oppression and violence at the hands of a cruel dictator.

QUESTIONS ON WRITING STRATEGY

1. By opening his essay with "I think of my mother" (par. 1) and closing it with "I think of her" (11), he frames his narrative in a dreamlike state of admiration. The device of introducing and closing the essay with variations on the same sentence creates a satisfying coherence.
2. Although he is telling someone else's story and relates the bulk of it in the third person, Díaz writes from a very subjective point of view: He imagines his mother's feelings as well as those of his grandmother, and he allows his own feelings to infuse most every line of the story. Given that the point of the story is the effect it had on him (par. 11), the choice seems highly appropriate.
3. He focuses almost exclusively on female characters and stresses the difficulties faced by girls in the Dominican Republic. Although male readers can certainly appreciate the story, Díaz's obvious admiration for women in general and the resilience of a young girl in particular seems intended to appeal to a female readership.
4. A convergence of circumstances opened the possibility of education for the author's mother: Trujillo decreed mandatory education for children her age, a teacher accepted her into the school when she "should have

laughed and sent her poor ass back to the hills" (par. 8), and the police intervened when her mother tried to pull her out of school—but it
was his mother's own action, Díaz stresses, that saved her. Astonish-
ingly, she deliberately ingested dirty water to make herself so sick that
her family would have to leave her behind, and then she walked to the
school and demanded an education. Although the education didn't help
her much and she did not realize her dream of becoming a nurse, she
passed her values on to her son, who did benefit from her daring by becoming a successful writer.

QUESTIONS ON LANGUAGE

1. Our dictionary doesn't define the idiomatic *ironwill*, but students
   should appreciate the implications of Díaz's adjective: It creates an image of his mother as a strong, stubborn woman.
2. *Horizon* can refer to the apparent convergence of earth and sky in the
   distance; it can also mean a person's goals and interests. Díaz uses the
   word in the second sense, but for most readers it will conjure an image
   of open space in the distance. By stressing the word, Díaz effectively
   creates a metaphor equating his mother's dreams with distant realities
   that are, eventually, illusions.
3. Fragments can be found throughout the essay. Díaz knows what he's
   doing: His heavy use of deliberately incomplete sentences—especially
   in paragraph 1—creates a brooding tone and rhythm; it also creates
   emphasis and, in some cases, a sense of indignation.
4. The second quotation is from a direct conversation Díaz had with his
   mother. The first is something he might have been told or have imagined she said, but since he didn't witness the conversation he reports it
   as dialog the way fiction writers often do, without quotation marks.

JUNOT DÍAZ ON WRITING

It seems to us that Díaz inherited a good streak of his mother's determination and willingness to make personal sacrifices—as indeed he suggests
in "The Dreamer" (p. 128). We like his comments both for the reassurance
they offer struggling writers and for their raw honesty. Although few students can imagine discarding hundreds of pages of manuscript, most should
be able to empathize with the frustrations of failed writing and the agony of
starting over. Incidentally, Díaz's comments bear comparison with Michael
Chabon's "XO9" (p. 208). Both portray the writing process as something of a
painful compulsion that nonetheless has healing qualities.

SHIRLEY JACKSON
The Lottery

"The Biography of a Story" by Shirley Jackson appeared in *Come Along with Me* (1968), a posthumous collection of sixteen stories, part of a novel, and three lectures, edited by Jackson's husband, S. E. Hyman. In the lecture Jackson discusses the writing and publishing of, and the public reaction to, "The Lottery." We have used excerpts in "Shirley Jackson on Writing," but you may find the entire lecture worth investigating.

Some students may know of Stanley Milgram's psychological experiments in obedience to authority. (We've directed students to Milgram's book in writing suggestion 3.) For the skeptics in your class, a brief discussion of Milgram's work could make Jackson's fiction more worthy of serious discussion.

Jackson reads "The Lottery" (and "The Demon Lover") on a Folkways recording made in 1963. Carol Jordan Stewart reads "The Lottery" on an Audio Partners cassette made in 1998. You can purchase and download the latter recording from *audible.com*. If you wish to screen a viewing of the story, a twenty-minute film version, produced by the Encyclopaedia Britannica Educational Corporation in 1968, is freely available on *YouTube*.

QUESTIONS ON MEANING

1. "The Lottery" makes sharp statements on human nature and the nature of society. It attempts to warn about the consequences of unthinking conformity to social practices.
2. The reader senses a problem in paragraph 45, when Mrs. Hutchinson objects. Full knowledge comes in paragraph 74 and is confirmed when Tessie is hit in paragraph 77.
3. It is a close-knit, rural community of farmers (pars. 3, 4). The villagers know each other well—all questions and instructions are mere formalities (13, 20, 50). It is a hardworking community—the lottery is rushed so that people can get back to work (10).
4. Villagers hesitate before touching the box (par. 4). They won't replace it, no matter how shabby it is (5). It is ignored throughout the year (6). And Mr. Summers gains in importance by resting his hand on it (7). It seems that the villagers respect their tradition but also fear it and feel ashamed of it.

QUESTIONS ON WRITING STRATEGY

1. By keeping her distance, Jackson heightens the suspense, for relating even one character's thoughts would doubtless reveal the lottery's nature. This point of view also emphasizes the complacency and hypocrisy of the townspeople—we mostly see and hear only their cheerful, bland interaction—and it intensifies the mystery of the lottery itself.
2. The references to rocks are puzzling but not the least alarming because of the conviviality and playfulness—the normalcy—surrounding them.

By the end of the story, the reader has forgotten all about the rocks until he or she is suddenly reminded in paragraph 74.

3. Through the characters' discussion of giving up the lottery, we get a hint that not everyone likes the ritual (some villages have stopped it), and we hear the most vehement defense of the practice from Old Man Warner.

4. The lottery is now merely tradition. It may have originated as a superstition to ensure a good corn harvest (par. 32), but it has long since lost that meaning even for its staunchest supporters.

QUESTIONS ON LANGUAGE

1. We would not know that the lottery is losing ground in some places or the more conservative defense of the ritual (pars. 31–34, 67), how Tessie Hutchinson feels about her fate (45, 49, 51, 59, 79), and how others feel (46, 47, 50, 67, 75). Other examples are possible.

2. The vocabulary in this story should not present much of a stumbling block to students. Even if they don't know all the words, contextual clues are numerous, and the suspense pulls the reader through any barriers.

3. "Snatched" suggests Mrs. Hutchinson's anger that her family has been chosen. She is following the rules but at the same time showing her defiance.

4. All the names seem British except for Delacroix and Zanini: Evidently, we are to think this is a British town or an American New England town. The non-British names indicate perhaps that immigrants have settled in the town, have been accepted (though the pronunciation of the Delacroix name has been altered in par. 2), and have in turn accepted the tradition. "Zanini," of course, gives a clear signal that the alphabet has ended (par. 42).

5. Figurative writing might have contradicted the plainness of the people and would certainly have mitigated the distance that Jackson establishes between herself and the story.

SHIRLEY JACKSON ON WRITING

We heartily recommend the rest of "The Biography of a Story" for the grace and humor of its author and for the numerous quotations from hostile readers.

Students should be interested to learn that the inspiration for such a story struck Jackson on her way home from grocery shopping. As writers frequently observe, inspiration often comes when least expected—in the shower, while driving, in a dream. Students should note, though, that Jackson didn't wait for inspiration to actually *write* the story: She sat right down and began work.

Is Jackson's surprise at readers' reactions naive or even disingenuous? Perhaps. Some students, even many, will think she asked for a harsh response.

NATIONAL GEOGRAPHIC

from The Pine Ridge Community Storytelling Project

In an extraordinarily ambitious undertaking, Aaron Huey, *National Geographic*, and the makers of Cowbird have collaborated with the residents of the Pine Ridge Reservation in South Dakota to create an extensive archive of multimodal oral histories documenting the lives, frustrations, and hopes of one group of Oglala Lakota Sioux. We had a difficult time picking out just a handful of the more than two hundred submissions made to date, and so we tried to select representative stories that hit on what seem to be the most common themes found among the collection—such as pride, politics, tradition, and community—without presenting a grouping that would paint the reservation as either romantic or tragic.

We settled on five narratives by four contributors. In "Unci Maka or Grandmother Earth," Marisa Snider recalls an important life lesson her grandmother taught her while planting flowers. Tom Swift Bird, in "First Racist I Ever Encountered," relates a painful childhood experience with a sense of befuddled humor. Monique M. Apple, in "Becoming a Lakota Woman," describes a traditional ceremony that had been long forbidden by the federal government. Leon Matthews tells a ghost story in "I See Spirits." And the final piece, "Faces I Do Not Worship," another entry by Marisa Snider, neatly encapsulates the community's longstanding issues with the American government.

A risk in offering only five stories is that the limited sample undermines one of the major goals of the storytelling project: to let the residents of Pine Ridge speak for themselves and express the full complexities of their experiences in ways that no reporters or editors could ever hope to accomplish. We would, then, encourage students to visit the project's home page at *ngm .nationalgeographic.com/2012/08/pine-ridge/community-project* and take in as many more stories as time and interest allow. We have no doubt that they will be fascinated and fully engaged by what's there.

QUESTIONS ON MEANING AND STRATEGY

1. The general tone might best be described as ambivalent. Although the storytellers express pride, hope, determination, and humor, there is also an underlying sense of resentment and struggle. Forcefully countering stereotypes of reservation Indians as desperate addicts, these stories portray the Pine Ridge Lakota as complex human beings who are deeply connected: to the earth and spirituality yes, but also to tradition, family, and community. They also reveal that the speakers are politically involved, very intelligent, and devoted to changing their circumstances in whatever ways they can.

2. Issues touched upon include education ("Unci Maka or Grandmother Earth," "First Racist I Ever Encountered"); racism and oppression ("First Racist I Ever Encountered," "Faces I Do Not Worship"); religion ("First Racist I Ever Encountered," "I See Spirits," "Faces I Do Not Wor-

ship"); hardship ("Becoming a Lakota Woman"); outlawed ceremonies ("Becoming a Lakota Woman"); land ownership ("Faces I Do Not Worship"); and broken treaties ("Faces I Do Not Worship"). The underlying theme, it seems to us, is a desire for sovereignty and respect. Students' interpretations may vary.

3. The Lakota have a long tradition of storytelling. Not surprisingly, then, the narratives abound in creative metaphors and analogies especially. There is, of course, the daffodil in Marisa Snider's "Unci Maka or Grandmother Earth," a tale of overcoming weakness; the ghosts of the past in Leon Matthews's "I See Spirits"; the understatement of Tom Swift Bird's "First Racist I Ever Encountered"; and the political and religious similes in Marisa Snider's "Faces I Do Not Worship." Students may well latch onto others as their favorites.

4. The integrated multimedia components bring depth and additional meaning to the texts; in some cases they *are* the texts. The speakers' voices, when offered, help listeners connect with the narrators as real people; we can hear their laughter and their pride. The singing and drumming in some instances juxtapose assumptions about native culture with the spoken words, often creating an intentionally jarring dissonance. And in most cases the photographs illustrate key points of the stories while allowing viewers to visualize both the beauty and the poverty on the reservation. None of the stories would have been as effective and powerful if they were limited to written words.

5
DESCRIPTION
Writing with Your Senses

Because most instructors make much of descriptive writing, this chapter offers an ample choice of illustrations. Students tend to think of descriptive writing as a kind of still-life painting in words: An apple or a banana sits on a table and you write about it. In this chapter we strive to demonstrate that, on the contrary, description can involve the testimony of all the senses. All the writers employ description in fresh and engaging ways. And the poet—Joyce Carol Oates—examines with careful eyes the smallest details of a painting, Edward Hopper's *Nighthawks* (reproduced along with the poem).

For our pairing in this chapter, we have chosen Brad Manning's "Arm Wrestling with My Father" (Manning wrote the essay as a college freshman) and Sarah Vowell's "Shooting Dad." Both authors look at their fathers, but otherwise their views (and their descriptions) are quite different. Note that each essay is followed by a "Connections" writing suggestion involving the other.

BRAD MANNING
Arm Wrestling with My Father

Manning's essay specifically addresses the male experience by exploring how masculine ideals (such as strong, silent, athletic) can affect father-son relations. Most students will have something to say about the general difficulties of parent-child communication, and you may want to extend discussion to how Manning's personal experience represents larger issues. That men communicate nonverbally and women verbally is a commonly held belief. Ask students whether they agree with this gender generalization. Is it easier, more common, or more acceptable for mothers to talk openly with their daughters than for fathers to do so with their sons? What about for mothers and sons, for fathers and daughters? (For a take on the latter relationship, see Sarah Vowell's "Shooting Dad," the essay following this one.) Students may need encouragement to complicate their answers to these questions with specific reasons for their generalizations.

To enhance class discussion, small groups could initially be asked to spend ten to fifteen minutes brainstorming stereotypes about a particular gendered parent-child relationship: one group working with fathers and sons, one with mothers and daughters, and so on (you could even throw stepparents into the mix). When the class reassembles, groups should both respond to each other's ideas and connect their claims to the relationship and standard of communication that Manning describes with his father.

QUESTIONS ON MEANING

1. Manning's father communicates through gestures rather than words.
2. They have learned primarily that they don't have to compete to express affection and that there are many different kinds of communication.
3. Clearly Manning has always felt loved, but he recognizes that these challenges *show* that his father loves him.
4. His purpose is definitely to express love for his father. In a larger context he also wants to suggest the strength of a nonverbal relationship between fathers and sons.

QUESTIONS ON WRITING STRATEGY

1. Manning begins with his bitterness to set us up for the emotional progress of the essay, which moves from frustration and anger to acceptance (all responses to various arm-wrestling competitions).
2. These options suggest that he believes they have both learned something about new avenues of communication. We aren't supposed to predict anything; just knowing options exist shows progress is being made.
3. Manning compares the thrill of hooking his first big fish (par. 10) to the sense of accomplishment he initially felt when he realized that he was going to win his first arm-wrestling match with his father. Although both events are exciting firsts that suggest the approach toward manhood, Manning is a little sorry in both cases to know that he can defeat (kill?) a worthy and longtime foe: "I wanted to win but I did not want to see him lose" (9); "when you finally think you've got him, you want to let him go, cut the line, keep the legend alive" (10). Still, these poetic and self-sacrificing impulses stand in contrast to the end of this wrestling match, which Manning, despite his regrets, won't lose on purpose (11).
4. The narrative progresses through events that demonstrate Manning's boyish powerlessness: his "whole upper body pushing down in hope of winning," his father would "grin with his eyes fixed on me," Manning would "start to cheat and use both hands," his brother once even tried to help, and yet "the man would win." The description emphasizes the contrast between the boy and the man in terms of size ("tiny shoulders" are no match for the man's "calm, unmoving forearm"); effort (the father "not seeming to notice his own arm" while the boy's "greatest efforts" were useless); and power (the father's arm moves "steadily . . . regardless of the opposition").

QUESTIONS ON LANGUAGE

1. *Competition* suggests sportsmanship, organized rivalry with a goal, rather than the discordant clash of wills that *conflict* suggests.

2. This reduces the father to just the arm, giving the reader a greater sense of how large a role the father's arms play in characterizing the man as a whole. The image of him as "the arm" suggests both his competitiveness and his protectiveness (par. 4).
3. Manning still feels competitive with his father but is loath to sacrifice his sense of being protected by a father who is stronger than he is.
4. *Mononucleosis* is a disease involving a high white-blood-cell count, causing fever, weakness, swollen lymph nodes, and a sore throat.

BRAD MANNING ON WRITING

Manning has some good advice for college writers, especially about taking the time to plan and revise and working for one's own voice. Students who struggle to write may dispute Manning's implication that writing can be a better means of self-expression than speaking. You might reinforce Manning's message that writing, unlike speaking, provides a chance to build and shape thought.

SARAH VOWELL

Shooting Dad

To begin discussion of this essay, consider the particular cleverness of Vowell's title: Her father is literally a "shooting dad" (a dad whose pastime is shooting firearms), and, in her conclusion, Vowell says that after his death the family will fulfill his request to bag his ashes and shoot them from his cannon (thus, the family will be literally "shooting Dad").

If you pair this with the previous essay, Brad Manning's "Arm Wrestling with My Father," consider asking students to compare and contrast the father-child relationships these two writers present. One interesting difference is that Manning focuses much more overtly on the love he feels for his father and his father's love for him than Vowell does in describing her relationship with her father. Why might this be less of an issue for Vowell? How would students characterize Vowell's feelings for her father and his feelings for her? Her portrait is for the most part quite affectionate, but she also treats her father with considerable humor, poking fun at his various foibles. Despite their differences, as Vowell has grown older, she and her father seem to have developed an easygoing relationship, with little if any of the unspoken baggage Manning describes between himself and his father. Do students think this a reflection more of gender, age, or basic family dynamics? (Note that Vowell's family seems far less "shy" than the family Manning describes.)

Another focus of discussion might be Vowell's highly polished comic tone, her delightful way of casually tossing in a verbal joke—having "to move revolvers out of my way to make room for a bowl of Rice Krispies" (par. 3), for example, or referring to the floor of her father's shop as "a tetanus shot waiting to happen" (7). You could divide students into groups, have each group analyze Vowell's essay for further examples, and then report on their findings and how the examples contribute to the persona Vowell presents in this essay. What relationship does she establish with her readers?

QUESTIONS ON MEANING

1. Throughout their lives, Vowell and her father have been at odds over political issues and divided in their interests—she the liberal, he the conservative; she antigun, he progun; she artistic, he mechanical. The division is made explicit in paragraphs 1–2, 5, 7–8, and 13.

2. Vowell writes that both her parents grew up in controlling households "where children were considered puppets and/or slaves" (par. 12). In reaction to the rigidity of his own parents, her father wanted his children to have the freedom to make their own choices. We see him, then, as fundamentally open-minded.

3. Vowell had reached a point in adulthood where she wanted to connect more closely with her father and decided that sharing in this major project of his was a good place to start—particularly since it represents "a map of all his obsessions" (par. 19). She isn't bothered by her father's cannon as she is by other guns because "it is a completely ceremonial object" (30), not a weapon that could readily be used to harm others. Also, she enjoys the noise it makes and the way its smoke fills the air.

4. Vowell's father is proud to be the descendant of reactionaries and renegades and enjoys recalling tales of his "nefarious" ancestors (par. 18). His slyly ornery streak helps explain his outspoken individualism.

5. Vowell's purpose seems to be to trace her evolving view of her father, from seeing him as her polar opposite to realizing that they have more in common—in terms of being "smart-alecky loners with goofy projects and weird equipment" (par. 29)—than she ever expected. She creates the impression of a man who is exasperating, obsessive in his beliefs and habits, but somehow endearing, finally, because of his idiosyncratic devotion to "his art" (31).

QUESTIONS ON WRITING STRATEGY

1. The anecdote demonstrates in a nutshell her father's penchant for guns and his tendency to behave as he sees fit. It also shows that, even at eleven, Vowell saw things completely differently and welcomed the restrictions that town life would place on her father's behavior.

2. The paragraph provides a bit of humor with its suggestion that boyfriends feared Vowell just might shoot them if they betrayed her. It also acts as a transition into the following paragraph, where Vowell admits that she has shot a gun only once in her life. While this aside doesn't contribute directly to the portrait of Vowell's father, it does bring in outsiders' views of her father's guns.

3. The final sentence suggests the depth of Vowell's feelings for her father: When he dies, she will and wants to feel pain. The double meaning of "hurt"—the pain of the cannon noise and the pain of loss—ties together the threads of guns and father and sharply etches Vowell's love for her father.

4. Comparison and contrast is found in paragraphs 1–2, 6–7, 13, and 29. The method is important to show how different Vowell believed herself and her father to be until she came to share one of his pleasures and realized that they were surprisingly alike.

QUESTIONS ON LANGUAGE

1. Shooting crows is clearly not "a national pastime, like baseball and apple pie." Vowell points up the irony of her father's statement by stating her own preference.
2. Our favorite concrete and specific words: *labyrinth, bagged, blue ballpoint pen, spiky, cramped,* the list of musical instruments, *penciled, pompous.* The words create two vividly real spaces, down to the writing on paper.
3. Repeating the word *six* asks the reader to focus on the young age of the twins when they were first allowed to shoot a gun. The short final sentence neatly summarizes, by contrast, Vowell's own bad experience with shooting.
4. In personification and similes, Vowell says the gun "kicked little me back to the ground like a bully, like a foe." It's not just big and heavy and dangerous to others but malevolent to her, "an evil presence."
5. *Pharaohlike* (par. 18) will not show up in students' dictionaries, though of course *pharaoh* will ("a king of ancient Egypt; a tyrant"). Vowell alludes to the biblical story of Moses, in which the ruler of Egypt ordered all Hebrew boy babies killed.

SARAH VOWELL ON WRITING

Most students won't share Vowell's experience of writing for radio and print, but they will know some frustrations of getting thoughts into writing and they may, like Vowell, have experienced distinct advantages and disadvantages in speaking and in writing. For instance, in speaking, as Vowell says, you can leave some things unsaid and can be a bit slapdash. But in writing you don't have to face your audience and can take time to work out your ideas.

ELIZABETH GILBERT

The Best Pizza in the World

An excerpt from one of the most widely read memoirs in recent memory, "The Best Pizza in the World" is great fun to read. Most of us have, at one point or another, experienced gastronomic delight of the kind Gilbert describes, but few could express it as forcefully or with as much originality as she does. Students should enjoy both Gilbert's infectious enthusiasm for her subject and her strikingly fresh figures of speech, many of which are irresistible.

You may want to spend some time considering Gilbert's overwhelmingly colloquial language (see question 2 on language). Such casual, everyday usage is normally frowned upon in formal writing, but in Gilbert's case it works quite well, creating a strong writer's voice, infusing a sense of intimacy with her readers, and forging an unmistakably clear emotional image of her joy at being in Naples.

Students interested in Elizabeth Gilbert's thoughts on the writing process can find several video interviews with the author at *bigthink.com/users/elizabethgilbert.*

QUESTIONS ON MEANING

1. The essay does not include an explicit thesis statement, but the dominant impression is of a breathless joy, even ecstasy, in the experience of chaos and sensory overload.

2. Gilbert means to entertain her readers, no doubt, but also, it seems, to persuade them to seek out pleasure for themselves. She appeals to readers directly in paragraph 9, enjoining them to not "even worry about it, just go," to "get there fairly early," and when "[y]ou try to take a bite off your slice and the gummy crust folds, and the hot cheese runs away like topsoil in a landslide . . . just deal with it." The suggestion is that readers should undertake the same journey Gilbert describes.

3. As Gilbert sees it, "[t]raveling-to-a-place energy and living-in-a-place energy are two fundamentally different energies" (par. 2). Travelers seek out new places "just to check [them] out" (1) and focus on novel experiences; temporary residents necessarily get caught up in the mundane aspects of real life, such as paying utility bills. Gilbert places herself in both categories: She's temporarily living in Rome but travels to Naples to reignite a traveler's sense of newness and wonder.

4. *Metaphysics* is the philosophical study of reality and being. The pizza is so good, and so beyond the realm of anything she's ever experienced, that it causes Sofie to question everything she ever knew — about pizza, about eating, about her place in the world, and perhaps even the meaning of life. The same is true for Gilbert.

5. The pizza represents everything that is good and special about Naples and serves as the embodiment of the "pure pleasure" (par. 11) Gilbert sought as a visitor to Italy.

QUESTIONS ON WRITING STRATEGY

1. Gilbert didn't go to Naples for the pizza, but it turned out to be the defining moment of her trip. The jump back to Rome serves as a transition between the two halves of Gilbert's essay: her description of Naples and her description of the pizza.

2. The irony is that, although Gilbert thinks she is abusing her body, she feels better than she has in a very long time. She seems to conclude that sometimes the healthiest thing a person can do is abandon all concerns about health and focus, instead, on pleasure.

3. Readers of a book titled *Eat, Pray, Love* would presumably expect and appreciate ecstatic descriptions of food that holds a special significance for the writer. Gilbert assumes that her readers are interested in traveling to new places and that, if they haven't done so themselves, they've at least read about exotic destinations (notice, for instance, her casual reference to "Tibetan prayer flags" in par. 4). She also assumes that they have some general idea of what Italy is like, yet she is careful to describe the specific experience of Naples with vivid and unforgettable images, such as a "crooked old woman seated at her window, peering suspiciously down at the activity below" (4) and pizza makers whose "sleeves are rolled up over their sweaty forearms, their faces red with

exertion, one eye squinted against the heat of the fire and a cigarette dangling from the lips" (10).

4. The first two paragraphs explain that Gilbert met somebody who was traveling for pleasure, and the encounter made her jealous, sparking a desire for adventure. The introduction establishes Gilbert's reasons for traveling to Naples and puts her experience in a broader context.

QUESTIONS ON LANGUAGE

1. *Similes*: "undershirts and brassieres flapping in the wind like Tibetan prayer flags" (par. 4); "The accent in Naples is like a friendly cuff on the ear," "It's like walking through a city of short-order cooks . . ." (5); "shoving for access like they're trying to get space on a lifeboat," "much the same way one shimmering movie star . . . ," "hot cheese runs away like topsoil in a landslide" (9); "looking for all the world like the boil-ermen in the belly of a great ship . . ." (10). *Metaphors*: "longing to travel while you are already traveling is . . . a kind of greedy madness," "a jones to hit the road" (2); "An anthill inside a rabbit warren . . . ," "A tripped-out, dangerous and cheerful nuthouse" (4); "I almost felt I was being inducted into a secret society" (7); "contact high of glamour" (9). *Hyperbole*: "There is not a street in Naples in which some tough little kid in shorts and mismatched socks is not screaming up from the side-walk . . . ," "Nor is there a building in this town that doesn't have at least one crooked old woman seated at her window . . ." (4); "I feared one of them might get shot" (6). We also particularly enjoy the writer's *personi-fication* of her pizza in paragraph 8, where she imagines that it loves her back. Every one of Gilbert's figures of speech is fresh, imaginative, and highly evocative.

2. Gilbert's diction is profoundly colloquial. Just a few examples include "gave me such a jones to hit the road" (par. 2); "tripped-out" (4); "so insanely psyched," "right up in your face," "flipped me the finger" (5); "don't even worry about it," "wannabe pizza twaddle," "deal with it" (9); "can barely cope" (10). Piled one on top of the next, her colloquialisms build a tone that is breathless and exuberant. She is utterly thrilled by Naples and can't contain her excitement, which she wants to share with her readers. Her choice of language therefore strikes us as not only ap-propriate but also effective.

3. The effect is one of intensity and immediacy. Students may have trouble finding a reason for the inconsistent use of quotation marks, but it seems that the girl's thoughts are directed at Gilbert, whereas the wom-en's (in italics) are more general, meant for everyone, and possibly mut-tered to themselves.

4. Students may have difficulty finding *nan* (sometimes spelled *naan*) in a general dictionary, but recipes abound online. The slightly sweet and aromatic leavened flat bread, similar to pita bread but fluffier and more flavorful, is common in south Asian cuisine.

SVEN BIRKERTS
Ladder

Anybody who suffers from a fear of heights, and of ladders in particular, will nod knowingly as they read Birkerts's amusing account of the physical and emotional panic he experienced as a hired painter. But his description is so precise and vivid that even readers who have no issues with wobbling up high on a narrow contraption can imagine his terrors for themselves.

The symbolism of the ladder as career trajectory and the deeper points of the essay will likely escape students on a first (or even second or third) reading. Encourage them to think carefully about and discuss the writer's meaning, focusing on the third and fourth questions on meaning and the third writing suggestion, labeled "Critical Writing."

QUESTIONS ON MEANING

1. The writer means to entertain, but also to mull over a defining moment in his life. The dominant impression he creates is a mixed sense of deep fear and shame as a young man.
2. He means that by abandoning his determination not to look down he suddenly lost his focus and became aware of the precariousness of his position. In other words, he panicked. (Some readers may recognize the somewhat vulgar slang usage of "breaking the seal," referring to the first trip to a bathroom in a night of drinking, which supposedly causes a person to need to urinate more frequently afterward. There's a slight implication that Birkerts may have wet himself in fear.)
3. As Birkerts explains in paragraph 1, he was young and unemployed. He sought out short-term menial tasks because he was broke but also, he suggests, because he didn't want or hadn't settled on a permanent job. The background details establish an aimlessness that sets up the ladder's function as a symbol (see the next question).
4. As we see it, the ladder symbolizes an adult career path (the proverbial "ladder to success"). Birkerts is afraid of responsibility. He is also afraid of getting old (like his employer) and dying.

QUESTIONS ON WRITING STRATEGY

1. Birkerts makes repeated self-deprecating remarks to establish humor and to make readers sympathize with and even like him. We think he succeeds quite well.
2. The essay is only four paragraphs long, with no formal introduction or conclusion. Birkerts takes a point of view that is simultaneously spatial and moving, and he arranges his description chronologically (with the exception of the end of paragraph 1, where he flashes back to provide the background to the story).
3. The unfocused structure of the last paragraph—and especially of the nearly 200-word sentence within it—conveys the author's feelings of panic, creating for readers the same sense of disembodiment and breathlessness that Birkerts experienced.

4. Birkerts compares the old man's appearance with and without teeth at the beginning of paragraph 1 and the end of paragraph 2. The striking difference creates humor; it also suggests that appearances can be deceiving and implies a not-so-flattering comparison between the employer (a successful man at the end of his career) and the author (an unsuccessful man at the beginning of his adult life).

QUESTIONS ON LANGUAGE

1. Notice the connotations of *lapping* in paragraph 3. Rather than describing the shingles with the more commonly used *overlapping*, Birkerts deftly chooses a word that also hints at competitive racing, wagging tongues, and the waves of the nearby ocean.
2. *Lady-killer* is a colloquial term for a man so attractive that women swoon over him. In using the term in both his introduction and conclusion, however, Birkerts seems to suggest that his employer's attractiveness and competence, especially compared to his own, left him feeling emasculated.
3. Students should have no difficulty finding examples: Birkerts masterfully employs vivid details and fresh figures of speech to render his sensations unmistakably clear. Some of our favorites include "a bump in my stomach" (par. 1); the "mouth . . . crimped like the top of a string bag" (2), "that first nervous heaviness in my legs" (3); "the time stream balked, then stopped and started backing up" (4); "the other hand feeling in its joints the cut of the handle, the weight of the bucket, the weathered shingles mere inches away" (4); and "shuddering my torso inch by inch down along the rungs" (4).

———

JOYCE CAROL OATES
Edward Hopper's *Nighthawks,* 1942

When assigning this poem, also ask students to look carefully at the reproduction and detail of Hopper's painting that accompany it. You might even ask students to complete a variation of the "Journal Writing" suggestion in which they jot down their own responses to the painting before reading the poem.

In class discussion, a central question for students is what they see as Oates's larger theme in the poem. Oates goes well beyond simply describing the scene of the painting and those peopling it—and even beyond imagining its characters' thoughts and feelings (although these are presented quite vividly). Implicitly, she is contemplating the painting as a work of art in which "time is never going to budge" (line 37), in which the word *still* has the connotations both of "not moving" and of "not changing," even being trapped in the moment the artist has created. In Oates's hands the image could be a metaphor for the human condition ("so why isn't he happier?" [60]).

Your library can probably provide you with other works by Hopper either in books about the artist or on slides, and numerous Hopper images can be found online. You may also want to bring to class a color reproduction of *Nighthawks* to share with students.

QUESTIONS ON MEANING

1. The couple are in the midst of an extramarital affair. The man has apparently left his wife (line 7), but he's done that before and gone back (15–19, 28–30, 39–41). He's relieved but, in the end, not happy (60). The woman's thoughts dwell on her mistrust of the man (7–8) as she works herself up not to be hurt by him again (37–41, 45–47).
2. Various interpretations are possible, of course. Perhaps the poem's speaker poses the question about the painting itself; none of the figures in the painting would seem to have this wider perspective. The setting of the picture seems to have the characteristics of a dream—"so much that's wide, still, mute, horizontal" (lines 23–24).
3. Two possible interpretations stand out. The figures in any painting are caught forever in a particular moment, still and silent, so Oates could be urging her readers to contemplate the larger idea of art and its permanency. And Oates also pictures a relationship that is stagnant, going nowhere (although the man is blind to this fact at the moment), which may be interpreted as a fact of the human condition.

QUESTIONS ON WRITING STRATEGY

1. Oates uses concrete language to describe the painting in lines 1–6, 8–10, 22–27, and 54–56. She uses these specific details as a springboard, imagining what they reveal about the characters or how the characters respond to them: for instance, "And she's thinking / the light in this place is too bright, probably / not very flattering, she hates it when her lipstick / wears off and her makeup gets caked" (30–34). Oates's purpose is not so much to render the physical details of the painting as to describe the situation those details could be illuminating, as well as to parallel the situation with the idea of artistic creation.
2. In lines 14–15 the woman thinks of her lover's guilt as "an actual smell, sweaty, rancid, like / dirty socks," and in lines 52–53 she recalls him "burying his hot face in her neck, between her cool / breasts." The man, in contrast, is "not the kind to talk much" (20), and his thoughts lack imagery: "he's thinking / thank God he made the right move at last" (20–21), "he's feeling pretty good, . . . this time he's sure / as hell going to make it work, he owes it to her / and to himself" (27–30), "he's thinking he's the luckiest man in the world" (59).
3. Oates runs sentences and phrases together with few pauses, in a stream of consciousness that builds to the italicized sentence ending line 44.
4. The man's thoughts and, particularly, the woman's thoughts are essentially narrative, and through them the reader can infer the larger narrative of their past relationship. The painting suggests a story to Oates, so she needs narration to relate it.

QUESTIONS ON LANGUAGE

1. *Rancid,* from the Latin *rancēre* ("to have a rank, unpleasant smell"), is a particularly effective word, its sound mimicking its meaning. One almost curls one's lip when saying it.

2. Oates clearly sees these two as a couple of tough characters, not at all refined or even admirable. Who else would be sitting in a cheap restaurant on a deserted street in the middle of the night?

3. "Relief" implies escape from a bad situation, whether from his unhappy home life or from his girlfriend's anger. It suggests looking back at something unpleasant rather than looking forward to something good.

JOYCE CAROL OATES ON WRITING

Both the prolific and the protean Joyce Carol Oates reveal themselves in her essay about her poem about a painting: Oates likes to communicate, and she has much to say in many different ways. This explicit analysis illuminates the painting and also Oates's description of it in her poem. Some students may at first have difficulty penetrating Oates's brief essay, but they should get the point that she wrote the poem for just the reason that most people write anything: to find meaning ("The poem enters the painting as a way of animating what cannot be animated; a way of delving into the painting's mystery").

JOAN DIDION
The Santa Ana

If there were any doubt about the lasting relevance of Joan Didion's *Slouching Towards Bethlehem*, Diane Keaton's 2012 reading for Audible should remove it. In a review of the audiobook for *Salon*, Kyle Minor exclaims that Keaton's performance reminds us that the value of Didion's writing "has only deepened with time." Didion remains, he says, "the most consistently interesting and quotable essayist in the English language." We tend to agree.

Like all of Didion's work, "The Santa Ana" offers an excellent example of descriptive writing. Her colorful yet unsettling images appeal to the senses—sight, sound, taste, and touch. Didion's precision permits the listener to share her sensual impressions of and experiences with the "persistent [and] malevolent" Santa Ana wind. Perhaps the most interesting question to begin discussion with your students is whether Didion admires the destructive force she writes about. Because it may remind students of some phenomenon that drives them crazy where they live, Didion's essay could start a discussion about such phenomena, leading into the first suggestion for writing.

QUESTIONS ON MEANING AND STRATEGY

1. The essay uses the Santa Ana to make a larger point about the craziness of life in Los Angeles. Didion seems to be responding to the problem she identifies: "It is hard for people who have not lived in Los Angeles to realize how radically the Santa Ana figures in the local imagination." The essay also has a self-expressive element: Such a potent force begs

to be written about and affords Didion the opportunity to explore its dramatic effects on herself and her surroundings.

2. The wind leaves the city dry, hot, and still. It makes people a little crazy, "drying the hills and the nerves to the flash point." "The baby frets. The maid sulks." It makes Didion testy and argumentative, causing her to "rekindle a waning argument with the telephone company." Natives used to throw themselves into the sea when the Santa Ana came. Didion's neighbor holes up inside, and the neighbor's husband runs around with a machete. People go to their doctors complaining of "headaches and nausea and allergies, about 'nervousness,' about 'depression.'" School-children become unmanageable. People have even committed murder.

3. A mechanistic view holds that human behavior is entirely controlled by outside forces (in this case, a force of nature). The opposite view would be that humans act of their own accord, that they have free will.

4. Didion's description relies on concrete examples because her subject, the wind itself, is nearly intangible. She is therefore limited to describing its physical and psychological effects: on nature (the Pacific, pea-cocks, the sky), on property (fires and property damage), and on people (see the second question on meaning and strategy). By describing these effects so vividly and thoroughly, she brings to life a phenomenon that people who have not lived in Los Angeles would otherwise have trouble understanding. Her examples are colorful and memorable and paint a vivid portrait for the outsider of what it's like to deal with such a malign phenomenon.

6
EXAMPLE
Pointing to Instances

Some essays in this chapter use only a few examples; others use many. They all show the ways examples can pin down and give meaning to generalizations.

Kellie Young's and Michael Chabon's essays are connected by theme as well as by method: Both treat obsessions—where they come from and how to deal with them. Anna Quindlen explores with a moving case the problem of homelessness. Juliet Lapidos takes a lighter touch, looking at words and phrases that have fallen out of use and pondering the fate of current slang terms. Brent Staples's personal memoir, "Black Men and Public Space," provides instances when the author aroused suspicion simply because of his skin color—anecdotes that generally arouse keen interest and lively discussion. And Luis Alberto Urrea's "Life on the Mississippi," an audio reading in the e-Pages, considers the ways "ritual nightly reading" of an American classic shaped one boy's view of the world.

Some students find difficulty in seeing the difference between giving an example and giving evidence to support a general statement. The latter is a larger concern, in which example is only one strategy. It may help to explain that, usually, an example backs up a general statement ("There have been many fine woman runners: Grete Waitz . . ."), but not everything supporting a general statement is an example. Statistics and other data, factual statements, expert opinions, and quotations also serve as evidence. The distinction may not be worth losing sleep over, but if a class has trouble seeing it, ask them to take a more painstaking look at "The Method" at the beginning of this chapter.

KELLIE YOUNG

The Undercurrent

Young's student essay on coping with dangers both real and imagined forms a pair with the next essay, Michael Chabon's "XO9." Both concern the effects that families have on mental health, as well as the ways we all tend to obsess over small things.

Students should enjoy Young's entertaining reflections on her anxious mother's incessant worries and their effects on her. For a generation raised by "helicopter parents," many will undoubtedly have similar tales to tell of overprotectiveness and nagging reminders. A good way to begin classroom discussion might be to ask students how Young's experience compares with their own. Why do parents worry so much about their children, especially after they leave home? Are they right to be concerned?

For students interested in learning more about emotional intelligence for the second writing suggestion (or simply for their own edification), the tenth anniversary edition of Daniel Goleman's *Emotional Intelligence: Why It Can Matter More than IQ* (2006) is an obvious starting point.

QUESTIONS ON MEANING

1. An *undercurrent* is a marine phenomenon in which a strong stream of water under the surface pulls back from the shore, often catching swimmers off guard and pulling them under and out to sea. (Warning signs on beaches usually advise bathers not to fight the current but to swim with it until it subsides.) According to Merriam-Webster's online dictionary, the word also refers to "a hidden opinion, feeling, or tendency often contrary to the one publicly shown." Young, a surfer, uses the concept as a metaphor for the nagging warnings from her mother that she hears in her head and struggles to overcome. As a swimmer must, she finds that the best approach is to follow the flow.
2. We outline Young's purpose in the essay headnote: Her essay is a response to a college composition assignment that specified she should reflect on events or emotions that shaped her into the person she is.
3. Her grandparents' relationship was not unusual for immigrant families in the mid-twentieth century. Young's widowed grandfather went to China to find a new wife to take care of his four teenage children; the wife brought a daughter from a previous relationship with her. Young doesn't make it terribly clear, but it seems that the couple had three children together after marriage. Because Young's grandmother was occupied with caring for her husband and his older children (the "first family," par. 12), it fell to her daughter to care for their younger children. Young's point is that her mother was laden with adult responsibilities from a young age and through hardships learned early the dangers of living.
4. Young seems to consider the influence somewhat mixed, as she states in paragraph 16: "My mother's voice in my head is something I cannot shake or hide from, but neither is it confining or oppressing. . . . Although at times her/my fears catch me, freezing me momentarily before I leap, she is me, and her voice steers me clear of jumps I realize I cannot make."

QUESTIONS ON WRITING STRATEGY

1. Young's description of surfing in the dark (pars. 1–3) and of the warnings in her head (4) is entertaining, surprising, and thoroughly engaging—a hook practically guaranteed to grab readers' interest in a personal topic that might otherwise seem irrelevant or abstract. At the same time, the story's focus, fears of injury or death while participating in an obviously risky endeavor, sets an ironic tone and establishes Young's overarching

point that while her mother's worries may sometimes seem overblown, the writer has learned that it's best to heed them.

2. The writer assumes an audience of peers: college students familiar with the struggles and ambivalent feelings that accompany growing up and away from a parent as they try to become independent.

3. Young covers a lot of ground in "The Undercurrent"; she maintains unity by ensuring that each paragraph includes a clear topic sentence that makes a generalization related to the thesis. Young is also careful to mark transitions among her paragraphs and to repeat key words such as *mother*, *hear*, *life*, and *danger*.

4. Young provides three anecdotes: the morning of pre-dawn surfing (pars. 1–5), the afternoon locked out in the rain (8), and the departure to Boston at the airport (15). The stories are meant both to amuse readers and to illustrate Young's point that her mother has good reason to worry about her.

QUESTIONS ON LANGUAGE

1. The quotations—both real and imagined—are essential examples of the voice and the warnings that have become engrained in Young's mind. Without them, the essay would contain only vague generalizations and would lose its effectiveness entirely.

2. "The Undercurrent" is loaded with examples of hyperbole, whether from Young's and her mother's overstatements of the dangers facing her—"*Get one shard in your toe and you're going to have to chop it off—the entire thing!*" (par. 4); "what if someone starts a mosh pit and you get crushed? (6); "if I were unfortunate enough to touch the seat with my bare skin, I would contract a disease and die too quickly for doctors to make a saving diagnosis" (10)—or from Young's predilection for exaggerated phrases, such as "risks that could (and would!) prematurely cut short our lives (6), "lightning bolts of doom" (9), "utter depths of poverty" (10), and " 'twenty seat covers and yards of toilet paper' " (10). The abundance of hyperbole is amusing, of course, but it also establishes a wry, self-mocking tone that lets readers know Young doesn't take herself or her worries too seriously.

3. *The American Heritage Dictionary* tells us that *maverick* can mean not only a stubbornly independent person but also an "unbranded range animal, especially a calf that has become separated from its mother." We don't know if Young intended the second meaning, but it seems especially fitting for her subject.

4. The repetition points out the parallels between her mother's behavior and Young's own.

MICHAEL CHABON
XO9

Chabon makes his living by undermining genre expectations while sticking to form. This ostensibly personal essay is no exception. Dwelling through most of it on the obsessive-compulsive disorders that have plagued many members of his family including himself, Chabon switches gear in his conclusion and transforms his musings into sly literary criticism aimed both at his own work and that of "every writer" (par. 5).

The essay also gives an opportunity to talk to students about control: Which parts of their lives do they have direct control over? What lies beyond their control? What can they gain from the latter? Does Chabon gain the upper hand in his concession to the "grip of XO9" (par. 5), or has OCD defeated him?

Kellie Young's "The Undercurrent" complements Chabon's essay. A "Connections" writing suggestion after each essay helps students compare them. In class, you might want to emphasize the differences in the writer's tones. Both write openly and honestly about their own psychological quirks, but while Young emphasizes humor, Chabon starts with mockery and quickly turns to compassion. Why do students think that is?

QUESTIONS ON MEANING

1. We have no idea where or how Chabon's son came up with the odd label (he doesn't tell us), nor can we guess what it might refer to (although we have tried, obsessively), but XO9 is the writer's family's name for obsessive-compulsive disorder.
2. Chabon's thesis, stated in paragraph 5, is that writing fiction is a kind of obsessive-compulsive disorder, comparable to his desperate need to fix anything that's broken. He does it because he feels compelled to.
3. Writing the essay is a kind of cognitive therapy for Chabon. His purpose, it seems, is to "feel better" (par. 2) about his own OCD by talking about it openly.

QUESTIONS ON WRITING STRATEGY

1. Each member of his family suffers from a different kind of obsession, or compulsion, and Chabon groups his examples around those types. For his grandmother, it's germophobia. His son has symmetry issues and a habit of repeating words (Chabon shares that tic). His father is compulsively organized. Chabon needs to fix things; he also needs to "rock" (par. 4).
2. Chabon takes his thesis very seriously and develops it thoroughly. Students should note that he leads to it carefully, laying out several examples of OCD that affect members of his family before turning the lens on himself and the ways the disorder manifests in his behaviors. He then makes a point of showing how his impulses as writer compare to his other impulses. To further verify his claim, he cites examples of

other writers whose "recurring tropes, motifs, and phrases" (par. 5) suggest that they, too, suffer from similar compulsions.

3. Clearly, Chabon assumes an educated audience of sophisticated fiction readers, especially fans of his own novels and stories. Although it would help to have a familiarity with the writers he mentions and their novels, he offers just enough information about each—an example or two of a recurring aspect of their work—to support his claim that many writers tend to return to the same ideas in their fiction.

4. Chabon compares the forms of OCD experienced by his family members and himself to show why his obsessions are real and to acknowledge that they cause him the same kinds of frustration and discomfort (albeit at a less extreme level). As he writes in paragraph 4, "My few collections are incomplete, I have braved hellish [toilets] without benefit or need of Lysol, and I have never experienced any bodily compulsions beyond those of my animal appetites. But I have this thing where I can't stop trying to fix something that's broken. . . ."

QUESTIONS ON LANGUAGE

1. *Daven* comes from the Yiddish *davnen* and refers to the ritualized recital of Jewish liturgy. For Chabon then, the act of rocking back and forth, especially while writing, is a form of prayer.

2. The most obvious metaphor, of course, is writing as obsession; notice also how neatly Chabon ties the lock metaphor of paragraph 5 back to his expressed need to fix things that are broken. As Chabon acknowledges in his conclusion, he is a writer particularly prone to simile. Some examples: "*pushed me like a dollyload of bricks,*" "she had to enter the stall like a fireman shouldering his way into a burning house (par. 1); "foliating like creepers though the kid's thoughts" (2); "as neatly as the pipes of a church organ" (3); "trapped like flies in the casements of my brain," "like a junkie who needs a fix, a madman on the subway, a devout Jew at prayer, a kid who really needs to pee" (4). Students' favorites will vary.

3. Chabon is openly mocking of his grandmother's germophobia in his introduction because he's writing from his perspective as a child. As an adult, he explains, he came to understand that she suffered from a disorder. His descriptions of his son's and his father's compulsions, accordingly, are highly empathetic, not least so because he has experienced them himself.

MICHAEL CHABON ON WRITING

Delivered off the cuff, this comparison of writing and cooking is both clever and illuminating. Students should have fun elaborating on the similarities between the processes: Some, for instance, might comment that reading, like eating, can provide sustenance (or indigestion); others might invoke vocabulary as ingredients, or grammar as recipes. Encourage them to be creative. You might discuss with students how to follow Chabon's example and "write the kinds of" essays they'd want to read.

ANNA QUINDLEN

Homeless

In this direct, personal essay, Quindlen uses detailed examples to explore what it is to be without a home. The third question on meaning provides a likely occasion for class discussion of the importance of a home and what a home is.

If you think your students may need more background on the issue of homelessness, the third writing suggestion gives them a chance to do research into and write about the rights of the homeless—to supplement the evidence of their own experience with facts, expert opinions, and so on. Students could research collaboratively, with small groups focusing on each of the following questions to cover more ground: How widespread is homelessness in your area? What are local attitudes toward homeless people? What provisions are made for the homeless? Is homelessness thought of differently on the national level? Each group could report its findings back to the class. (If this sort of research is something you'd like to have students do fairly regularly, you might consider rotating the responsibility so that just one group works and reports on any given essay.)

If students already have enough background on the issue, you might use Quindlen's essay as a springboard for discussing practical measures to help solve the problem. Working in groups of three or four, students could discuss the practicalities of Quindlen's claim that nothing but a home will solve the problems of the homeless: With this as a premise, what can be done to achieve this goal? Fifteen minutes of collaborative brainstorming on this question should give students enough time to prepare for a whole-class discussion of the issues Quindlen raises.

QUESTIONS ON MEANING

1. Quindlen's thesis (in pars. 8–9) is that abstraction from particular human beings to "issues" may distance us from problems and impede their solution—in this case, solving homelessness with homes.
2. The key is in paragraph 8: Use of the term "the homeless" distances us from the problem suffered by particular people with particular needs.
3. Having a place to live makes you "somebody" (par. 2); it provides "certainty, stability, predictability, privacy" (4), and "pride of ownership" (7). Students' opinions about the importance of a home will vary. This question and the fourth writing suggestion provide good opportunities to discuss just what a home is, anyway: a house or an apartment? a room in a dorm? a heating grate?

QUESTIONS ON WRITING STRATEGY

1. Quindlen might have begun with a statement of her opinion (among other options), but the story of Ann draws the reader in and illustrates Quindlen's point. It also, perhaps even more important, reinforces

Quindlen's argument that we should focus more on particular people
with particular problems.
2. The examples bring Quindlen to earth and magnify the loss suffered by
the homeless.
3. The author assumes that the reader has a home and feels strongly
about it. Some students may not feel as strongly about having a home
as Quindlen does. In paragraph 7 she addresses readers' likely assumption that shelters are better than the streets.
4. The second through fourth sentences enumerate examples and could
be parallel simple sentences, but Quindlen varies their structures and
complexity (notice the distribution of subordinate clauses), building to
the brief, poignant fragment spoken by the mother.
5. She wants readers to agree that nothing short of homes will solve the
problems of homeless people.

QUESTIONS ON LANGUAGE

1. It invests her opinion with passion and urgency.
2. Not only do our hearts reside in and take nourishment from our homes,
but we can show heart by providing homes for those who lack them.
3. *Crux* is a Latin word meaning "cross." In English it is a critical point or
essential feature.

ANNA QUINDLEN ON WRITING

Analyzing the differences between Quindlen's essay and a conventional
news report (the second question for discussion) may engage students. To
us, the myriad differences come down to "My God" (par. 9): Such a fervently
personal exclamation would never appear in straight news, not even in feature writing. Other examples include statements of belief, such as "You are
where you live" (par. 2) and "That [a home] is everything" (4), or personal
details, such as the Irish grandfather (3) and the beloved hot-water heater (4).

JULIET LAPIDOS

That's So Mysto: What Makes Slang Stick?

In this brief essay journalist Juliet Lapidos examines the life cycle of
slang, making the point that most nonstandard English usages lose their
appeal for speakers rather quickly. The essay is wonderful proof that researched writing need not be dry. In Lapidos's hands the academic field of
linguistics becomes a source of entertainment.

For a fun classroom exercise you might try a small-scale replication of
Connie Eble's research, which Lapidos cites in paragraphs 3–5: Ask each
of your students to record examples of slang they hear on campus over the
course of a few days and submit a list—to a message board if you have an online course space or in print if you don't. Write their examples on the board,

and invite students to comment on the terms' potential "stickiness." What terms pop up more than once?

QUESTIONS ON MEANING

1. Lapidos writes to reflect and inform by exploring a question that intrigues her.
2. Lapidos says she became interested in slang after reading *The Electric Kool-Aid Acid Test* and noticing that most of the slang terms from the 1960s "have fallen into disuse" (par. 1). She is most intrigued by the question of why some words and phrases come and go quickly, while others last for decades, but she also considers what defines slang (2), who generates it (3), and how it gains popularity (6–8). Whether students share her fascination will vary.
3. They were too clever and complex to gain widespread acceptance or longevity.
4. The author's purpose is more to ponder than to support a thesis, although she does organize her thoughts around a general principal, stated in paragraph 8: ". . . a slang word's long-term survival is more the exception than the rule."

QUESTIONS ON WRITING STRATEGY

1. The writer seems to imagine an audience of savvy, educated older readers. (Most students will not fit this description, so we gloss the author's allusions to help them along.) Lapidos introduces her subject with glancing references to Tom Wolfe and Robert Heinlen, writers popular in the 1960s, returning to Wolfe and the Merry Pranksters (and bringing up the 1940s jazz musician Charlie Parker) in her conclusion. Her references to popular films from more recent decades hint that she also assumes those readers keep up with the times. Students might point out that Lapidos doesn't seem to include any current slang terms or recent pop-culture productions, reinforcing the idea that she's not writing with teenagers or young adults in mind.
2. Lapidos opens with a set of outdated words—*dig, trippy, groovy, grok, heads, hip, mysto,* and *cool*—tightly associated with the "psychedelic" (par. 1) hippie counterculture of the 1960s.
3. The examples come from Lapidos's reading (both for pleasure and from research) and from interviews with experts. Her sources are, for the most part, academic.
4. Lapidos makes six broad claims: "The very definition of slang is tenuous and clunky" (par. 2); ". . . young people, seeking to make a mark, are especially prone to generating such dignity-reducing terms" (3); "most slang is . . . ephemeral" (3); the "most frequently submitted slang words could often be classified as judgments of acceptance or rejection (5); "For a slang term to really succeed, it also helps to have influential proponents" (6); and "Once a word gets to the level of general understanding, it's still subject to caprice (9). How persuasive readers find her will vary, but students should note that each generalization is supported with just a handful of examples.
5. A tentative definition of *slang* appears in paragraph 2. Citing the work of scholars Bethany Dumas and Jonathan Lighter, Lapidos proposes that slang is a word or phrase that is informal, understood only by members of a particular group, unacceptable for use with some people,

and a synonym for an existing word. She then questions the usefulness of that definition, however, preferring to focus on what she sees as the most defining aspect of slang: that it "is ephemeral" (3). The examples she provides are all intended to support that point.

QUESTIONS ON LANGUAGE

1. *Psychedelic* is commonly used to describe the bright colors and surreal aspects associated with hippie counterculture; its literal meaning is "hallucinogenic" and refers to effects of the experimental drugs, especially LSD and psilocybin, that were popular with the Merry Pranksters and their ilk. Students would probably be surprised to learn that at the time, those drugs were legal and touted by researchers for their psychological benefits.
2. Lapidos avoids using the term (aging) *hippies*, which itself is 1960s slang and would imply judgment—especially of those readers she expects to understand her allusions to Tom Wolfe, Robert Heinlein, and the Merry Pranksters.
3. Lapidos combines formal, academic vocabulary with casual words and phrases. The mixture of objective, almost scholarly language—such as "sounds taboo in ordinary discourse" (par. 2) and "Another positive indicator is brevity" (5)—with lively terms such as "stickiness" (1), "fizzled" (4), and "thrown around" (7) seems meant to show that the author is knowledgeable about her subject but not stiff or impersonal; it helps her to connect with her readers.

BRENT STAPLES

Black Men and Public Space

As Brent Staples demonstrates, the most gripping and convincing examples are often brief anecdotes. In this essay examples of Staples's discovery—of the "alienation that comes of being ever the suspect"—take up most of the room. In addition, Staples gives examples of "tough guys" who died in street violence (par. 7) and precautions he takes to appear less threatening (11–12). His vivid opening paragraph, with its first sentence pretending that he is a killer, deserves special scrutiny.

For collaborative work on this essay, we suggest focusing on just what public space is and what happens to us when we enter it. Students might try to define *public space* by coming up with examples and discovering what the examples have in common. How do they feel different in private and in public space? Once they have their examples and definitions, the groups could reassemble as a class to arrive at a generally accepted definition.

As an alternative, you could encourage students to explore their own feelings about public space. Are there places they feel more or less welcome, safe, at home? The "Journal Writing" prompt after the essay gives students an opportunity to explore such questions. They might also find it helpful to generate a list of generalizations in small groups. What does it mean to be a student, a woman, a man, a member of a particular religious or ethnic group, and so on, in American public spaces? Working in small groups, students will probably feel freer to discuss their experiences; you might even consider dividing the groups along gender lines for those women and men who might be reluctant to speak up otherwise.

QUESTIONS ON MEANING

1. Students will state the author's purpose variously. Staples writes to communicate his experience as a black man of whom others are needlessly frightened. He writes to explain his discovery that, when mistaken for a criminal, it is wiser not to react with rage but to take precautions to appear less threatening. However the writer's purpose is put, this is personal experience and observation; we do not see Staples trying to predict the future or proposing any long-term solutions.
2. If we keep on reading, we find Staples acknowledging that women are often the victims of street violence, some of it perpetrated by young African American males. He believes, though, that reports have been exaggerated. He takes pains to make clear that he isn't dangerous. He considers himself not a tough guy but a "softy" who hates to cut up a raw chicken (par. 2); he has shrunk from street fights (6); his own brother and others have been killed in "episodes of bravado" (7).
3. By using it in this context, Staples gives the word *survivor* fresh connotations. Usually it suggests rugged strength, ability to endure, and so on, but here Staples helps us to understand that, in an area of gang warfare, knifings, and murders, timidity is a form of self-preservation.

QUESTIONS ON WRITING STRATEGY

1. Staples convinces by giving examples: anecdotes from his own experience (pars. 1, 5, 8, 9) and that of another African American male (10).
2. The examples are set forth in detail too rich to seem a mere bare-bones list. The similar nature of all the examples lends the essay coherence, and to give it even more Staples uses transitions skillfully. In nearly every paragraph, the opening sentence is transitional, and transitional phrases indicate time: "One day," "Another time," "a couple of summers ago."
3. Beginning with the scene of a near-empty street at night and a frightened woman fleeing him, Staples dramatizes his thesis and immediately sets forth a typical, recurrent situation.

QUESTIONS ON LANGUAGE

1. As we have seen, Staples's essay uses a narrative hook at the start, and to make the hook grab hard, the writer deliberately misleads us. The word *victim* leads us to take him for a self-confessed criminal. By the end of the paragraph, we doubt our impression, and in his second paragraph, Staples explains that he is harmless; he can hardly take a knife to a chicken. If we look back on the opening paragraph, we see the discrepancy between the word *victim* and reality. In truth, the fleeing woman is mistaken and fearful, a person on whom the innocent narrator has no designs. This discrepancy makes clear the writer's ironic

attitude. As the essay proceeds, he expresses a mingling of anger, humor, and resignation.

2. We admire Staples's use of that fine old formal word *constitutionals*, "walks taken for health." Like the expression "robust constitution," though, it seems a throwback to another era.

3. Students will have fun defining *dicey* ("risky, unpredictable"), recalling that shooting dice is, of course, a game of chance.

BRENT STAPLES ON WRITING

Staples provides a clear and enlightening illustration of how writing generates ideas, instead of simply recording them, as most inexperienced writers seem to believe. His comparison of essay- and news-writing is related: The work begins in the details, in the data, the observations, the feelings—in the facts, as Staples says. The big picture depends on the details.

LUIS ALBERTO URREA
Life on the Mississippi

Luis Alberto Urrea is known for his disarming ability to portray bleak circumstances with an uplifting tone, a skill he applies in full force to this lyrical essay on the strategies he used to cope with living in a rough neighborhood as a child. Literature, he suggests, is a saving force. We strongly encourage you and your students to listen to Urrea's audio performance of the piece; his cheerful, unassuming voice brings the work to life—just as his imagination brought to life the stories he read in his youth.

Sherman Alexie, in "Superman and Me" (p. 582), also writes about the life-saving power of reading; we point out the link between the two selections in the writing suggestion labeled "Connections" following Alexie's essay. Students may be interested to know that Urrea and Alexie are friends.

QUESTIONS ON MEANING AND STRATEGY

1. Everything to do with the Mississippi River is, of course, the product of Urrea's childhood imagination as fueled by reading *The Adventures of Tom Sawyer*. A dirt alley becomes a river, rickety porches transform into docks, and disabled cars turn into boats. (The same happens in Urrea's conclusion, where the front stoop morphs into the wilds of Rudyard Kipling's *The Jungle Book*.) The real world of his urban neighborhood is bleak and rife with crime; the imaginary world is Urrea's salvation.

2. Urrea's purpose goes beyond offering examples of childhood adventures. His essay is a hymn to the transformative power of literature—reading, he implies, let him escape the deprivations and all too real dangers of his neighborhood and very likely saved his life.

3. No doubt Urrea assumes intimate familiarity with Twain's *The Adventures of Tom Sawyer* and Kipling's *The Jungle Book* (1894), both classic works of literature for children. He alludes to Sawyer's famous fence-painting ruse, to Becky Thatcher, and to several of the friends' adventures and scrapes in Twain's novel. Clearly, too, Urrea assumes that readers know that Mowgli is a boy raised by wolves and that Rikki-Tikki-Tavi is a mongoose adopted to protect a family from poisonous snakes. Even if readers aren't familiar with these works, however, Urrea offers enough detail to get across his point that the stories (and presumably many others) colored his imagination and shaped his view of the world around him.

4. Students may not catch at first that Urrea describes a neighborhood plagued by gangs—or, in his mind, the "river urchins and cut-pockets" that swarm the back alleys. He implicitly compares the black and red ants in constant, futile battle with the neighborhood's competing gangs; the analogy supports Urrea's understated claim that "[m]ost of the strife in that little dirt alley world was racial."

7
COMPARISON AND CONTRAST
Setting Things Side by Side

Many students dread the method of comparison and contrast, perhaps because of meeting it on essay examinations. We do our best to reassure them (in "The Method") that it is manageable with a little planning. The chapter offers extra help with outlining; we try to take some of the mystique out of it, and we urge the student not to feel a slave to a mere charting of letters and numerals. For a short paper, the formal outline—of the Roman numeral *I*, capital *A* variety—is surely more trouble than it's worth. But in writing any paper that compares and contrasts, a plan to follow, at least a rough plan, is especially useful.

Suzanne Britt's "Neat People vs. Sloppy People" is easy reading, but it makes sharp comments on human behavior. We've paired it with another humorous piece on human behavior, Dave Barry's "Batting Clean-Up and Striking Out." Both essays contrast neatniks and others, but they explain the differences differently.

Keeping up the humor, David Sedaris amusingly contrasts his dull life in an American suburb with his partner's garishly textured life as the child of a nomadic diplomat, and Fatawesome uses analogy to compare pets and friends. The remaining selections in this chapter are more serious, though not somber. In "We're Not . . . ," student writer Andrea Roman contrasts her Bolivian heritage with her American upbringing. Bruce Catton's "Grant and Lee: A Study in Contrasts" remains a classic example of a method clearly serving a writer's purpose. And Fatema Mernissi's "Size 6: The Western Women's Harem" uses comparison to argue that the Muslim harem has its parallels among supposedly liberated Western women.

For introducing the method of comparison and contrast, here's a lightweight illustration possibly worth reading to your class. At least it suggests that in comparing and contrasting, a writer has to consider a whole series of points. Craig Hosmer, a Republican and, at the time, representative from California's thirty-second district, introduced the following advice into the *Congressional Record* for October 1, 1974. (We found this item in *American Humor: An Interdisciplinary Newsletter*, Fall 1983, and offer it in a slightly abbreviated version, the better to illustrate comparison and contrast.)

How to Tell Republicans from Democrats

Republicans employ exterminators.
Democrats step on bugs.

Democrats name their children after popular sports figures, politicians, and entertainers.
Republican children are named after their parents or grandparents, according to where the money is.

Republicans tend to keep their shades drawn, although there is seldom any reason why they should.
Democrats ought to, but don't.

Republicans study the financial pages of the newspaper.
Democrats put them in the bottom of the bird cage.

Democrats buy most books that have been banned somewhere.
Republicans form censorship committees and read them as a group.

Democrats give their worn-out clothes to those less fortunate.
Republicans wear theirs.

Democrats raise Airedales, kids, and taxes.
Republicans raise dahlias, Dalmatians, and eyebrows.

Democrats eat the fish they catch.
Republicans hang them on the wall.

Republicans sleep in twin beds—some even in separate rooms.
That is why there are more Democrats.

SUZANNE BRITT

Neat People vs. Sloppy People

Whatever Suzanne Britt believes, she believes wholeheartedly. Then she merrily sets out to convince her readers that she's right. A danger in teaching this essay, perhaps, is that students without Britt's skill may be inspired to emulate her slapdash unreasonableness without quite achieving the desired effect. Some students, though, just might surprise you with the delightful writing they can produce with this essay as their inspiration.

Small groups can be useful for helping students through the brainstorming part of writing an essay. Students might appreciate having time to talk about the points of comparison they have come up with in preparing to write an essay for either of our first two writing suggestions. Group members can help each other expand their lists of comparative points and find the details that will bring these points to life.

QUESTIONS ON MEANING

1. Whoever said it failed to perceive Britt's humor.
2. Britt is hardly impartial. It's easy to see that her sympathies lie with sloppy people and that she considers herself one of them. Mostly, she writes to amuse and entertain.

3. "As always" means what it says. Yes, Britt is saying—with tongue only partially in cheek—the distinctions among people are moral.

QUESTIONS ON WRITING STRATEGY

1. Britt's tone is blunt, assured, and, of course, hyperbolic. The tone is established from the start: "Neat people are lazier and meaner than sloppy people." Words and phrases that illustrate the tone abound throughout the essay.
2. Britt finds no similarities at all between the two. Had she mentioned any, her essay would be less exaggerated and would therefore lose some of its force. Writers who aren't exaggerating might give short shrift to similarities, too, if they are obvious or irrelevant.
3. These broad statements are generalizations because they make conclusive assertions on the basis of some evidence—although, of course, Britt is deliberately exaggerating whatever evidence she has. By using so many generalizations, Britt compounds the outrageous nature of her essay. Her humor derives from her being unfair to neat people and finding no fault at all with their opposites.
4. Britt constantly clarifies her subjects by repeating *sloppy people* and *neat people*.
5. The examples do specify the kinds of behavior Britt has in mind, but they are themselves generalizations about the two kinds of people. They illustrate behavior but not particular persons.

QUESTIONS ON LANGUAGE

1. *The American Heritage Dictionary* tells us that *métier* is a word that began as the Latin *ministerium* ("occupation") and then became the Vulgar Latin *misterium* and the Old French *mestier* before assuming its present spelling and meaning ("specialty") in modern French and English.
2. The word is not to be understood literally, but humorously, as are *rectitude, stupendous* (par. 2), *excavation* (5), and *vicious* (9). Students may argue for one or two others that they perceive are not to be taken literally.

SUZANNE BRITT ON WRITING

Here are some responses to the questions for discussion.

1. Britt doesn't offer much specific advice for the student assigned to write about Guatemala. But the method she urges, it seems, is to study the subject long enough to discover some personal connection or interest in it.
2. Britt's first paragraph yields at least two metaphors ("you have to suck out all the marrow of whatever you do" and "My answer is rock bottom and hard") and a simile ("silence falls like prayers across the room"). More colorful still are the similes two paragraphs later, in which the student is advised to gather "your life around you as a mother hen gathers her brood, as a queen settles the folds in her purple robes." There's hyperbole, too, in the next paragraph: "an interminable afternoon in a biology lab."

3. What is the tone of Britt's remarks? Though she regards writing with
    humor and zest, and doesn't take it in grim earnest, clearly she deeply
    cares about it. In the end, she equates it with an act of faith.

DAVE BARRY
Batting Clean-Up and Striking Out

Dave Barry is one of America's best-known and most prolific humorists,
and his essay makes a perfect companion piece to Suzanne Britt's. Both writers rely on exaggeration and generalization to make readers laugh.

Students respond differently to humor based on stereotypes. While some
will see this kind of humor as cathartic, others will be annoyed or even an-
gered by it. The second through fourth writing suggestions all ask students
to respond to Barry's use of stereotypes for their humorous potential. In addition, you might want to give students a chance to express their reactions
in class. Encourage those who were offended by the essay to voice and clarify
their objections; encourage those who enjoyed the essay to defend it.

QUESTIONS ON MEANING

1. Barry's purpose is to entertain and amuse. His humor is characterized
    by broad generalizations (such as the first sentence); tall tales (the
    "hormonal secretion" and the Pompeii example, par. 2); exaggeration
    ("clumps large enough to support agriculture," 2; "bacteria you could
    enter in a rodeo," 3); self-effacement ("an important project on the Etch-
    a-Sketch" and the pajamas anecdote, 4); and a tongue-in-cheek tone
    ("my specific family unit" and "Standard Male Cleaning Implements," 3;
    "a sensitive and caring kind of guy," 4; "human relationships or some-
    thing," 8).
2. Barry is anything but objective. He is clearly writing from a male point
    of view, and he understands male behavior. However, his tone is far too
    facetious for the essay to be taken as a justification of boorish behavior.
    He makes as much fun of himself as of anyone else.
3. Barry seems to take the differences between the sexes as a given. He
    is less interested in reconciliation than in exploiting gender misunder-
    standings for their humorous potential.

QUESTIONS ON WRITING STRATEGY

1. A subject-by-subject organization would have undermined Barry's ex-
    amples, which depend on the interaction of women and men to make
    their point.
2. From the first ironic sentence we know to take everything Barry says
    with a grain of salt.
3. The second half of Barry's thesis sentence is in paragraph 5: "The oppo-
    site side of the dirt coin, of course, is sports. This is an area where men

tend to feel very sensitive and women tend to be extremely callous."
Students (and teachers) may disagree over whether the divided thesis
sentence helps or hurts. A single, early sentence might have tied the
parts together, but it also would have stolen an element of surprise from
the essay.

4. Barry effectively appropriates the force of Poe's story, giving his own anecdote an added dimension. The incongruity of Poe's horror story and
   Barry's domestic scene produces a comic effect.
5. He uses the phrase "the opposite side of the . . . coin."
6. This example is obviously invented. Its purpose is not to persuade but,
   like everything else in the essay, to amuse.

QUESTIONS ON LANGUAGE

1. Students sensitive to its connotation may object to Barry's use of
   prattled to describe the women's talk, even though he clearly intends it
   humorously. The word means "to talk idly or meaninglessly" and comes
   from a Dutch word, *praten*, with the same meaning.
2. The breathless, digressive nature of the sentence adds to the humor of
   the anecdote. It has the oral quality of someone gossiping on the telephone.
3. Again, the orality of the text is increased. We can hear the emphasis in
   Barry's voice, the near hysteria of "*during a World Series Game*" (par. 6),
   the sports-announcer tone of "Annual Fall Classic" (8).
4. By using *males* and *male*, Barry creates an anthropological distance
   between himself and his subject.

DAVE BARRY ON WRITING

Writing is a serious job for this humor writer, and students may be surprised at how difficult it can be for a funny man to wring a laugh from a
reader. We appreciate Barry's observation that writing is, to quote Edison on
genius, "one percent inspiration and ninety-nine percent perspiration." We
also appreciate Barry's insistence that experience helps, a lesson that students may learn themselves as they gain more practice writing.

ANDREA ROMAN

"We're Not . . ."

This engaging and well-written student essay is sure to resonate with
many students who have shared Roman's frustrations with a parent's opposi-
tions to their quest for independence, as well as those who have struggled to
shape their own identities. For students who are children of immigrants, the
essay may be especially affecting because cultural differences often exacerbate the normal parent-child conflicts, as Roman demonstrates.

Two possible approaches to discussing this essay: Focus on how your
students define *American* and the degree to which their families contribute

to that definition, directly or indirectly; or focus on how differences between parents and children nourish or thwart the children. For either approach, students will be drawing on their own experiences, so small groups may encourage freer discussion than a whole-class setting. Hearing their classmates' experiences and ideas will broaden students' own perspectives and prepare them for work on the second, third, and fourth writing suggestions.

QUESTIONS ON MEANING

1. Roman states her thesis in paragraph 1: "One would think that language would create the biggest barriers for immigrants but in my mother's case, the biggest obstacles were the small cultural differences." The last sentence of the paragraph reiterates that idea.
2. Roman's purpose is to explain the differences between her mother's Bolivian cultural assumptions and her own American assumptions. She makes it clear in her conclusion that she considers neither cultural heritage superior to the other: "Through my mother's multiple rules, I had become comfortable enough with my identity and culture that showing pride in another country would not take away from my heritage" (par. 27).
3. To her mother's Bolivian eye, borrowing clothing indicated to others that the Roman family was too poor to provide for their children. It was, in other words, a source of shame. She punished Roman not for the borrowing but for having the audacity to question her mother's rules, for "talking back."
4. Each flag—one Bolivian, one American—represents an important part of the author's identity.

QUESTIONS ON WRITING STRATEGY

1. Although we have included Roman's essay as a model of comparison and contrast, it is also an episodic narrative (see question 5, below), an assignment we have noticed is becoming increasingly popular in college writing courses. The blank spaces separate the three major episodes Roman recounts, breaking the essay into its parts and lending a reflective quality to her story.
2. Roman's basis of comparison, identified in her introduction, is "that certain unacceptable acts in [Bolivian] culture were quite acceptable here in the States" (par. 1). Her points of comparison focus on three of those acts: borrowing clothing (2–3), attending sleepover parties (4–11), and working on Sundays (12–24).
3. Roman is writing for her peers—other students at Boston College, specifically her hall mates who asked why she displayed a large American flag in her dorm room. The essay answers their question, which had become her own. To some extent, then, Roman is also writing for herself.
4. In her concluding paragraph Roman not only explains the significance of her thesis but circles back neatly to each of the major points in her essay without resorting to dull summary: "I now borrow clothes, have sleepovers, and do a ton of work on Sundays, but I have not left behind that little Bolivian girl who received the mouth-washing with dishwasher soap, no matter what flag hangs on my wall."
5. Dialog lends immediacy and vibrancy to each episode and expresses each participant's lack of understanding better than summary or explanation could. In Roman's case it also reveals the linguistic and cultural

differences she asserts in her introduction. The conversations mingle English and Spanish for both mother and daughter.

QUESTIONS ON LANGUAGE

1. In almost every instance Roman restates the Spanish phrase in English, usually within the space of a sentence or two. There are two exceptions. The opening quotation from her mother is translated in paragraph 3 (we provide it in a gloss note as well because students may not recognize the relationship). She doesn't translate *"Te dije qué no,"* but most readers can figure out its meaning by context.
2. "We're not poor, Andrea. Why do you have to borrow clothes?" (par. 3); "We're not American, Andrea. Why do you want a sleepover?" (4); "We're not American, Andrea. We don't do that in Bolivia" (10). The repetition gives the essay coherence, but it also does more: In repeating her mother's continued assertion that she's not American, Roman emphasizes the cultural conflict she felt and is able to conclude with some defiance that she is, indeed, American.
3. Notice the paradox in Roman's statement that the specifics of her mother's objections "invariably changed" (par. 1): *invariable* means unchanging, constant.

ANDREA ROMAN ON WRITING

Although Andrea Roman may not have thought she's "all that interesting," we have to disagree. Her comments offer useful points about the personal benefits to be derived from writing—and from seeking and accepting feedback. Her advice to draft from the heart should prove especially useful to other students struggling with the pressures of writing for an audience. Being "true" to themselves and then letting others help refine their work can help them work through their own difficulties, as Roman illustrates.

BRUCE CATTON

Grant and Lee: A Study in Contrasts

If ever that weary term *classic* applied to an essay, this is it. Where can you find a neater illustration of comparison and contrast? First Catton contrasts the two generals, then he compares them—gracefully moving from broad generalizations to specific evidence. Introducing the essay, you might remind students that they know a good deal about Grant and Lee already (or reveal that they need more knowledge). If your campus is far from Virginia, you may wish to acquaint the class with the connotations of *tidewater Virginia* (old family name, wealth, landowning, patrician). (See the third question on language.) A small group of students could research Virginia, the generals, and the Civil War and present their findings as a counterpoint to Catton's observations. (Note: If this sort of research is something you'd like to have students do fairly regularly, you might consider rotating the responsibility so that just one group works and reports on any given essay.)

QUESTIONS ON MEANING

1. Catton's central purpose is to explain how Grant and Lee stood for opposing social forces. Though he remarks in paragraph 13 that the two generals differed in personality, he doesn't expand on this observation. The qualities he cites (daring, resourcefulness, and so on) seem traits not of personality but of character.

2. Lee, an aristocrat from tidewater Virginia, believed in a leisure class of landowners responsible to their community and obliged to be models of strength and virtue. Grant, son of a frontier tanner, held with self-reliance, competition, and a society in which the most resourceful will rise. Lee's first loyalty was to his native soil; Grant's was to the nation. Lee's commitment was to the agrarian society of the past; Grant's, to an urban industrial future.

3. Both had "utter tenacity and fidelity," "daring and resourcefulness." Most important, both possessed the ability to turn quickly from war to peace. They made possible a reconciliation of North and South, for which all later Americans are indebted to them.

4. Each by nature was a warrior of "utter tenacity and fidelity" (par. 14), who fought for the ideals of his people (10–11).

QUESTIONS ON WRITING STRATEGY

1. *The American Story* is a collection addressed to general readers with a special interest in American history. Catton doesn't assume a profound knowledge of the Civil War on their part, but he does assume that the campaigns of Petersburg, Second Manassas, Chancellorsville, and Vicksburg (in pars. 14–15) will be at least somewhat familiar to his readers.

2. Catton rounds out his essay by so doing; he stresses his point (made in his opening paragraph) that at Appomattox "a great new chapter" in American life began.

3. By arranging the essay to show that Grant and Lee, despite their profound differences of background and outlook, agreed on one essential, Catton saves his most important point for last. This structure makes the point more effectively than if Catton had begun by asserting that Grant and Lee were much alike and had then spent the body of his essay differentiating between them. Important points often stand out more when the reader is left with them.

4. Nearly every paragraph begins with a sentence containing some transition: sometimes no more than a word or phrase, such as "these men," "they," "each man," referring back to both Grant and Lee. Some transitions are explicitly comparative, such as "on the other hand" (par. 11). The most crucial sentence of transition is the one that opens paragraph 13: "Yet it was not all contrast, after all"—announcing the start of Catton's comparison.

5. The tone is sympathetic, admiring, and respectful. By imagining Lee with lance and banner, Catton hints that he finds the general's chivalric ideals a bit preposterous. But he is referring back to the point he makes in paragraph 5: Lee's way of life descended from "the age of knighthood." That he thinks its values outdated doesn't mean he finds them silly, nor that he mocks Lee for being their representative.

6. The classification broadens the significance of the comparison from two generals to the whole population. The analysis provides Catton with his points of comparison, his differences and similarities.

QUESTIONS ON LANGUAGE

1. Like most figures of speech, Catton's add vigor and concreteness to his prose. They include the metaphor of "two conflicting currents" (par. 3); the metaphor of an age "transplanted" (5); the metaphor of the "past that had settled into grooves" (8); the metaphors of the nation's expanding horizons and of the "dollars-and-cents stake" (9); the metaphor of Grant's seeing the Union as the ground under his feet (11); the personification of Grant as "the modern man emerging," the metaphor of the stage, and that of Lee as a knight with banner and lance (12); the metaphor of Grant and Lee as two battered boxers, each able to "remain on his feet and lift his two fists" (14).

2. *Poignant*, from the French verb *poindre* ("to sting"), means "sharply painful to the feelings; piercing or wounding." Clearly it is a stronger and more energetic word here than *touching, sad,* or *teary.* You might care to remind students (if you aren't tired of it) of Twain's remark about the right word being the lightning; the almost right word, the lightning bug.

3. Eastern Virginia's tidewater region, the low-lying coastal plain bisected by Chesapeake Bay, is so named because tidal water flows up its bays, inlets, and rivers. It is the area of the oldest colonial settlements (including Jamestown, Yorktown, and Williamsburg), where large plantations were established.

4. *Aristocratic* refers to a privileged class responsible for the well-being of the people it served as leaders.

5. Context will supply these meanings almost as well as a dictionary. This might be an opportune moment to point out that you don't expect students to interrupt their reading of an essay fourteen times to rummage through a dictionary. They usually can figure out the sense of words they don't know if they pay attention to other words in the neighborhood. Those they can't figure out they can circle and save up for a one-time trip to the dictionary.

DAVID SEDARIS

Remembering My Childhood on the Continent of Africa

This essay is humorist David Sedaris's account of the exotic childhood and adolescent experiences of his partner Hugh—who grew up in various African outposts as the son of a US diplomat—as contrasted with Sedaris's far more mundane youth in suburban North Carolina. Students may initially have some trouble with Sedaris's subtle irony. You could begin discussion by asking class members whether they think Sedaris truly wishes he could have traded places with Hugh, whose youth, while "fascinating" in retrospect (par. 13), was in fact marked by some pretty gruesome and dangerous events. Sedaris admits that he can't acknowledge this fact because it means "I should have been happy with what I had" (21). Instead he retreats into fantasy, safely appropriating the stories he has heard from Hugh as memories of his own.

To pursue this question further, you could divide the class into small groups and have each group analyze the essay for evidence of Sedaris's clear awareness that Hugh's childhood was "not as glamorous as it sounds" (12). In reporting back their findings to the class, each group could consider what Sedaris seems to be suggesting about his own personality.

Sedaris's reading of *Me Talk Pretty One Day*, from which this essay comes, is available on CD and for download. Students may enjoy his distinctive delivery, familiar to anyone who has heard him on National Public Radio.

QUESTIONS ON MEANING

1. Sedaris contrasts his own "unspeakably dull" middle-class American childhood (par. 8) with the much more exotic and eventful childhood of his partner Hugh, who, as the son of a diplomat, grew up in various countries in Africa.
2. The thesis might seem to be that Sedaris's life was dull compared to Hugh's (par. 8) or that Sedaris makes up for his dull life by appropriating Hugh's (21). But hovering over all, just hinted, is the larger idea that Hugh's childhood, while much more exciting than Sedaris's and food for resentment and imagination, had terrible costs that Sedaris would not have wanted to pay.
3. Sedaris's envy is essentially ironic because many of Hugh's childhood experiences seem pretty lonely and harrowing, beginning with the field trip to the slaughterhouse. This is true even when Sedaris writes of something that one might indeed be envious of: For example, Hugh's family had servants, but they included guards with machetes (par. 11), suggesting that the family was always in danger. In paragraph 21 Sedaris notes that while he was longing for more exotic adventures as a child, Hugh ("[s]omeone unknown to me" at the time) was probably longing for something more normal.

QUESTIONS ON WRITING STRATEGY

1. Sedaris's point-by-point organization can be outlined as follows: comparison of field trips (pars. 1–7); of daily life (8); of access to popular culture, specifically movies and the circumstances of viewing them (9–10); of servants and security (11); of dangerous experiences (12–13); of meeting a celebrity (14); of Sedaris's ten-day visit with his senile grandmother and Hugh's two years living with strangers (15–19); and of vacations (20–21).
2. Transitions include "[w]hen I was in elementary school" (par. 7), "[w]hen I was seven years old" and "[w]hen he was seven years old" (8), "[u]nlike me" (10), "but" (11), and "[a]bout the same time" (16).
3. A monkey is a particularly exotic pet that many children might long to own. Hugh's monkey comes to represent for Sedaris everything that he envies about Hugh's childhood.
4. The opening conversation establishes the relationship between Sedaris and Hugh and particularly the fact that Hugh seems unfazed by his odd experiences. This opening also makes clear that Sedaris has had many such conversations with Hugh, on which he bases his knowledge of Hugh's experiences.
5. Sedaris narrates stories from his own life and from Hugh's to point up how different their experiences have been.

QUESTIONS ON LANGUAGE

1. The second and third, fourth and fifth, and sixth and seventh sentences in the paragraph are parallel in structure, which highlights the contrast that concludes each sentence. As Sedaris wittily puts it, "The verbs are the same, but [Hugh] definitely wins the prize when it comes to nouns and objects."
2. The term "petty thief" emphasizes the self-deprecating portrait that Sedaris has presented throughout. His use of Hugh's memories represents no "spiritual symbiosis" but is merely a way for Sedaris to live vicariously through the other man's experiences.
3. Almost any paragraph will provide examples of specific, concrete language. In paragraph 6 examples include "low-ceilinged concrete building," "small white piglet," "its dainty hooves clicking against the concrete floor," "class gathered in a circle," "turned from face to face," "drew a pistol from his back pocket, held it against the animal's temple, and shot the piglet, execution-style," "Blood-spattered, frightened children wept."
4. *Symbiosis*, from the Greek word for "living together," implies the intimate union of two dissimilar types.

DAVID SEDARIS ON WRITING

You might take a poll of the students in your class: How many have ever used a typewriter? Sedaris's animus against the computer and love of the typewriter probably grows quainter by the day, but we like what he says about the feel of writing, the sense "that you're actually building something."

FATEMA MERNISSI

Size 6: The Western Women's Harem

Mernissi, a Moroccan intellectual, comes to a rather startling conclusion in this essay. Discovering that she is overweight by American standards, she suggests that the invisibility imposed on women in Muslim cultures—being housebound in harems and completely veiled in public—has its counterpart in Western norms of female attractiveness: Western women who don't conform to an ideal of youthful beauty are ignored and devalued. Encourage students to discuss the extent to which the "norm is everywhere," as the saleswoman encountered by Mernissi says in paragraph 9. How often do TV shows, movies, or fashion or cosmetics ads feature obviously mature or heavyset women?

If your classes are ethnically diverse, you could have students discuss how standards of attractiveness differ among cultures, not only internationally but within the United States as well.

QUESTIONS ON MEANING

1. Mernissi compares attitudes toward women in Western and Muslim cultures. She first states her thesis in paragraph 1 ("That distressing experience made me realize how the image of beauty in the West can hurt and humiliate a woman as much as the veil does when enforced by the state police in extremist nations such as Iran, Afghanistan, or Saudi Arabia"). She repeats it in paragraph 13 ("I realized for the first time that maybe 'size 6' is a more violent restriction imposed on women than is the Muslim veil"), elaborates on it in paragraph 14 ("Unlike the Muslim man, who uses space to establish male domination by excluding women from the public arena, the Western man manipulates time and light. He declares that in order to be beautiful, a woman must look fourteen years old"), repeats it in paragraph 15 ("This Western time-defined veil is even crazier than the space-defined one enforced by the ayatollahs"), and again elaborates on it in paragraph 17 ("Framing youth as beauty and condemning maturity is the weapon used against women in the West just as limiting access to public space is the weapon used in the East"). For Mernissi the objective is the same in both situations: "to make women feel unwelcome, inadequate, and ugly" (par. 17).
2. The saleswoman is initially superior and condescending. She later takes an interest in Mernissi's life and finally seems almost envious of a culture where size 6 is not the norm. Her change in attitude suggests the tyranny of size 6 for Western women.
3. Western attitudes are "more dangerous and cunning" because aging is inevitable ("that normal unfolding of the years," par. 15) and the Western stricture is "masked as an aesthetic choice" rather than "attacked directly" (16).

QUESTIONS ON WRITING STRATEGY

1. In paragraphs 6–7 Mernissi depicts herself as self-confident, impervious to attitudes about the way she looks within her own culture. It is only within Western culture that she feels humiliated by her physical attributes.
2. In paragraph 16 Mernissi first compares the Chinese custom of foot binding with the expectation that she shrink her hips (the transition here is "Similarly"). She then compares the month of fasting for the Muslim holy time of Ramadan with the perpetual dieting of the Western woman ("but").
3. The narrative (pars. 1–5, 8–13) draws readers into Mernissi's complex comparison and confronts them, as she was confronted, with the physical ideal imposed on Western women. She may have considered, too, that many of her readers might have had similarly humiliating experiences shopping for clothes.

QUESTIONS ON LANGUAGE

1. *Deviant* suggests not just a differing from the norm but also shamefulness, even immorality.
2. The veil is figurative in Western cultures, "wrapping [mature women] in shrouds of ugliness." In Muslim cultures, of course, it is literal, masking women in public.

3. Students may be unfamiliar with the sense of *generous* to mean "amply proportioned." Note that in context the word also has positive connotations.

FATAWESOME
Cat-Friend vs. Dog-Friend

With more than 13 million views on *YouTube* as well as national media attention for the piece, there's a good chance that many of your students have seen "Cat-Friend vs. Dog-Friend" before. But they probably haven't thought of this highly entertaining video as the excellent model of comparison and contrast it is. Clearly ordered point by point, the video is especially effective in that it makes two distinct comparisons—of dogs and cats, and of pets and friends. You might wish to spend some time in class having students tease out the implied meaning of Fatawesome's central analogy, a mental exercise we encourage with the third question on meaning and strategy. You could also extend that analogy by asking your students what other sorts of animal characteristics can be ascribed to humans. What characteristics would they like to see more—or less—of in their friends, their family, and others?

Students who enjoy "Cat-Friend vs. Dog-Friend" might be pointed to *fatawesome.com* for additional works. The comedy team regularly posts new videos, comics, and sketches and also gives on-campus performances by appointment.

QUESTIONS ON MEANING AND STRATEGY

1. "Cat-Friend vs. Dog-Friend" is clearly meant to entertain, but notice *how* it entertains. The actors portray human characters with animal qualities, implying a secondary focus on how human friends interact. Students might express the thesis as some variation of "dogs make better pets than cats do" or "friends who act like dogs are better than friends who act like cats," but Fatawesome offers a more nuanced thesis in the *YouTube* tagline for the video: "If your friends acted like your pets, you might not keep them around" (see the first suggestion for writing). Students might paraphrase the thesis as "people who are overly needy or overly independent do not make desirable friends" or, from another perspective, "we wouldn't accept our pets' quirks and behaviors if they were human."

2. The cat-and-dog comparison is structured point by point, and the points of comparison focus on behavior. For example, dog-friend greets his human friend enthusiastically, while cat-friend runs away; dog-friend cuddles on the couch, but cat-friend nonchalantly walks all over; dog-friend regrets spilling the milk, but cat-friend spills it deliberately; and so on. Dog-friend comes off as the better companion, although certainly not without flaws. (The portrayals of sniffing a person's rear, sulking over spilled milk, and volunteering to eat vomit are clearly negatives, although such behaviors are encouraged with "That's a good boy!" at the end.) At

the same time, cat enthusiasts might argue that cat-friend's indifferent independence is preferable to dog-friend's overeager enthusiasm.

3. Viewers who have any familiarity with cats or dogs will not need the captions to grasp which actor plays which role, but the graphic cues help clarify the comparison from the start. The analogy, too, is simple enough: In comparing two unlike things (pets and people), the video makes concrete the abstract notion that behaviors acceptable or even endearing in animal companions would be irritating (or worse) coming from human friends.

4. Students' choices will, of course, vary, but each example illustrates an easily understood (if unstated) generalization. The coming-home scene, for instance, illustrates the idea that dogs are loyal and enthusiastic while cats are independent and rebellious; the spilled-milk scene could be said to exemplify the point that dogs are more attuned to disapproval than cats are; and the vomit scene suggests that both animals eat things they shouldn't. Such generalizations are somewhat stereotypical, of course, but that's where the humor lies.

8
PROCESS ANALYSIS
Explaining Step by Step

This chapter provides a good sampling of process analyses, ranging from the directions in Linnea Saukko's "How to Poison the Earth" and June Melby's "How to Make a Sno-Cone" (albeit directions that are not to be followed) to the informative analyses in Dan Koeppel's "Taking a Fall," Jessica Mitford's "Behind the Formaldehyde Curtain," and Dove's "Evolution." Mixing both types is Firoozeh Dumas's personal reflection in "Sweet, Sour, and Resentful," which opens the chapter and is paired with Melby. Both essays treat processes of food preparation—for houseguests in Dumas's case, customers in Melby's.

Incidentally, the opening of this chapter explains the *analysis* part of process analysis. We continue to introduce process analysis *before* analysis (Chap. 9) because we expect that many students find the former easier to understand. Process analysis thus becomes a way into analysis. But if you'd rather cover analysis itself first, nothing in the text discussion or essays will impede you.

FIROOZEH DUMAS

Sweet, Sour, and Resentful

Popular humorist Firoozeh Dumas has made it her mission to humanize Iranian people in the American consciousness, a mission that seems especially important in the context of political unrest and wars in the Middle East, nuclear proliferation, and terrorism.

Younger readers may not be familiar with the Iranian revolution to which Dumas refers or with the ensuing exodus of Iranian families to America and Americans' distrust of them in the 1970s and 1980s. We encourage students to research this background in the second writing suggestion, but you may also want to flesh out the basic outline provided in the gloss note on page 293: In the late 1970s fundamentalist Muslims fostered political and religious unrest in the country, culminating in a coup and the exile of American-backed Shah Reza Pahlavi. In his place revolutionaries installed Ayatollah Ruhollah Khomeini, who was determined to jettison Western influence and restructure Iranian culture and politics around strict interpretation of Islamic religious rule. In 1979, Khomeini supporters captured fifty-three Americans at the US embassy in Tehran, precipitating a hostage crisis that lasted 444 days and ended in a botched rescue attempt and embarrassment for the Carter administration; the hostages were released upon Ronald Reagan's inauguration in 1981. (During the same period Iran was attacked by Iraq, leading to a brutal war that lasted until 1988.) Backlash against Iranians in the United States—the vast majority of whom had fled the violence and repression in their country—was severe and included general hostility, physical attacks, and demands for universal deportation.

We have paired "Sweet, Sour, and Resentful" with June Melby's "How to Make a Sno-Cone" because both writers examine the frustrations that seem often to accompany the task of feeding others. But if you assign Amy Tan's "Fish Cheeks" (p. 110), another short piece about a family tradition surrounding food, you might prefer to have students compare and contrast Dumas's essay with Tan's. Both writers, whose families immigrated to the United States in the wake of political unrest, explore the difficulty of keeping a tradition alive in their new country. Whereas Tan's difficulty stems from a desire to fit in with her American peers, Dumas's mother's difficulty is purely logistic. Nevertheless, the two essays make a similar point about the importance of maintaining family tradition and cultural ties. And although both writers focus on the difficulty of adjusting to American life, Dumas states her thesis explicitly while Tan leaves it up to readers to work out the significance of her story.

QUESTIONS ON MEANING

1. The dinners provided an opportunity to orient recent Iranian immigrants to life in California; they also allowed the hosts to share "the hospitality that Iranians so cherish" (par. 3) as well as stay connected to their roots. For both the hosts and the guests, the elaborate and traditional Persian meals helped to maintain a sense of community; they also served as a bittersweet "reminder of the life [they] had left behind" (10).

2. "As I watched my mother experience the same draining routine week after week, I decided that tradition is good only if it brings joy to all involved. . . . Sometimes, even our most cherished beliefs must evolve" (par. 12).

3. Dumas wants to share a belief that she developed as a witness to her mother's exhaustion and resentment—the importance of adapting tradition and beliefs when circumstances demand it. To some extent, she is also relating the impetus behind her own assimilation into American culture.

4. Dumas suggests potluck, or requiring guests to contribute to the meals by bringing food with them. Based on the way Dumas characterizes her (traditional, diplomatic, judgmental of inadequate or lazy cooks, perfectionist, and controlling), we doubt her mother would have relinquished the role of hostess, no matter how much it strained her. However, Dumas does relate the process in the past tense, so it's possible that her mother did, indeed, scale back her efforts—or that the number of guests dwindled after the first wave of Iranian immigration in the late 1970s and early 1980s.

QUESTIONS ON WRITING STRATEGY

1. The introductory paragraphs establish the context behind the elabo-rate weekly meals: The guests who came to the author's parents' condo every weekend were reluctant immigrants, possibly even refugees, dis-placed from their "real home" (par. 1) by war. At the same time, the introduction indicates the parallels between Iranian culture and Ameri-can culture to help make Iranians seem less "foreign" to readers—one of Dumas's overriding goals as a writer.

2. "Sweet, Sour, and Resentful" was, as the introduction to the essay indi-cates, first published in the now-defunct *Gourmet*, an upscale magazine for "foodies" (par. 5) that often featured complicated recipes and travel essays. Dumas could reasonably assume, then, that her readers held a strong interest in food and culture. Most readers of the magazine would have had some experience preparing elaborate dishes, hunting down elusive ingredients, and hosting large gatherings, so it's likely they could empathize with the difficulties and stresses the author's mother endured—if not, perhaps, her resentment.

3. Although Dumas identifies the "first step" as "preparing the herbs" (par. 6), the process actually began with her father taking phone calls and extending invitations to near strangers. Next came menu planning (on Mondays) and softening the neighbors with gifts of food (par. 4), fol-lowed by Tuesday shopping trips that usually ended in frustration. With all ingredients corralled, by midweek the author's parents began the simultaneous tasks of chopping by hand and frying herbs and onions (6); mixing, cooking, and rolling the contents of stuffed grape leaves (7); and preparing homemade yogurt and other side dishes (8). The guests would arrive on the weekends, at which time Dumas's mother cooked and drained the rice. The meals would then be served "buffet-style" (10) and consumed in a matter of minutes (11). The final step was "fielding thank-you phone calls from . . . guests" (12) and extending more invita-tions. With several overlapping stages occurring over the course of a week, Dumas ensures coherence by providing clear time-markers and transitions throughout her analysis, then circling back to the first stage in her conclusion, implying that the process never ended.

4. By comparing bucolic local market days in Abadan with frustrating car-dependent shopping trips in California, Dumas harkens back to her in-troduction and underscores her point that adjusting to life in the United States was challenging and unpleasant for Iranian immigrants. At the same time, she emphasizes how much additional trouble her mother went to in order to give her guests a taste of home.

QUESTIONS ON LANGUAGE

1. Characteristically, Dumas's ironic tone in this essay borders on sar-casm but is nonetheless good-natured and appreciative. She tempers the implied criticism of her parents' and guests' behavior with sev-eral self-deprecating remarks, which is where most of her humor lies. You might ask students how the writer's attitude toward her parents would have come across without the mocking comments about her own abilities.

2. Dumas provides the Persian names for most of the dishes her mother prepared and served to guests every week. In doing so, she emphasizes

the sense of home those meals provided for both her family and their guests. She ensures that American readers will understand the meaning by renaming each dish in an appositive phrase, such as "*fesenjan*, pomegranate stew with ground walnuts" (par. 4) or "*qormeh sabzi*, herb stew" (6).

3. In its literal sense a "litmus test" is a chemical process that measures the pH level of a substance to determine where it falls within a range from base to acid; colloquially, the phrase refers to a basis for making a judgment. Dumas uses the term in its colloquial meaning, but we like the echo of "sweet" (base) and "sour" (acidic) with the title and the concept's effectiveness in evoking her mother's bitterness about performing her tasks.

4. *Locavore*—a combination of *local* and the Latin *vorare*, "to eat"—is a recent coinage and does not appear in all dictionaries. The word refers to a politically and environmentally motivated movement advocating a preference for organic, local foods, rather than those that have been processed or shipped long distances. Students may be interested to know that Barbara Kingsolver (p. 494) is a strong proponent of local eating.

FIROOZEH DUMAS ON WRITING

Many students may identify with Dumas's childhood memory of soaking up observations in a room full of adults. Fewer will relate to her experience of feeling almost intoxicated with the inspiration to write them down. One way to simulate the experience is to have students write for ten minutes from observation or from a prompt. Try having them write about their favorite Halloween costume or the first time they can remember feeling guilty. The only rule is to keep the pencil moving (or the fingers typing) until you call time.

JUNE MELBY

How to Make a Sno-Cone

In this excerpt from a forthcoming comic memoir about her family's failed mini-golf course, June Melby combines tongue-in-cheek process analysis with personal reflection to contemplate a childhood living on and working in a lowbrow tourist attraction. We pair this essay with the work of another humorist, Firoozeh Dumas, because both "How to Make a Sno-Cone" and "Sweet, Sour, and Resentful" touch on food, family, and resentment in telling and insightful ways.

As we point out in the headnote and in the fourth writing topic, Melby's essay is a work in progress. An earlier draft is available on the author's Web site: *junemelby.com/artwork/2472512_Take_a_Break_for_a_Delicious_Sno _cone.html*. It might be instructive to spend some classroom time examining her revisions and discussing Melby's writing process in general. What has she changed, and why? What further revisions might she make?

QUESTIONS ON MEANING

1. Readers could certainly follow Melby's instructions (assuming they had access to an industrial ice grinder and flavoring syrups), but this essay comes from her memoir-in-progress. The writer's purpose is to reflect on her experiences as a child.
2. The statement is meant both literally and figuratively. Although there is a real risk of injuring customers with plastic shards mixed in with ice, the warning and Melby's follow-up statement, "Don't make them choke . . ." (par. 1), reveal her feelings of hostility toward those customers.
3. The portrait is not a flattering one. Melby portrays her customers as clueless tourists who are easily fooled (pars. 1, 13), who "like to feel important" and exude a sense of privilege (pars. 1, 8, 9), who don't know a good Sno-cone from a bad one (6, 8), and who could be litigious (14). At the same time, however, she reveals feelings of jealousy in her tender description, in paragraphs 9–12, of a vacationing father's loving relationship with his daughter.
4. Melby's thesis, it would seem, is that she hated working in her parents' Snack Shack and would have preferred a more typical childhood.

QUESTIONS ON WRITING STRATEGY

1. The essay mingles both points of view. The present tense and the references to "Mom" and "Dad" indicate a child's perspective, but the vocabulary of the first paragraph and the detachment of the last, along with the insights into customers' needs and emotions, suggest an adult reflecting on the past. The choice seems appropriate, although some readers may find the mixture confusing: It shows that Melby is still coming to understand her experience and has not yet finished maturing.
2. In the instructive passages (pars. 1–8, 13) she is giving instructions to a new employee—specifically, one of her sisters (students may need to be reminded to read the headnotes before the essay to grasp this information). The more reflective paragraphs (9–12, 14) seem to be addressed to herself.
3. The instructions are clear enough, if presented in a deliberately muddled order. To make a Sno-cone, a person should grind enough ice for one serving (par. 5) while being careful not to damage the plastic scoop (1), pack the ice into a ball if necessary (6, 8), ask the customer what flavor he or she wants (2–3), apply three squirts of flavoring slowly and in stages (4), hand the finished product to the customer slowly (8), and wipe the machine clean as necessary (13).
4. Melby's intention is to step back and reflect on the implications of her experience, implying a judgment that her parents probably shouldn't have had their children making Sno-cones. Some readers will likely find the conclusion unsatisfying. As an excerpt from a longer work, the last paragraph does feel somewhat lingering, yet we think it creates a nice, dreamlike closing impression.
5. Melby's descriptions appeal to every sense but smell.

QUESTIONS ON LANGUAGE

1. Paragraphs 1–4, part of 6, 8, and 13–14 are written in the second person; paragraphs 5–7 are in the first-person plural, 9 is in the third person, and 10–12 are in the first-person singular. The shifts are problematic

and some readers will find them jarring (we encourage students to try resolving them in the fourth writing prompt, labeled "Critical Writing"). Melby does seem to have a logic to the shifts, however: The instructions themselves are written in the imperative, mixing in *we* when Melby refers to her family; the first-person singular passage reverts to a specific memory. Overall the effect is conversational and creates a sense of daydreaming, which we imagine the author did a good bit of while working the stand.

2. Melby gives the machine human qualities in her introduction and her conclusion: "ice can stick like a wet tongue on a swing set" (par. 1), "The roar of hungry blades" (14). As personification tends to do, these figures of speech make the machine seem alive—and in Melby's case, threatening.

3. Melby uses *wafts* to describe the transmission of sound (an appropriate usage), but most readers will associate the verb with smells. It could be argued, then, that her descriptions in this essay (see question 5 on writing strategy) appeal to all five of the senses.

DAN KOEPPEL

Taking a Fall

Students should enjoy Koeppel's highly entertaining romp into survival strategies for those unlucky enough to fall from an airplane unexpectedly. In just a few pages the author traces the physical and biological processes of free-fall, at the same time providing details from physics and aviation history and showing what research has taught us about statistical probabilities. It sounds unreadable, but Koeppel pulls it off wonderfully. In his hands what could be dry, impenetrable science turns amusing and informative, even life saving.

At the same time, Koeppel offers glorious proof that researched writing need not be dull or mechanical (we encourage students to analyze his use of sources in the fourth writing topic). Drawing on sources both popular (*Mythbusters*, even!) and scholarly, his essay is a model of synthesis. Koeppel paraphrases and summarizes materials in such a way that anybody can follow their ideas, and quotes only the most delectable language. At no point does he lose his delightfully insouciant voice.

In case some of your students resist science writing, even comical science writing, you might start off by dividing the class into small groups to work on the first and third questions on meaning. When they see clearly *why* Koeppel goes the trouble of explaining the intricacies of terminal velocity, students will be able to relax and enjoy the ride.

QUESTIONS ON MEANING

1. Koeppel writes to explain and to entertain. His use of the second person for an informative process analysis is unusual, but by addressing readers directly he engages them in a process that might otherwise come

across as theoretical and dry. He doesn't expect that readers will actually need to use the information, as he makes clear in his thesis and in the middle of the essay: "Granted, the odds of surviving a six-mile plummet are extraordinarily slim, but at this point you've got nothing to lose by understanding your situation" (par. 5); "here's some supplemental information, though be warned that none of it will help you at this point" (17).

2. A "wreckage rider" is somebody whose fall is cushioned and slowed by virtue of "being attached to a chunk of the plane" (par. 5). Such crash victims have a higher chance of survival.

3. As Koeppel explains it, *terminal velocity* is the point at which a faller reaches the highest speed of descent. (The word *terminal,* in this case, refers to a limit, rather than an end.) If a person hits that limit while still falling, the possibility of slowing ("drag") and reducing the intensity of impact comes into play. This is why, Koeppel says, a person is more likely to survive a fall from an airplane than a fall from, say, a tall building.

4. Judging by the time-markers in the essay's headings, the fall Koeppel analyzes takes three minutes and twenty-five seconds—almost as much time he estimates it should take a person to read the essay (pars. 8, 17). (Note that a few minutes might be enough for a first quick read, but we would argue that students should take significantly more time to fully digest his work.) The connection helps make it clear just how long three and a half minutes actually is, while also stressing to readers that Koeppel is unfolding events in (almost) real time.

5. Koeppel's straightforward thesis appears in paragraph 5: "Granted, the odds of surviving a six-mile plummet are extraordinarily slim, but at this point you've got nothing to lose by understanding your situation." One might say that his point is to have fun with some useless information.

QUESTIONS ON WRITING STRATEGY

1. Koeppel opens and closes his essay by having readers imagine themselves sleeping on an airplane. By putting them in the situation he means to explore, he makes a potentially abstract concept concrete and understandable. At the same time, the framing device reassures readers that the rare horrors he examines were nothing but a dream.

2. The headings break the process into its stages, both in terms of time and height.

3. Koeppel's analysis of what a person endures in a six-mile fall shows that he assumes a general audience. He explains the process carefully and with no small amount of cheek, using simple language and humor to convey complicated scientific concepts. He defines certain physics terms, such as *terminal velocity* (par. 7), and he draws comparisons to sports, such as martial arts (13) and cliff diving (15) to help clarify his points. He does assume, however, that his audience is well educated and somewhat knowledgeable about science, using terms such as *hypoxia* (4), *friction* (12), *cranial* (16), *tonus* (19), and *subcutaneous* (19) without defining them.

4. Koeppel cites eight examples of people who have survived falls from airplanes: Vesna Vulovic (pars. 5, 18), Alan Magee (6, 11), an unnamed sky diver (11), Yasuhiro Kubo (14), Mohammed el-Fateh Osman (18), Bahia Bakari (18), Nicholas Alkemade (20), and Juliane Koepcke (21–23). Ranging in detail from quick mention to extended consideration, the

examples prove his claim that survival is possible and help him to illustrate each of his recommended moves; they're also quite gripping and morbidly entertaining.

QUESTIONS ON LANGUAGE

1. The connotations of *banzai* for most readers will bring up images of reckless attack, as Koeppel intends. Students may enjoy learning that according to *The American Heritage Dictionary*, the Japanese battle cry translates into "(may you live) ten thousand years!"—a nice touch of irony, we think.
2. Koeppel deftly overshadows formal, scientific language and technical terms with giddily colloquial expressions, conversational sentence structures, and black humor. Taken together, the writer's language choices clearly communicate the details of a complicated scientific process while making that process surprisingly entertaining and easily understandable, even for general readers with no background in science.
3. The allusion is to acrobatics, which Koeppel first brings up as good training for fall survival in paragraph 13. In gymnastics (and also in figure skating) "sticking the landing" means completing a jump gracefully, without wobbling or falling down.
4. Although Koeppel uses a few figures of speech, such as the metaphor "a semiprotective cocoon of debris" (par. 6) and the simile "[h]itting the ocean is essentially the same as colliding with a sidewalk" (11), he relies much more heavily on literal images which are no less vivid (although admittedly gruesome) for being real. Some of our favorites include Vesna Vulovic "wedged between her seat, a catering trolley, a section of aircraft, and the body of another crew member, landing on—then sliding down—a snowy incline" (5); "Magee's landing on the stone floor of that French train station . . . softened by the skylight he crashed through" (11); the "mucky, plant-covered surface" of swamps (11); the clear description of the classic sky diver pose (12); and Juliane Koepcke waking "on the jungle floor, strapped into her seat, surrounded by fallen holiday gifts" (21).

LINNEA SAUKKO

How to Poison the Earth

It won't take students long to realize that Saukko's essay is an impassioned plea for sanity on the part of those whose actions are contributing to the pollution of the earth. Though it is mainly a directive process analysis, no one is expected to follow the directions. Clearly what the author hopes is just the reverse: that readers will make every effort to stop those who are already, and all too effectively, poisoning the earth.

Students might be asked to do a little research into the issues Saukko addresses—questioning why environmental destruction is permitted, whom it benefits, what its elimination might cost, and what its alternatives are. (The second writing suggestion can be helpful in this regard.) If students are themselves well informed about the issues, the discussion that results might be one of the liveliest of the year.

Saukko's technique—giving advice precisely opposite to what she really hopes will happen—is so effective that students may find themselves inspired to imitate her. While the method can be particularly forceful, duplicating her deadpan irony will not be so simple. You can give students practice at managing this tricky tone by asking them to work in pairs or threes to write a short how-to essay of their own. Have them consider carefully *why* Saukko's essay works so well and then try their own hands at giving advice in this backward way. (You may need to remind them that they will likely be more successful if they choose a subject they know a lot about.)

QUESTIONS ON MEANING

1. Saukko's purpose is to warn readers about threats to the future of our planet, and she has done her homework. She has taken the trouble to collect statistics and other information. She knows the names and strengths of the pollutants she mentions. She is familiar with the methods by which wastes are disposed of, oil wells are drilled, pesticides are applied, and bombs are tested. Her satire is all the more biting for being buttressed by facts.
2. Students will find the mechanisms explained succinctly in paragraphs 5–7.
3. Saukko mentions disposal of nuclear wastes and toxic chemicals through deep-well and shallow-well injection, the location of dumps and landfills where their poisons can spread, pesticide use, ocean dumping, industrial air pollution, and nuclear bomb testing as practices detrimental to the environment.

QUESTIONS ON WRITING STRATEGY

1. Clearly Saukko doesn't expect individual readers to carry out her instructions. Her point is that these dangerous exercises are already routine—practiced by corporations and by local, state, and federal governments on our behalf—and ought to be stopped.
2. Saukko introduces her essay effectively with some generalizations about poisoning the earth and then, starting with paragraph 2, moves more or less geographically, as water does, from land to ocean to air. The organization is effective because it corresponds with a natural order.
3. Saukko uses the first-person plural *we* almost throughout, though she shifts to the imperative in paragraphs 7 and 8: "make sure" and "be sure."
4. The examples Saukko uses—nuclear wastes, PCB, DDT, nuclear fallout—are perhaps the most poisonous. Among the pollutants she doesn't mention, lead emissions from automobiles, carbon particles from smokestacks, and carbon dioxide from diverse sources come immediately to mind.

QUESTIONS ON LANGUAGE

1. All are dripping with irony. Typically, satire depends on such irony to attack its subject.

2. One of the things students would do well to note about the word *nuclear* is its pronunciation. A number of people in the United States still speak of "nucular" war, "nucular" power, and the like, just because they've heard it wrong and never looked closely enough at the word to get it right.

LINNEA SAUKKO ON WRITING

Perhaps one of the reasons that Linnea Saukko's essay won a Bedford Prize for Student Writing was her feeling for the subject. Those writers who pick a subject about which they care passionately tend to write well. Students who know that are off to a running start.

JESSICA MITFORD

Behind the Formaldehyde Curtain

For that soporific class that sits and looks at you, here is a likely rouser. If Mitford can't get any response out of them, they're in a league with her Mr. Jones, and you might as well devote the rest of the course to silent study periods. Sometimes, it is true, a class confronted with this essay will just sit there like people in whose midst a large firecracker has been hurled, watching it sputter. Give them time to respond with five or ten minutes to freewrite about whatever Mitford's essay first inspires them to say. Then have them trade papers in groups of three or four, read the papers, and discuss their responses with each other. You can turn these smaller group discussions into a whole-class conversation whenever it seems appropriate.

Teaching Mitford's essay invites one possible danger: that someone in the class, having recently experienced the death of a loved one, will find Mitford's macabre humor cruel and offensive. We once received a painful letter from a student in Wenatchee, Washington, who complained bitterly about this "hideous" essay. "My husband was crushed in a logging accident," she wrote. "If Mitford also learned a little about grief, she would know that those people who view a body have an easier time with grief than those who don't. She wouldn't hate funeral directors. I guess Mitford would have had me view my husband's mangled body, but I'm glad the funeral director prepared his body for viewing."

How can you answer such a protest? Before assigning this essay for reading, you might ask the class whether anyone present has suffered a death in the family. At least warn students what to expect. Anyone recently bereaved might be given the option of skipping both Mitford's essay and the class discussion. If a student in mourning reads Mitford's essay anyway and protests its seeming callousness, you might see whether that student feels impelled to write a personal response to Mitford and her essay—as our correspondent did so effectively. The first and fourth writing suggestions may be helpful.

The painstaking legwork that Mitford did before she wrote *The American Way of Death* is documented in *Poison Penmanship: The Gentle Art of*

Muckraking (1979). Much of her information came from professional journals, such as *Casket & Sunnyside, Mortuary Management,* and *Concept: The Journal of Creative Ideas for Cemeteries.* While laying stress on the value of such research, Mitford adds that a muckraker profits from sheer luck. A friend happened to recall a conversation with an undertaker when she was arranging for her brother-in-law's funeral. She had insisted on the cheapest redwood coffin available, but the undertaker objected. The deceased was too tall to fit into it; a costly coffin was required. When she continued to insist, the undertaker said, "Oh, all right, we'll use the redwood, but we'll have to cut off his feet." This grim example of high-pressure sales tactics supplied Mitford's book with one of its "more shining jewels."

When Mitford first showed her analysis of the embalming process (as a manuscript chapter for *The American Way of Death*) to her British and her American publishers, "it was met with instantaneous and thunderous disapproval from the editors on both sides of the Atlantic; this chapter is too revolting—it must go, they said." She insisted on keeping it, and lost the publishers. A year after Simon & Schuster brought out the book, she recalls, "those self-same embalming passages were chosen for inclusion in a college textbook on writing. Well! Of course I felt vindicated. The obvious moral is that although *some* editors can *sometimes* perform wonders in improving your work, in the last analysis your own judgment must prevail" (from *Poison Penmanship*, pp. 22–23).

QUESTIONS ON MEANING

1. In case anyone finds this essay repulsive and resents your assigning it, we suggest you begin by inviting reactions of all kinds. Let students kick the essay about, and, if they hate it, encourage them to say why. Almost certainly some will find it hilarious and will defend it as humor. Others will probably say that they didn't like it, that it's unpleasant, but that it tells truths we ought to know. You'll usually get more reactions if you are slow to advance your own. If the sense of the meeting should be vehemently against this essay, you may care to stick up for it (or you may want to skip on to the next selection in a hurry). But if, as is likely, most students are intrigued by it, they'll indicate this by their reactions, and your ensuing class discussion can ride on this momentum.
2. She speculates that perhaps undertakers keep it secret for fear that patrons, knowing what it is, wouldn't want it done (par. 6).
3. "To make the corpse presentable for viewing in a suitably costly container" (par. 2). Most of the usual obstacles to presentability are itemized in paragraphs 14–18: the effects of mutilation, emaciation, and disease.
4. If the subject was not dead, the undertaker will have killed him.
5. Her purpose is to attack the custom of embalming (and to chide the society that permits it). Mitford finds Americans "docile" and "ignorant" in tolerating such a procedure (par. 4). From her concluding paragraphs (23–27), we infer that she would urge Americans not to embalm, to admit the fact of death, and to bury the dead in closed coffins, as is done in much of the rest of the Western world.

QUESTIONS ON WRITING STRATEGY

1. Mitford's tone is cheerful scorn. Her verbs for the treatments inflicted on the corpse—"sprayed," "sliced," "pierced," "pickled," and so on—clearly show that she regards the process as ridiculous. The ironic phrase "suitably costly container" strongly hints that she regards morticians as racketeers.
2. She is determined to show that if we knew what embalming and restoration entailed—its every detail—we wouldn't stand for it.
3. The body becomes a character in her drama—whether it is that of an adult or a child.
4. Mitford's opening sentence indicates the start of a time sequence, and students should easily be able to find the ensuing time-markers. Her favorites are the small words "next" and "now," and most of the paragraphs about Mr. Jones contain one or the other.
5. Her audience is American general readers, whom she distinguishes from "funeral men" in paragraph 6.
6. The quotation in paragraph 3 suggests that embalming (and all it entails) may be illegal; the one in paragraph 10 suggests that dolling up the corpse is more important to the mortician than possibly saving a life. Mr. Kriege (quoted in par. 22) makes the undertaker sound like a funeral football coach, in whose hands the corpse is a helpless ball. In offering these quotations, Mitford hangs the ethics and professional behavior of morticians by their own words and once more questions the desirability of embalming.
7. Mitford's passive verbs are to us very effective. They keep the focus on the grisly process, and they undermine her target actors, funeral directors.
8. The groups are "surgery" tools, tissue chemicals, restorative cosmetics and plasters, and props and stabilizers. The groups make the catalog of equipment and supplies more intelligible and reinforce Mitford's point about the pretentions and absurdities of the process.

QUESTIONS ON LANGUAGE

1. By alluding to the Prince of Denmark's speech with skull in hand (*Hamlet* 5.1), Mitford suggests that perhaps Yorick's "counterpart of today" is another luckless jester or clown. This theatrical allusion also enforces her metaphor of the drama that begins and the curtain that must be lifted.
2. Mitford delights in citing undertakers' euphemisms. The morticians, she implies, dislike plain words—in paragraph 20 she quotes one who warns against creating the impression "that the body is in a box" (which, of course, is fact). There seems an ironic discrepancy between the attitudes expressed in the last two sentences and Mitford's own view. A funeral, she implies, shouldn't be a "real pleasure" but an occasion for grief. Death isn't an opposing football team.
3. To the general reader, these brand names carry unpleasant connotations, and a lively class discussion may be devoted to unraveling what these are. Lyf-Lyk tint seems cutesy in its spelling, like some drugstore cosmetic item. Other brand names seem practical and unfeeling: Throop Foot Positioner, Armstrong Face Former and Denture Replacer. Porto-Lift and the Glide Easy casket carriage stress slickness and efficiency. Classic Beauty Ultra Metal Casket Bier seems absurdly grand.

Mitford's purpose is to attack our sympathy and tolerance for the undertaker's art, and certainly these names rub us the wrong way.

4. "Dermasurgeon" (par. 8) is a euphemism Mitford especially relishes.
Although it tries to dignify the mortician, Mitford points out how (unlike
the surgeon he imitates) the embalmer acquired his training in a quick
post–high-school course.

JESSICA MITFORD ON WRITING

Surprisingly often, authors are in total agreement when they discuss the
art of writing. Mitford takes the common view that to write well, you have to
care deeply about your subject. (We love that British phrase "besotted by.")
Like so many writers, both amateur and professional, she knows that writing
is hard work. Like George Orwell, muckraker Mitford sees writing as a valuable tool for righting the world's wrongs.

From what Mitford says about her research for *The American Way of
Death*, students can learn how important it is to get the facts straight when
doing an exposé. The author makes clear as well that in writing, as in most
other activities, a sense of humor is a valuable asset.

DOVE

Evolution

In this clever bit of viral marketing, Dove reveals the extent to which images of women are manipulated by the media, arguing that (other) advertisers have created false standards of beauty. Although most of us are aware
that photographs are routinely tweaked for publication, the degrees of altera-
tion in "Evolution" will surprise—and possibly even outrage—many viewers. Others, accustomed to digital manipulations by the media, might not be
troubled by the practice at all.

For the most part Dove's "Campaign for Real Beauty" has been met with
praise for showcasing "real" women in its advertising and for attempting
to redefine beauty with more realistic criteria. (The campaign worked, too:
In just the first year after its launch Dove's sales increased by some 5%.)
Yet some of your students may raise the criticism that many viewers have:
Dove's parent company, Unilever, has been known to use blatantly sexist images in ads for other products, such as Axe body spray. You might use this
point to spark discussion of the contradictions inherent in the campaign:
Although Dove questions contemporary standards of beauty promoted by
advertisers, the company itself makes and advertises beauty products. What
do your students make of the paradox? How, if at all, can it be resolved?

QUESTIONS ON MEANING AND STRATEGY

1. The video's purpose is to expose and criticize the manipulations, both
physical and digital, that advertisers use when creating images to pro-

mote beauty and fashion products. The "perception of beauty" that results, claims Dove, is "distorted"—not only entirely false but also unat-
tainable. (Judging from comments attached to the video on *YouTube*, a
surprising number of viewers miss the point entirely, mistaking this for
an actual advertisement for the fictional "Fasel" makeup named in the
billboard at the end. We expect your students are more savvy than that.)

2. Seconds 0:19 to 0:39 show how a team of makeup artists and hair styl-
    ists transform a woman's physical appearance; the next ten seconds
    show how a photograph of the resulting look is further transformed
    with computer software (such as *Photoshop*). Most viewers will be
    startled by the digital alterations that take an already attractive image
    and render it completely divorced from reality—particularly the length-
    ening of the model's neck, the enlargement of her eyes, and the slim-
    ming of her shoulders.

3. The word *evolution* alludes to Darwin's theory of the gradual process,
    over several generations, of a species' biological improvement. The
    irony in the title is that the supposed perfection achieved for the model
    is quick and illusory; the video suggests that our standards of beauty
    are actually degrading to humans.

4. The video contrasts three versions of the model's face: a natural look,
    a glamorized look, and a digitally enhanced look. The final, billboard
    image bears no resemblance to the woman's actual appearance (and
    not much resemblance to the original photograph). The comparisons
    support Dove's thesis, stated in the frames from 1:00 to 1:05, that "our
    perception of beauty is distorted."

9
DIVISION OR ANALYSIS
Slicing into Parts

Division and classification have long been combined and confused in composition textbooks, so it is no wonder that some authors, some teachers, and many students cannot tell them apart. The true loser has seemed to be division. Indeed, some texts dispose of division as the mere servant of classification, the operation required to sort (divide) things into classes.

At the same time, first-year writing classes are absorbed in critical thinking, reading, and writing. Scholarly journals, textbooks, and teachers are inventing and experimenting with ways to teach these crucial skills. Yet all along we have had the means to introduce the skills through the Cinderella of the division and classification pair. Though generally treated, when treated at all, as a simple cutting operation, division is of course *analysis*. And what is analysis but the basis of criticism?

We have tried to rescue division/analysis and give it useful work in the composition course. We have, most noticeably, given the method its own chapter (and classification its own), in which we stress analytic thinking and discuss critical thinking. We have also made much more explicit the analytical underpinnings of the other methods of development, including (but not only) classification. (Two of these related methods—comparison/contrast and process analysis—continue to be covered before this chapter on the theory that they may be more familiar and accessible to students, even without explicit discussion of analysis. Of course, you may change the order of chapters if you see it differently.)

The magic of e-Pages allows us to bring back Jamaica Kincaid's provocative short story "Girl"—as read by the author herself. We now pair "Vampires Never Die" by Guillermo del Toro and Chuck Hogan with "Our Zombies, Ourselves" by James Parker, for what students should find an irresistibly fascinating look at monster legends in the media. Robert Lipsyte's "Jock Culture" forms a bridge from simple division to critical analysis, illustrated by Francine Prose's "What Words Can Tell" and student Laila Ayad's "The Capricious Camera."

GUILLERMO DEL TORO AND CHUCK HOGAN
Vampires Never Die

Students may be surprised to discover that the creators of such pulp fiction as *Hell Boy*, *Blade II*, and *Prince of Thieves* are also capable of writing a poetic, sophisticated, and seriously academic literary analysis of a trend in popular culture. In just a few pages, del Toro and Hogan survey the complete history of vampire lore and offer a fresh take on what it reveals about the human condition, especially within contemporary culture. Some of their literary and philosophical allusions, as well as their unstated reliance on the psychological theories of Carl Jung, may wash over students, yet the analysis as a whole remains compelling and understandable. (We've glossed those allusions that seem most important to following the authors' ideas; others we leave to students to investigate if they're so inclined.) Fans of current vampire stories will surely be interested to learn of the legacy behind them and be intrigued by the idea that those stories could mean anything more than just good entertainment.

"Vampires Never Die" forms a pair with James Parker's "Our Zombies, Ourselves," an examination of similar monster mythologies on television and in the movies. You may wish to begin class discussion with the question likely to be on many students' minds: Does popular culture, especially something as seemingly trivial as vampire fiction and zombie lore, merit academic study? Why, or why not? What can we learn from analyses such as these? Or, as an alternative, you might consider encouraging students to find and share criticism of del Toro's and Hogan's own literary and filmic productions. To what extent has their creative work been the subject of similar kinds of interpretation? And does "Vampires Never Die" make readers more—or less—inclined to read the authors' collaborative vampire novels for pleasure?

QUESTIONS ON MEANING

1. There's no question that "Vampires Never Die" serves as clever and well-conceived publicity for the authors' vampire trilogy. However, the authors also examine the larger cultural meanings of vampire stories in general, over time and across cultures. The essay is a sophisticated psychological analysis of one particular literary genre.
2. "Monsters, like angels, are invoked by our individual and collective needs. Today, much as during that gloomy summer in 1816, we feel the need to seek their cold embrace" (par. 7).
3. The authors posit that the concept of vampiric immortality fills a universal psychological and spiritual void. By tapping into deep-seated fears and desires, vampire stories both reassure us and "provide the possibility of mystery in our mundane . . . lives" (par. 16). The particulars of those fears and desires might change over time and across cultures, but the basic truths of death and sexuality do not. Vampires, say del Toro and Hogan, represent a powerful mixture of the two most profound aspects of human existence.

4. Students should be able to infer from the context that a *social construct* is any custom, taboo, philosophy, or law designed to govern human conduct by repressing base urges. (The idea also refers to any cultural infusion of meaning onto abstractions, but the authors aren't using it that way.) The concept is important to del Toro and Hogan's analysis because they see the vampire character as one released from the pressures of civilization, who allows human beings to reconnect vicariously with their primal instincts.

5. Although science appears to be rational and objective, new technologies can seem mysterious, even ominous to laypersons. Even those with a scientific mindset tend to embrace innovation and understanding as a faith in itself and, in so doing, to "experience fear and awe again, and to believe in the things [they] cannot see" (par. 15).

QUESTIONS ON WRITING STRATEGY

1. Writing for the *New York Times*, del Toro and Hogan assume an audience of well-educated readers with wide-ranging interests. At the same time, they assume a familiarity with popular culture, from classic novels to *American Idol*, and an immersion in communication technologies. Some students may object that several of the authors' allusions go above readers' heads, but other students will surely appreciate the apparent respect for their intelligence.

2. Their principle of analysis is the question of what makes vampires appeal across time and culture. The two basic elements identified by del Toro and Hogan are lust and death, introduced as "romantic hero" and "undead monster" (par. 4) and reiterated in the conclusion as "Eros and Thanatos fused together in archetypal embrace" (16). Subsets of those elements include primal fear (6), immortality (8), adaptability (10), uncertainty (13–14), superstition (15), and spirituality (16).

3. Their point is that the folklore taps into something deeply personal—yet primal and universal. That the first written story might have stemmed from deep-seated emotional, psychological, and sexual tensions is therefore highly significant (even if students don't recognize Jung's theory of the collective unconscious lurking behind the authors' assumptions).

4. The single word *forever* evokes immortality, both of vampires as individual characters and as a universal cultural need. Coming on the heels of a paragraph about faith and spirituality, it also echoes the concluding sentiment of Christian prayers: *Amen.*

5. The authors compare two eras "of great technical revolution" in paragraphs 13–15. Both in the early nineteenth century and now, people were confronted with "new gadgets . . . , various forms of communication . . . , and cutting-edge science" (par. 13). Del Toro and Hogan name those new technologies in the case of the nineteenth century but leave it to readers to fill in the details for the twenty-first. In either case, such innovations were both liberating and disorienting, leaving us "still ultimately vulnerable to our fates and our nightmares" (15).

QUESTIONS ON LANGUAGE

1. For a definition of *mash-up*, students may need to turn to the Internet or to a recent dictionary of slang. The term, similar in meaning to *remix*, applies to the creative process that combines elements of multiple ex-

isting productions (songs, film clips, video clips, and the like) to create something new, a technique often used by avant-garde musicians and filmmakers. We find it interesting that del Toro and Hogan manage to apply a cutting-edge (and controversial) creative trend to "ancient myth" and folklore.

2. Traditionally, *twitter* means to chirp or speak excitedly, but the word also refers to the recent and fast-growing social networking application. The verb is especially effective, given that del Toro and Hogan are writing about the psychological effects of fast-paced technology and overwhelming torrents of communication.

3. *Alchemy* refers to medieval beliefs that an as-yet-undiscovered chemical process could transform base metals, lead in particular, into gold; the hope was that such transformations would form the foundation for an elixir for everlasting youth. The metaphor fits the vampire subject very well, both in the idea that commingling of blood would transform both biter and victim into something better and that the transformation would enable immortality; it also reinforced the suggestion that science is superstition (see par. 15). The authors return to the metaphor in the next paragraph (9).

GUILLERMO DEL TORO AND CHUCK HOGAN ON WRITING

Del Toro and Hogan provide valuable insight into their collaborative writing process. Their committal "bro-hug" and their banter during the interview indicate a rapport between the two men. Is a friendly relationship a prerequisite for the deep (and sometimes ruthless) revision del Toro and Hogan do? Students may want to discuss best practices for giving feedback and ways to approach suggested revisions with an open mind, especially if peer revision is part of your course.

JAMES PARKER
Our Zombies, Ourselves

With its abundance of allusions and jargon drawn from literary criticism, Parker's whimsical essay may prove difficult to students. And yet they should have fun with "Our Zombies, Ourselves," even if much of Parker's meaning eludes them. Who doesn't enjoy a good look at zombies these days?

We pair this selection with "Vampires Never Die," by Guillermo del Toro and Chuck Hogan, for what should be obvious reasons. Vampires and zombies pervade popular culture at the moment (even the normally staid Centers for Disease Control and Prevention circulated a tongue-in-cheek guide to surviving a zombie apocalypse). We expect that college students will find both essays interesting and relevant, maybe even entertaining. It may surprise students that such characters can support academic study, but the authors of these two pieces do an exemplary job of lending intellectual rigor to a potentially frivolous topic.

A good place to begin discussion is to focus on the journal prompt. Zombies, in some cultures, are taken to be very real. Why would anyone believe they exist? What kinds of folk tales or urban legends have students heard in their hometowns or at school? How do they compare to zombie stories? Campus folklore can be especially evocative: If a popular legend or rumor circulates at your school, encourage students to investigate it, perhaps visiting the site involved or searching the campus newspaper's archives for details, and then report on what they learn.

QUESTIONS ON MEANING

1. Parker reveals his purpose in paragraph 3: He was prompted to write about zombies by the DVD release of the first season of *The Walking Dead*, "the surprise cable smash" of 2010 (and still one of the most popular programs on television). His essay is an oblique review of the show, which readers can see he admires and enjoys.

2. Although the first appearance he cites seems to be the shuffling masses in T. S. Eliot's poem *The Waste Land* (1922), and although he acknowledges that zombies figured in the book *The Magic Island* (1929) and the movie *White Zombie* (1932), Parker claims that the "modern zombie" of popular culture was born in George A. Romero's cult favorite film *Night of the Living Dead* (1968) and really took off at the start of the twenty-first century. He seems to think that the character should have been able to gain traction with the postwar industrialization of the early twentieth century, but suggests that the subject required a "trash visionary" (par. 1)—a less serious artist than someone like Eliot—to grasp the interest of a broad audience.

3. In Romero's film, zombies are the result of "radioactive contamination from an exploded space probe" (par. 5). Parker's point is that modern technology is the impetus behind and the propagator of today's cultural sense of not living fully, of a general zombified malaise, much as Guillermo del Toro and Chuck Hogan (p. 335) argue that new technologies explain the popularity of vampires in the late nineteenth century.

4. Zombies, Parker says, have been seen as metaphors for "the consumer, the mob, the Other, the proletariat, the weight of life, the dead soul" (par. 6), but he argues that they have no meaning: "A zombie is *always* just a zombie" (8). At most, he suggests, zombies represent the current national mood—a generalized sense of exhaustion and purposelessness in life.

5. Parker's thesis appears in paragraph 8: "The blow-'em-all-away success of *The Walking Dead* is no mystery: The show, and the comic-book series by Robert Kirkman on which it's based, mark a triumphant return to zombie orthodoxy, to the non-galloping zombie and his icons." He withholds it because he spends his time in the essay building to this idea, broadening his focus beyond *The Walking Dead* to establish what he means by "zombie orthodoxy" and to explain its appeal.

QUESTIONS ON WRITING STRATEGY

1. As we mention in the headnote to this essay, Parker was writing for his entertainment column in *The Atlantic Monthly*, a fairly intellectual magazine focused on culture and politics. Accordingly, he assumes a well-educated audience grounded in literary theory and basic history, but who also happen to enjoy "trash" (par. 1) media productions, pos-

sibly as guilty pleasure. Students will probably fit the latter part of his assumptions, if not the former.

2. Students may not recognize the allusion to the (supposedly) Freudian disclaimer that "sometimes a cigar is just a cigar" (see the first question on language), but Parker is saying that zombies carry no deep symbolic meaning; they just are. He outlines the basic elements of zombiedom in paragraph 5: "the wobbliness of the zombie, the terrible mobility of the virus, the pockets of survival, the squall of information as the grid collapses." Each of these elements is elaborated on in more detail in the rest of the essay. Zombies, as Parker portrays them, walk unsteadily (pars. 1–2), cannot be stopped easily (3), lack free will (4–5), crave "human flesh" (5), cannot speak (6), and multiply their number by taking victims (7).

3. For evidence Parker cites multiple media productions centered on zombie lore: George A. Romero's *Night of the Living Dead* (pars. 2, 5), a spate of parodies and video games (3), the novel *World War Z*, the Béla Lugosi movie *White Zombie* (4), a punk song from the 1980s (6), and the movies *28 Days Later, Dawn of the Dead*, and *Shaun of the Dead*. We know he takes his subject seriously because he also draws on literary and quasi-scholarly works (T. S. Eliot's *The Wasteland*, 1, and William Seabrook's *The Magic Island*, 4), claims that "zombie studies" is an emerging academic field (4), and uses terminology from literary theory (see the second question on language). But as serious as he is, readers can tell that Parker is also having fun.

4. Parker uses topic sentences as transitions that preview clearly the focus of each paragraph; repeats key words such as *zombie* (and our favorite invented variation, *zombificently*, in par. 4), *shuffle/wobble/plod/bumble/lurch, slow*, and *dead*; and deftly circles back to his introduction with his concluding sentences: "He crookedly advances. He's taking his time. But he'll get there" (8).

5. Parker compares the movies, examples of two distinct variations on the classic zombie popularized by *Night of the Living Dead*, to lead to his point that the show *The Walking Dead* and the comic-book series it's based on "mark a triumphant return to zombie orthodoxy" (par. 8).

QUESTIONS ON LANGUAGE

1. The allusion to *The Waste Land* is obscure; we include the full stanza with the question because students undoubtedly won't catch it (it blew past us on the first few readings, and then we had to look it up). Parker seems to expect that the one line will evoke for readers an image of the walking dead and his implication that Eliot somehow presaged the emergence of zombies in fiction; we think that's unlikely. The same may or may not be the case for his several other allusions. These include his title, a reference to the 1970s self-help book *Our Bodies, Ourselves*; his oblique reference to World War I in the introduction (which we have glossed for students); "the Age of Aquarius" (1); the Jungian theory of the collective unconscious (3); the "horror-flick tradition" in which immorality and irreverence are punished (5); the concept of "the Other" (6); the sly reference to Freud with "sometimes a zombie is just a zombie" (8); and of course the zombie films and books Parker brings up. Students may catch some of these allusions, and will probably miss most of the non-zombie ones, but they certainly reveal the depth of Parker's analysis and show that he knows his theory.

2. Notice how many of Parker's words hail from literary criticism: *proverb, metaphysically, alienated* (from the Marxist school), *canons, postmodernity, semiotic, proletariat* (Marxism, again), *existential, pathos.* Parker's allusions to Carl Jung (par. 3) and Sigmund Freud (8) add the psychological school of theory to the mix.
3. Parker mixes academic vocabulary and colloquial expressions with a dose of cliché (see James Parker on Writing, p. 347); his tone strikes us as simultaneously lyrical and fun. Neither the diction nor the tone are appropriate for a formal analysis, but Parker doesn't mean to be formal. He's having a good time and means for his readers to enjoy themselves, as well.

JAMES PARKER ON WRITING

Parker makes an interesting, if debatable, point that some clichés convey depths of meaning more effectively and more efficiently than fresh language is capable of. A risk of exposing students to his argument, of course, is that they may fail to make distinctions between those phrases that are "laden with experience" and those that are merely trite. You might ask them to dispute his claims, arguing among themselves for the benefits of fresher, creative language.

ROBERT LIPSYTE

Jock Culture

While sports are an integral part of American culture, Robert Lipsyte argues in this compelling essay, the values instilled by competition are harmful and counterproductive, both for those who embrace them and those who don't.

The sports fans in your class will likely have a strong reaction against the writer's negative assessment of "Jock Culture," while the indifferent will probably be relieved to find a sympathetic friend—especially if your school has a vibrant athletic program. It may be worth reminding both camps that although Lipsyte self-identifies as a "Puke," he has made his career writing about sports.

"Jock Culture" is one of several pieces in *The Bedford Reader* that touch on sports (albeit the only one that's overtly critical). To appease students hostile to Lipsyte's criticisms, you may wish to assign his essay in conjunction with one or more of the following: Maya Angelou, "Champion of the World" (p. 104); Annie Dillard, "The Chase" (p. 122); Brad Manning, "Arm Wrestling with My Father" (p. 156); Dave Barry, "Batting Clean-Up and Striking Out" (p. 248). How well does Lipsyte's analysis hold up when compared with the positive feelings others have derived from watching or participating in athletics?

QUESTIONS ON MEANING

1. Lipsyte describes an interview he held with Columbia University's crew coach in the midst of student occupations of the school's buildings in protest of the Vietnam War. It would seem that Stowe was involved in breaking up the demonstrations. The student occupations are relevant to Lipsyte's subject for several reasons. First, his interview with Stowe introduced him to the concept of Jocks and Pukes: Stowe, of course, is an example of the former; and Lipsyte (and the protesting students) of the latter. By placing his analysis in the context of the Vietnam War, Lipsyte also highlights the conflicts between athleticism and intellectualism and previews his claim that Jock Culture can be blamed, at least in part, for violence and warfare.

2. Jock Culture is the set of values instilled by devotion to overly competitive team sports: "submission to authority, winning by any means necessary, and group cohesion" (par. 4). Sports themselves, Lipsyte acknowledges, are beneficial (5), but Jock Culture debases them through "greed and desperate competition" (6) that turn people against each other in other aspects of life, particularly business, school, and government. It pits aggression against cooperation and results in "the cheating, the lying, the amorality" (12) that seems to mark contemporary society.

3. Lipsyte introduces his thesis in paragraph 4: "Boys—and more and more girls—who accept Jock Culture values often go on to flourish in a competitive sports environment that requires submission to authority, winning by any means necessary, and group cohesion." Implied in this statement and developed in the rest of the essay is Lipsyte's claim that those values are damaging to society as a whole. In a culture focused on winning, everybody—Jocks, Pukes, men, women, business leaders, workers, professionals, artists, intellectuals, and children especially—loses.

4. "Jock Culture" is an argument against aggressive, competitive values in American business and leisure. Lipsyte aims to persuade his readers to question those values and, perhaps, to support "de-emphasizing early competition and redistributing athletic resources" (par. 6), especially in schools (16).

QUESTIONS ON WRITING STRATEGY

1. Using the "myths of masculinity and power" (par. 4) instilled by competitive team sports as his principle of analysis, Lipsyte identifies several elements of Jock Culture, among them "greed and desperate competition" (6); "bullying, violence, and the commitment to a win-at-all-costs attitude that can kill a soul" (7); division into "winners and losers" (8); "coachlike authority figures who use shame and intimidation to achieve short-term results (8); expectations for people "to be tough, stoical, and aggressive, to play hurt, to hit hard, to take risks to win in every aspect of their lives" (9); desires to "pursue . . . jock dreams no matter the physical, emotional, or financial cost" (10); and "misogyny" (13). The positive aspects of sports—"entertaining, healthful, filled with honest, sustaining sentiments for warm times and the beloved people you shared them with" (5); "a once safe place to learn about bravery, cooperation, and respect" (7); learning teamwork and developing the ability

to reach a goal despite setbacks (9)—are completely overshadowed by the damaging effects of Jock Culture.

2. As he indicates, Lipsyte is writing to other Pukes like himself—educated, politically aware readers of *The Nation* who "were often turned off or away from competitive sports" (par. 4). He assumes his audience consists of liberals who "question authority and seek ways of individual expression" (4), and anticipates that many of them identify as artsy misfits, whether they work in "business, medicine, the law," or in "symphony orchestras, university philosophy departments, and liberal magazines" like *The Nation* (8). He seems to want them to understand that even if they think they live apart from Jock Culture, it permeates every aspect of their lives and affects them more than they may realize.

3. Although the 9/11 example may seem gratuitous to some readers, it neatly encapsulates the entirety of Lipsyte's analysis. It shows, first of all, that Jocks—both male and female—have an advantage in business yet also are harmed by that advantage. It reinforces his implication, in paragraphs 1–4, that competitive values lead to military action and outright war. It hints at why "submission to authority" (4) is a dangerous trait. And it lets Lipsyte show empathy for those who embrace the values he disdains.

4. By quoting the "affable *ur*-Jock" (par. 2) in his introduction, Lipsyte establishes the position that he intends to counter while simultaneously distancing himself from terms that some readers will find offensive. Returning to Stowe four decades later in his conclusion, Lipsyte circles back to his introduction (creating unity) and reveals that even a devoted athlete has changed his mind about the value of sports and come around to the author's way of thinking.

5. Lipsyte starts off with Bill Stowe's binary classification, which ascribes positive characteristics to Jocks: They are, he claims, "brave, manly, ambitious, focused, patriotic, and goal-driven" (par. 1). Pukes are exactly the opposite: "wooly, distractible, girlish, and handicapped by their lack of certainty that nothing mattered as much as winning" (1). In Lipsyte's own reckoning, however, the characteristics are different. As he presents them, Pukes "question authority and seek ways of individual expression," while Jocks are conformists who do whatever is asked of them (4).

QUESTIONS ON LANGUAGE

1. Although Stowe uses the word *Jock* approvingly, both words have derogatory connotations, especially *Puke*, which brings up images of sickliness and weakness. If nothing else, the labels capture readers' attention and stress the different personalities more colorfully than *athlete* and *intellectual* would.

2. No doubt Lipsyte himself would describe his tone as "Puke-ish" (par. 2)—in a good way. His words are calm, reasoned, intellectual, and infused with empathy.

3. Lipsyte's invective against sport mentality is riddled with sport metaphors. Some examples: "mental conditioning" (par. 4); "arenas of elite athletes," "cockpit of bullying" (7); "'cut' from the team early" (8); "pushed the envelope" (9); "our lives outside the white lines" (12). Taken together with Bill Stowe's mixed metaphors/clichés in paragraph 16 ("It's time to give up the torch. . . . I'm not running it up the flagpole anymore"), they show that while the author might reject Jock Culture, he understands it fully—and probably better than Jocks do.

4. *Wonkish* is a relatively new coinage and could be counted as slang. The word refers to a student or analyst (a *wonk*) who focuses excessively on a particular subject.

FRANCINE PROSE
What Words Can Tell

Francine Prose's book *Reading like a Writer* holds that thoughtful reading is the key to good writing. This excerpt from Prose's best-selling writing guide both reinforces our own assumptions about the benefits of close reading and serves beautifully as a model of such reading. We hope students will be inspired by Prose's example to attempt similar analyses of both the fiction and the nonfiction included in *The Bedford Reader*. As Prose demonstrates, even a few sentences of a quality work reveal much meaning and have much to teach about the value of words.

Students who want to read "A Good Man Is Hard to Find" can locate it in many venues. Flannery O'Connor's marvelous collection *"A Good Man Is Hard to Find" and Other Stories* is available in almost any library, and it can also be found online via the University of Central Florida at *pegasus.cc.ucf .edu/~surette/Goodman.html*. The critical writing topic following Prose's analysis invites students to read the story and then respond to Prose's interpretation of its opening paragraph. This topic could also spark class discussion as students share their responses to Prose and to the story itself.

QUESTIONS ON MEANING

1. Prose examines the paragraph to demonstrate just how informative and rewarding it can be to "slow down and read every word" (par. 2) of an enduring writer's work.
2. The author's thesis is stated in paragraph 3: "All the elements of good writing depend on the writer's skill in choosing one word instead of another. And what grabs and keeps our interest has everything to do with those choices."
3. Prose admires the passage for O'Connor's skill in establishing every character's personality, setting the tone, and foreshadowing the plot in a "highly concentrated . . . model of compression from which it would be hard to excise one word" (par. 12).

QUESTIONS ON WRITING STRATEGY

1. Prose's intended audience is made clear in the title of her book: *Reading like a Writer: A Guide for People Who Love Books and for Those Who Want to Write Them*. Her use of the language of literary criticism further suggests that she imagines her readers to be well educated, or at least somewhat experienced in reading literature.
2. Given that Prose has no qualms about including spoilers, she does seem to assume that most members of her audience have read O'Connor's

short story. Yet she is careful to reprint the full passage under analysis and to alert readers to its connections with later plot developments. Even those who have never read "A Good Man Is Hard to Find" learn enough about it from Prose's essay to follow her examination of its introduction. (And we hope that those who have not yet had the pleasure of reading O'Connor's masterful story will be inspired by Prose's analysis to track it down for their own enjoyment.)

3. Prose ties her analysis together in paragraph 13: "Skimming just won't suffice" to "teach us about how to use the language."

4. By giving a close reading of one short passage from a famous story, Prose proves her point that writers can learn a lot by reading the masters.

QUESTIONS ON LANGUAGE

1. Figures of speech in the lead-in to Prose's analysis include her analogy of wiring to explain how readers need to relearn their approach to fiction (par. 1) and her similes comparing a writer's words to a composer's notes and an artist's paints (2). Each of these turns of phrase demonstrates the author's appreciation for colorful, meaningful writing and encourages her readers to think in creative terms.

2. The switch in address reflects Prose's switch in emphasis and purpose. The introductory paragraphs are meant as instruction for the readers who are the subject of Prose's lesson, so the second person is appropriate. In the analysis itself, however, Prose is more interested in the intricacies of reading and thinks of her audience (and herself) as the objects of O'Connor's efforts, hence the third-person *we*.

3. The allusions stress that Flannery O'Connor is part of a community of revered literary masters whose work continues to influence contemporary writers.

4. Notice that many of Prose's word choices—*psychic, archetypal, infantilizing, egocentrism, narcissism*—reveal her interest in the psychological school of literary criticism.

FRANCINE PROSE ON WRITING

Prose's statement about grammatical errors may puzzle those students who have been taught that errors are always wrong. Her point, we think, is that Philip Roth can get away with what might be considered a textbook error because he knows what he's doing—the error is deliberate—and because his meaning is clear. What distinguishes his error from that of a less experienced writer is his control and clarity.

LAILA AYAD
The Capricious Camera

This documented student essay is complex in both its ideas and its organization. It analyzes a photograph taken during the Nazi occupation of Poland during World War II: an image of a young girl surrounded by soldiers. Ayad makes two overlapping points—one about the Nazis' *Lebensborn* experiment (the attempt to create a master race through breeding and adoption) and another about the ambiguities of photography.

Ayad assumes her readers will have some familiarity with the Nazi agenda, so before you begin discussion you may want to explore what students know about Nazi Germany, its occupations, and the Holocaust. Showing students photographs from the era could help them put Ayad's analysis in context. Your library may even have the book by Clay and Leapman that was Ayad's source.

QUESTIONS ON MEANING

1. Ayad's dual theses are as follows: "It is not merely people of other persecuted races who can become victims in a racial war, but also those we would least expect—the persecuting race itself" (par. 1); and "Unlike hand-made art, which in its very purpose begs to be viewed through various interpretations, photography, and particularly photojournalism, . . . demands to be viewed alongside its agenda, for without this context, it may never be fully understood" (par. 8). The two come together in the final paragraph: "[E]ven if the original photographer saw the image as artistic, subsequent events compel us to try to see the image of the Polish girl with Nazis as journalism. In this endeavor, we must uncover as much as possible about the surrounding context. As much as we can, we need to know this girl's particular story."

2. Ayad focuses on the Nazi *Lebensborn* experiment, in which "[c]hildren who possessed strong Nordic or Aryan qualities were systematically taken from their native countries, adopted by German parents (who were paid by the Nazi regime), taught to forget their families and former lives, and raised to breed not only many children of their own but, above all, families that would uphold Nazi ideology" (par. 11). Thus the Nazis persecuted their own "race" as well as others.

3. Ayad seems to want to show both the limitations of and the opportunities in photojournalism. It must be viewed in context, but that analysis can be very revealing.

QUESTIONS ON WRITING STRATEGY

1. Ayad focuses extensively on the photograph to show the ways it can be interpreted out of context and to demonstrate that without context we cannot truly understand the image.

2. Ayad seems to assume a general familiarity with Nazi Germany: In paragraph 1, for example, she uses "Hitler," "Aryan," "anti-Semitism," and

"Holocaust" without explanation. However, she does not assume familiarity with the *Lebensborn* program, which she explains in detail (pars. 1,
9–12).
3. The conclusion brings the essay full circle and (as noted in the answer to the first question on meaning) weaves together the essay's two
threads. The last two sentences freeze the image of the girl in readers'
minds, capturing the poignancy of her unknown fate.
4. Ayad uses description in paragraphs 2–6, giving readers the information
they need to see the photograph as she does.

QUESTIONS ON LANGUAGE

1. Ayad is clearly moved by the girl's plight, as evident in language such
as "overwhelming," "the magnitude and force of the oppressing men,"
"innocence and helplessness of the lone girl," "both cruel and terribly
frightening," "menacing and unjust" (par. 4), "symbols of oppression,
producing an eerily suffocating effect" (5), "dramatic," "wistful and innocent," and "heads . . . hang in almost shameful disgrace" (6).
2. The quotations from Hitler, Gunther, and Himmler chillingly prove the
Nazis' racism and their goals of racial purification. The quotation from
the Polish woman provides an eyewitness account of what happened to
many children, including, perhaps, the girl in the photograph.
3. *Targeting* conveys a sinister intent, as in targeting prey.
4. *Aryan* originally referred to a Northern tribe that conquered much of
Asia around 2000 BC. German racialists began—some spuriously—to
trace Northern Europeans back to these ancestors in the nineteenth
century, and the Nazis found further reason to apply the term to themselves because of that people's idealization of conquest.

JAMAICA KINCAID
Girl

The writer Stephanie Vaughn has said that Kincaid's story "spills out in a
single breath. . . . Its exhilarating motion gives . . . the sense of a writer carried
over the precipice by the energy of her own vision." Even so, students may
need a little guidance on how to follow and understand this evocative piece of
fiction. They may complain that as a story, it unfolds much less clearly and
logically than, say, the narrative essays in Chapter 4. For those who resist
the unorthodox style, you might ask students to compare Kincaid's spoken
version with the written transcript. The story's form, especially when read
out loud, helps emphasize the mother and daughter's relationship.

Students will certainly notice that this story is not set in the United
States. Encourage them in small groups to locate the details that make this
fact obvious. How does the foreignness of the location help or hinder understanding of the story? Are there things in "Girl" that suggest the universal
experience of growing up? How would they rewrite this story to capture the
lessons their parents repeat?

QUESTIONS ON MEANING AND STRATEGY

1. These are any boys who hang around without enough to do—boys without motivation. She should avoid them because, presumably, they would be interested in "ruining" her.
2. A life full of risk, danger, and vigilance—risks including miscooked food and bad sex, dangers including becoming pregnant and becoming a "slut," vigilance with household chores, social obligations, health, and personal morality.
3. This advice lightens with a little laugh the heavy sense of obligation conveyed by all the other advice. If it were the last line, it might detract from the seriousness of the rest of the piece.
4. The categories include how to wash, cook, sew, iron, sing, grow food, sweep, smile, set the table, interact with men, and make medicine. The categories show that the roles of women are methodical, not random, and should be appreciated for their subtlety, efficiency, and complexity.

10
CLASSIFICATION
Sorting into Kinds

In our general comments on Chapter 9, we explain our reasons for divorcing the hoary pair of division and classification. Our reasons have mainly to do with salvaging division/analysis, but benefits accrue to classification, too. For one thing, it doesn't have to compete for attention (ours, yours, students'), so it's much clearer. For another, we can provide more illustrations.

The selections in this chapter range from humorous to serious, reflecting the classifications we find in the publications we read. Deborah Tannen and William Lutz look at miscommunications inadvertent and deliberate, respectively. Russell Baker contributes a well-known humorous piece of curmudgeonly confusion over our material possessions. Student writer Ashley Herzog takes aim at what she believes to be counterproductive political correctness on college campuses. Adventure writer Jeff Wise uses psychology to group mistakes that can lead to death, or at the very least embarrassment. And in the e-Pages, a compelling infographic from the US Census Bureau shows the changing face of American immigration.

Troubleshooting: All our efforts to keep division/analysis and classification separate and equal are hampered by the inescapable fact that *divide* is sometimes taken to mean *classify*, as in "Divide the students into groups." You might want to point out this issue directly to students if you think the terminology will confuse them. We maintain that division/analysis treats a singular, whole, coherent subject (a camera, a theory, a poem), whereas classification treats a plural, numerous subject (cameras, theories, poems).

The confusion between division and classification may account for the tendency of some students to "classify" by taking a single item (say, the television show *Survivor*) and placing it in a category (say, reality shows). We'd explain that they haven't classified anything; they have just filed an item in a pigeonhole. If they'll remember that classification begins not with one thing but with several things, they may avoid much perplexity.

DEBORAH TANNEN
But What Do You Mean?

The linguist Deborah Tannen came to national prominence with *You Just Don't Understand*, a book about misunderstandings between men and women in conversation. Since then, she has continued to disseminate much of her research through the mass media, trying to help people solve the communication problems of daily life. Oliver Sacks, another intellectual who often addresses a general audience, wrote of *You Just Don't Understand*: "Deborah Tannen combines a novelist's ear for the way people speak with a rare power of original analysis. It is this that makes her an extraordinary sociolinguist, and it is this that makes her book such a fascinating look at that crucial social cement, conversation."

This is one essay that students should be able to apply easily to their own lives, although the men in your class may be more resistant than the women. The essay will certainly evoke a wide range of student response, which should lead to lively class discussion. Here is an in-class exercise to test Tannen's theories: Ask students to bring in dialogs that illustrate conflict from novels, plays, or movie scripts, deleting characters' names and direct references to gender. Have students read the dialogs out loud and try to guess characters' genders, justifying their choices. Encourage students to look for instances of Tannen's seven categories of miscommunication in the dialogs. (A variation is to cross-cast the dialogs, with women reading men's lines, and vice versa, and see if they are still believable.)

While Tannen examines innocent misunderstandings, William Lutz, in the next essay, takes on language that misleads on purpose. The "Connections" questions following both essays will help students consider what both kinds of miscommunication have in common, as well as how such confusions might be avoided.

QUESTIONS ON MEANING

1. Tannen is pointing out the areas of communication in which misunderstandings between the sexes are most frequent. She seems to hope that a better understanding of how men's and women's communication styles differ will help eliminate such misunderstandings. A secondary purpose is to show women how their problems in the workplace may be linked to their style of communication.
2. Much of what we say is based on pure protocol, which serves as a kind of social cement. We're not so much communicating facts as establishing a rapport with the other person. This speech is often so automatic and predictable that we aren't even aware of what we're saying. (See also the journal prompt and the first writing suggestion.)
3. "Many of the conversational rituals common among women are designed to take the other person's feelings into account, while many of the conversational rituals common among men are designed to maintain the one-up position, or at least avoid appearing one-down" (par. 2).
4. "Thank you" is not always used as an expression of gratitude, but is simply a ritual, "an automatic conversation starter and closer" (par. 15).

An answer of "You're welcome" results in an imbalance between the speakers.

QUESTIONS ON WRITING STRATEGY

1. Tannen uses these characters as examples of the points she is making. She adds variety to the essay by referring to people alternately by their first names (real or fictitious) and by their functions ("a well-known columnist," par. 4; "[a] woman manager I know," 13). These characters are ciphers, empty vessels in the service of Tannen's argument, and as such do not need to be described in detail. Tannen reveals only what is relevant to her point. (See also question 4.)
2. Because the essay appeared in *Redbook,* a women's magazine, Tannen uses *you* to address women readers: "What's important is to be aware of how often you say you're sorry (and why), and to monitor your speech based on the reaction you get" (par. 9); "Although you may never enjoy verbal sparring, some women find it helpful to learn how to do it" (19). (Tannen takes a broader approach for a male *and* female audience in *Talking from 9 to 5*, the book from which this essay was excerpted.)
3. Tannen begins by redefining women's apologizing not as self-deprecation but as a "way of keeping both speakers on an equal footing." She then offers an extended example of this redefinition and expands on it further through a brief dialog that reveals apologizing as "a mutual face-saving device." In paragraphs 6 and 7, she gives an example of a woman whose constant apologies may have limited others' perceptions of her competence. Finally, she poses a contrast: the negative response women may get if they don't use "ritual apologies."
4. That the columnist is well known makes her apology all the more unexpected, less likely to be chalked up to insecurity.
5. (1) *Apologies*: Women apologize more than men do. They see apology as a way of keeping both speakers on an equal footing, of sharing responsibility. Men take apologies at face value, seeing them as self-deprecating. (2) *Criticism*: Women tend to soften criticism more than men do. Men prefer "straight answers." (3) *Thank-yous*: Women say "thank you" more often, as a ritual. Men take "thank you," like "I'm sorry," more literally. (4) *Fighting*: Men see conversation as a battleground, stating their ideas and criticizing those of others in the strongest possible terms. Women often perceive this approach as a personal attack. (5) *Praise*: Women often assume that the absence of praise is the equivalent of criticism. For men, in contrast, praise is often implied when no criticism is given. Women who ask for criticism may really be asking for praise, but men will give them what they ask for. (6) *Complaints*: Women complain as a way of bonding with others. Men see these complaints as a call for a solution. (7) *Jokes*: "[T]he most common form of humor among men is razzing, teasing, and mock-hostile attacks, while among women it's self-mocking. Women often mistake men's teasing as genuinely hostile. Men often mistake women's mock self-deprecation as truly putting themselves down."

QUESTIONS ON LANGUAGE

1. The humor here relies on exaggeration. It usually refers to finishing off a suffering animal.
2. Tannen uses the metaphor of a gun: criticism as shooting.

3. These verbs liven up the essay and inspire a strong visual or auditory impression. Other examples are "*leapt* into a critical response" (par. 10) and "*poke* holes" (17).

4. Note Tannen's vocabulary of physical and verbal conflict: "contentious," "hedge," "sparring," "rebuttal," "retorted," as well as "disadvantage" (par. 2), "attack" (18), and "enemy" (19). You might discuss whether Tannen loads her case with such words, perhaps exaggerating the conflicts between genders.

DEBORAH TANNEN ON WRITING

Students may not be aware of the debate about the personal in scholarly writing, but many have probably been told at some time not to use *I* in their academic papers. Tannen suggests why and also argues in favor of the first person on scholarly grounds. Students in the natural and applied sciences may be more likely than others in the class to resist Tannen's argument, contending that they don't write about personal interactions. Uncovering resistance and getting a discussion going are of course the aims of the first follow-up question. For the second one, collaboration in small groups is ideal: Working together, students will find it easier to draft the third-person or first-person passage and then revise it, seeing firsthand what the differences are.

WILLIAM LUTZ
The World of Doublespeak

William Lutz is a leading figure in the campaign against the dishonest language that he (and others) call doublespeak. This essay, extracted from the first chapter of his book-length treatment of the subject, both defines the term and classifies its varieties. The many, many examples will leave students in no doubt about the meaning of doublespeak and should make it relatively easy for them to spot it.

One problem with doublespeak is that it often relies on multisyllabic words and complicated syntax. As a result, the most example-heavy parts of Lutz's essay may be difficult reading for some students. Lutz himself practices what he preaches, writing clearly and concisely, but you may want to warn students that some passages in the essay require patience.

Probably the best way to make this essay immediate and significant for students is to have them locate doublespeak in what they read and hear. Indeed, you may want to ask them to try the journal-writing assignment as soon as they've read the essay and to bring their examples to class. Even if each student contributes only one or two examples, you'll have a good collection. Working as a whole class or in small groups to sort their examples into Lutz's categories, students will be writing a continuation of the essay.

We pair Lutz's essay with the previous one, Deborah Tannen's "But What Do You Mean?" While Tannen deals with gender communications and Lutz with a subtle form of deception, both authors look at how our uses of language can hinder understanding. The fifth writing suggestion following each essay can be used as an assignment or to spark discussion.

QUESTIONS ON MEANING

1. Lutz's thesis might be stated briefly as follows: The four kinds of doublespeak all include language "that avoids or shifts responsibility, language that is at variance with its real or purported meaning" (par. 2). The thesis accumulates over paragraphs 2–3, with the addition of the intention to classify in paragraph 5.
2. Paragraph 4 offers the following questions: "Who is saying what to whom, under what conditions and circumstances, with what intent, and with what results?" These questions locate the motivation for dishonesty that would indicate doublespeak.
3. The greatest danger is that, as in Orwell's *Nineteen Eighty-Four*, doublespeak will lead to the "control of reality through language" (par. 23). Doublespeak "alter[s] our perception of reality and corrupt[s] our thinking. . . . [It] breeds suspicion, cynicism, distrust, and, ultimately, hostility" (22). It can "infect and eventually destroy the function of language" (23).
4. Lutz clearly assumes an educated reader, someone able to perceive the fundamental dishonesty in his examples. At the same time, his careful classification, scores of examples, and extensive discussion of the dangers indicate that he believes his reader probably is not sensitive to doublespeak and needs help to recognize it.

QUESTIONS ON WRITING STRATEGY

1. Lutz's principle of classification is the intention of doublespeakers. Those who use euphemisms are trying to "mislead or deceive" (par. 7) with inoffensive words. Those who use jargon seek to give their words "an air of profundity, authority, and prestige" (10). Those who use gobbledygook or bureaucratese are bent on "overwhelming the audience with words" (13). And those who use inflated language seek "to make the ordinary seem extraordinary; . . . to make the simple seem complex" (17).
2. Lutz begins by offering a definition of the category. Then he offers examples of euphemisms used to spare others' feelings or to avoid language regarded as taboo—euphemisms he finds acceptable. Finally, he contrasts these kinds of euphemism with three examples of euphemism used by government agencies to "mislead or deceive"—in which case it becomes doublespeak.
3. Greenspan's second comment is surprising because he acknowledges that he is deliberately unclear. With the quotation Lutz shows that doublespeak is intentional.
4. Many of Lutz's examples are dated, and some students may at first think that doublespeak is an old, not a current, problem. The first writing suggestion, asking students to find current examples of their own, should help them see that doublespeak is no less a problem now than it was more than two decades ago.
5. Definition appears mainly in paragraphs 2 and 3 and in the explanations of each kind of doublespeak (pars. 5, 7, 9–10, 13, 17). Cause and effect also figures in the explanation of categories, as Lutz gives the inten-

tions of doublespeakers, but mainly it develops the last section of the essay (20–23). The definition, of course, clarifies Lutz's subject and his categories. The cause-and-effect analysis shows what is at stake with this dishonest language.

QUESTIONS ON LANGUAGE

1. Lutz's language provides a good foil to the quotations of doublespeak: He uses plain language and relatively simple syntax.
2. The words listed all have negative connotations, suggesting undesirable or even dangerous effects of doublespeak. More neutral language would not make Lutz's point as sharply. For just a few examples, see paragraph 1.
3. *Taboo* now refers to a prohibition against the use or practice of something. The word comes from the Tongan word *tabu*, an adjective meaning "set apart, consecrated to a special use or purpose." Captain Cook traveled to Tonga in 1777; his widely read narrative of his experiences, including an explanation of *tabu*, brought the term into common use in England.

WILLIAM LUTZ ON WRITING

Students may be encouraged to see recognizable behaviors, particularly procrastination, in a successful writer. Students aren't writing whole books for their classes, of course, but Lutz's advice, scaled down, should remind them that they needn't try to write an essay all at once, only a few paragraphs. The longer students wait to write a paper, the greater the chance they will have to do it in one sitting and will be daunted by the task.

The writer and humorist Fran Lebowitz once joked that being a writer was a bit like being a perpetual student . . . except you can't write a book the night before it is due. "I know," Lebowitz deadpanned, "because I tried twice."

RUSSELL BAKER

The Plot against People

In this essay, the well-known humorist Russell Baker makes a common use of classification—for humor. Baker takes a wry look at the universal human feeling that the material world is conspiring against us. Ask the class to come up with more examples of things that "have it in" for people.

Writing humor is difficult, as students who have tried can attest. Give students an opportunity to try their hands at a collaborative essay modeled on Baker's. What conspiracy theories can the class generate? (These might include the school's conspiracy to keep students from registering for any of the classes they most need, the local market's conspiracy to run out of Diet

Coke when you most need one, and so on.) Make a list of ideas on the board, and have small groups of students write a short essay describing this conspiracy in detail. You might ask the groups to read their finished products.

Students who enjoy Baker's approach can be encouraged to look into some of his collections, such as *Poor Russell's Almanac* (1972) and *So This Is Depravity* (1980).

QUESTIONS ON MEANING

1. Baker's thesis is stated in paragraph 1. His larger meaning is that inanimate objects conspire to frustrate humans.
2. The reason may be that objects are doing humans a favor (par. 11) or that they are "incredibly stupid" (12).
3. He may also want to point out how ridiculous we are when we become infuriated with inanimate things.
4. By not working, thus "conditioning him never to expect anything of them" (par. 16).

QUESTIONS ON WRITING STRATEGY

1. Baker classifies objects by the ways they thwart human wishes. He might have included things that work for a while and then break, or even things that work fine; but his use of extreme cases adds to the essay's humor.
2. Baker begins by contrasting the category with the previous category. Next he provides two examples (pliers and keys) and then an additional example (women's purses). Finally, he again contrasts things that break down with things that get lost, using the examples of a furnace and a woman's purse.
3. "[A]ny object capable of breaking down at the moment when it is most needed will do so" (par. 2); "A furnace . . . will invariably break down . . ." (10); "Thereafter, they never work again" (13). (Students will, of course, find others.) Hyperbole establishes Baker's comic tone of exasperation.
4. His pseudoscientific classification, with its dogmatic assertion of the three categories of objects, is a parody of intellectual authority. The pseudophilosophical discussion of spiritual "peace" in the conclusion reinforces the essay's mock-serious tone.
5. Baker's little stories (the cunning automobile of paragraph 3, or paragraph 8's climbing pliers) capture the reader's attention. Shared experiences provide a sense of recognition and help make the essay funny.

QUESTIONS ON LANGUAGE

1. The vocabulary words highlighted here all contribute to the essay's mock-serious tone. In general, the essay's diction is quite simple.
2. Clever, malicious, plotting. Its effect is to personify the automobile.
3. The general terms make the shared experiences more universal. Had Baker used *I*, he might have seemed more of a crank, less persuasive.

RUSSELL BAKER ON WRITING

What do lead pencils, Shakespeare, eternal quests, cave writing, dreaming, Luddites, and cornpone politicians have to do with computers? In Russell Baker's fertile mind, everything and nothing. In addition to enjoying the fun of the piece, students may be interested in noting how he cleverly shows a mind in the act of composition. Stream-of-consciousness writing has been used more often in confessions, but with some behind-the-scenes crafting, Baker demonstrates its humorous potential.

ASHLEY HERZOG

College Classes for Conservatives to Avoid

Political columnist Ashley Herzog certainly likes to provoke, as this essay—written when she was a senior at Ohio University—makes unmistakably clear. Writing for the very conservative *Townhall.com*, Herzog puts forth her objections to the liberal politics typical on college campuses and seems to question the value of a liberal arts education in general. No matter your own students' political leanings, her complaints are sure to get a rise out of your class.

Discussion might open with the question that will be on many students' minds: What is the purpose of a college education? (See the journal prompt and the first writing suggestion.) Are your students in school simply to earn a degree or to gain a particular set of marketable skills, or have they enrolled for other reasons, such as developing critical-thinking abilities and enhancing their personal development? Is it worthwhile to study the liberal arts, or do more "practical" disciplines—such as math, science, or a technical trade—seem more useful? Should students really avoid classes that challenge their beliefs? Why, or why not?

QUESTIONS ON MEANING

1. Herzog's thesis and purpose are stated in paragraph 2: "As an Ohio University senior who has sat through plenty of college junk courses—many of which were required for graduation—I've compiled a list of classes for incoming freshmen to avoid." She is writing in the hope that she can spare incoming freshmen "from wasting their precious time and money on the politically correct, non-educational classes that have become so common on our campuses" (8). A secondary purpose, it seems, is to criticize those classes and question their worth.
2. She thinks it's worthless nonsense, even dangerous nonsense. Forms of political correctness Herzog cites include claims that some groups have experienced oppression (pars. 3, 5), revisionist history (4), "negative attitude[s] toward religion, law enforcement, morality, marriage, and families" (5), multiculturalism (6), and cultural relativism (6).

3. Herzog asserts that such classes are "non-educational" (pars. 1, 8) and thus a waste of money and time.

QUESTIONS ON WRITING STRATEGY

1. Herzog is writing for politically conservative college freshmen (and by extension, their parents), whom she assumes share her views and her hostility to liberal thought. She seems to expect that her readers object, especially, to political correctness and multiculturalism and that they are proud Americans (par. 6) who embrace traditional values such as "religion, law enforcement, morality, marriage, and families" (5). At the same time, Herzog assumes her readers are serious students who would rather work hard than "earn A's without putting forth any intellectual effort" (7).
2. She names her principle of classification in her title: "College Classes for Conservatives to Avoid." All of her groups list humanities and social sciences courses (or entire disciplines) that take an unabashedly liberal perspective.
3. We might summarize her categories as "Gender Studies" (par. 3), "Social History" (4), "Sociology" (5), "Cultural Studies," and "Popular Culture" (7). Students may well come up with their own terminology.
4. Herzog draws her examples from her own experience at Ohio University, from a published research study (par. 4), and from listed course titles at other schools (both of which, incidentally, were lambasted by the media at the time she wrote). Students will likely find her personal examples most effective, although some may point out that some of them—like her characterization of Howard Zinn's *A People's History of the United States*—seem suspect, or at least hyperbolic. Students might also notice that Herzog offers no examples to support her claims, in paragraph 5, about teachers' expectations of students in introductory-level sociology classes.

QUESTIONS ON LANGUAGE

1. Herzog comes across as hostile and condescending, even sarcastic. Some students might find this tone appropriate, but we would argue that it puts off any readers who don't already share her conservative point of view. A more moderate tone might win her more converts.
2. Cultural relativism is more or less the opposite of American exceptionalism. "Relativists" take the position that no one culture is inherently better or worse than another, but must be assessed in its own context. Herzog indicates that she finds this school of thought ridiculous by enclosing it in scare quotes, as she also does to distance herself from the concepts of "queer theory" (par. 1) and "sex/gender system" (par. 3). Other times she uses quotation marks to set off titles and words used as words.
3. By addressing her readers directly while bringing up her own experiences, Herzog makes it sound like she's having a heart-to-heart conversation with the reader—a senior counseling a freshman.
4. A *prism*, as Herzog uses the word, is a medium that distorts, not merely a lens. Her word choice here underscores her disapproval.

JEFF WISE

Deadly Mind Traps

Mixing academic psychology with a morbid sense of humor in this blog post turned essay, journalist Jeff Wise effectively offers practical tips for overcoming common cognitive errors while keeping his readers thoroughly entertained.

"Deadly Mind Traps" is one of several selections in this book that use humor, sometimes dark humor, to impart scientific information to a general audience. We point to one, Dan Koeppel's "Taking a Fall," in the writing suggestion labeled "Connections." Others include Jessica Mitford's "Behind the Formaldehyde Curtain" (p. 313), Dan Ariely's "Why We Lie" (p. 440), and Bonnie Berkowitz and Laura Stanton's "Roller Coasters: Feeling Loopy" (in the e-Pages, at *bedfordstmartins.com/thebedfordreader*). You might want to ask students what it is about hard science that leads some writers to look to irreverence as a way to hook readers in. And why do people writing about death (Wise, Koeppel, Mitford) so often turn to gallows humor? Are such attempts to amuse ever appropriate? Why do students think so?

QUESTIONS ON MEANING

1. Wise gives two reasons in paragraph 7: Altruism is a "deep-seated emotion" that is difficult to control to begin with, and in an emergency situation panic kicks in and causes irrational thinking. Essentially, instinct overpowers reason.
2. He cites our "irrational assessment of risks and rewards" (par. 12). Most people, Wise explains, would rather risk a large loss when there's a potential for gain than take a certain small loss. But they fail to consider the real possibility of losing when there's any chance for gain.
3. Situational blindness is "the failure to remain aware of one's environment" (par. 16), or not paying attention; confirmation bias, or "bending the map" (19), is the failure to recognize an incorrect theory or assumption in the face of new evidence. The terms come from psychology.
4. Wise is referring to the foreclosure crisis: the housing market collapse and credit meltdown caused by a rash of risky mortgage lending and securities bundling in the late 1990s and early 2000s. His point is that confirmation bias can affect enormous groups of people at once and cause widespread disaster.
5. If the limits were set for safety reasons, you could die. In less serious situations "redlining" (par. 28) simply causes people to lose their way and miss whatever goal the limits were meant to define.
6. Wise's thesis, stated in paragraph 3, is that potentially deadly cognitive errors generally fall into one of a few simple categories. His purpose is to inform readers of what those categories are and to show how an awareness of them can be applied to less harrowing aspects of daily life; he also means to entertain.

QUESTIONS ON WRITING STRATEGY

1. Absolutely. Even if readers won't ever find themselves in one of the life-or-death situations he recounts, Wise explains that the general concepts he delineates can be applied to everyday life and offers examples of such applications in the sections labeled "Avoid the trap."

2. Each category starts off with a brief, real-life narrative that illustrates the consequences of the error for one person or group of people, moves to an explanation of the psychological concept at hand, and ends with suggested real-life applications for the knowledge. We think the strategy is very effective: The stories are engaging, the explanations are clear and to the point, and the applications are practical and useful. Also, the predictable pattern pulls readers along and gives the essay unity and coherence.

3. It may interest students to know that in his first draft of this essay, published in his blog for *Psychology Today*, Wise used a different order and concluded with "Bending the Map." In this revised version he seems to order his categories of errors from those least to most likely to apply to readers' own lives. In essence, he starts with the most compelling point and ends with the most relevant one. Many readers will wish, however, that the essay didn't end quite as abruptly as it does.

4. Wise, a journalist, quotes experts in psychology to lend authority to his explanations and to give them a bit of extra color.

5. We'd say that "Deadly Mind Traps" is as much a cause-and-effect analysis as it is a classification. In each category of his essay, Wise identifies a specific type of cognitive error and examines both why it happens and what might result. Without the cause-and-effect analysis, his classification would seem a rather hollow exercise.

QUESTIONS ON LANGUAGE

1. Examples of colloquial language include the phrases "suck three buddies to their doom" (par. 1), "keeled over" (5), "no big deal" (11), and "in a hole" (13); the comments "take a breath" (4), "you'll be completely clueless about what to do next" (17), and "We look at clouds and see sheep" (19); and the casual vocabulary, such as "boneheaded" (2), "screwup" (3), and "bushwhacked" (21). Some students may like the playful tone for its humor and accessibility; others may find that it detracts from the seriousness of Wise's subject or inappropriately makes light of real human tragedies.

2. *Hydrogen sulfide*, a poisonous gas emitted by rotting organic matter and typically smelling of rotten eggs, is something of a euphemism for "sewer gas" in the context of Showalter's demise. It is heavier than air and thus tends to float just above its source.

3. Some metaphors: "autopilot" (par. 3), "mental traps from which there is no escape" (3), "blind faith" (16), "the human maze" (18), "Our minds are wired to find order in randomness" (19), and "windows of good weather can shut abruptly" (25). Some understatements: "mistakes best described as boneheaded" (2); "each one died in turn" (5); "another goes in after him, then another" (5); "a jump would cause serious injury at best" (11); "the gamble that he might be able to ride the gondola safely back to the ground seems preferable to a guaranteed pair of broken legs" (12); "In this particular case, the water had to be flowing uphill" (20); "it was too late" (26); and "Today his body remains where

he sat" (27). The metaphors, of course, bring freshness and vibrancy to Wise's prose. And as they often do, the understatements lend a sense of (dark) humor to his subject.

US CENSUS BUREAU

America's Foreign Born in the Last 50 Years

Immigration continues to be a contentious topic in American politics and culture, and this multilayered infographic from the US Census Bureau might help to explain, in part, why that is. Students may be surprised to learn that in their grandparents' time, most immigrants to the United States came from Europe, Canada, and the Soviet Union. Today, in contrast, foreign-born residents *look* foreign. They're also more likely to live next door.

To engage your students in the topic before they get into the data, you might begin discussion by focusing on their assumptions about recent immigrants. What, if anything, do they know about them, and what have they heard? Are they immigrants or children (or grandchildren) of immigrants themselves? Would they ever consider moving to another country? Why, or why not?

QUESTIONS ON MEANING AND STRATEGY

1. The first bar graph puts the immigrant population at 40 million. Some students may add up the numbers for the top ten countries of origin (23.8 million), but that graphic doesn't account for the total number of immigrants. The percentage has increased since 1960, from 5.4% to 12.9%. Interestingly, however, the percentage today is lower than it was at the beginning of the twentieth century (and for the second half of the nineteenth).

2. In this particular infographic the Census Bureau classifies immigrants by country of birth. The vast majority of foreign-born residents are from Latin America (Mexico, El Salvador, and Guatemala, as well as Cuba and the Dominican Republic), followed by Asia (China, India, the Philippines, Vietnam, and Korea). In contrast to the past, Europe accounts for a relatively small portion of immigrants today.

3. The West and the South have the most foreign-born residents today, with pockets in Florida and the Northeast (New York and New Jersey, especially). California, the Census Bureau reports, has the highest concentration of immigrants in the country, at 27% of the state's population.

4. The immigrant population today is far more diverse than it was half a century ago. Although most foreign-born residents in 1960 were white Europeans who shared a common cultural heritage with the native-born majority, now they tend to be Latino or Asian. They are younger (in their early forties, compared to late fifties), and they've settled across a broader swath of the United States.

11
CAUSE AND EFFECT
Asking Why

As you know, the matter of cause and effect can plunge a class into many complexities, and it can sometimes lead to fruitless wrangles. Still, many instructors find that this chapter leads to unusually satisfying results.

We start off with two complementary essays, Chitra Divakaruni's "Live Free and Starve" and student Marie Javdani's "*Plata o Plomo*: Silver or Lead" (Javdani's essay is documented), both examining effects of globalization. Then Dan Ariely's "Why We Lie" explains how small-scale cheating wreaks wide-scale damage, and Christopher Beam's "Blood Loss" considers inter-related trends in crime and journalism. Chris Anderson's "The Rise and Fall of the Hit" probes the effects of new technology and media on the business of popular culture. And in the e-Pages, Bonnie Berkowitz and Laura Stanton make clever use of Web technology to immerse readers in the physics of a roller-coaster ride.

We have endeavored to clarify the difference between process analysis and cause-and-effect analysis, a frequent source of confusion for students. Process asks *how*; cause and effect asks *why*. Further, process deals with events that are repeated or repeatable or even just theoretically repeatable (like the creation of the Grand Canyon); cause and effect deals with singular events, one-time happenings.

Studying cause and effect can lead to a discussion of common errors in reasoning, as we indicate in this chapter when we touch on the fallacy of *post hoc*. If you wish to bring up logical fallacies, a few are listed, defined, and illustrated in Chapter 13, on argument and persuasion (pp. 515–17). Perhaps it is enough at this point merely to call students' attention to them. Cause and effect may be complicated enough without trying to tackle logical fallacies at the same time.

CHITRA DIVAKARUNI

Live Free and Starve

Both Chitra Divakaruni's "Live Free and Starve" and the essay we pair it with, Marie Javdani's "*Plata o Plomo*," tackle globalization—specifically, the effects that policies or actions in the United States can have on those in the developing world.

Divakaruni focuses on the drastically limited choices of child laborers: If they don't work, even under terrible conditions, they starve. Divakaruni argues that Americans should not try to stop child labor abroad without also taking responsibility for the terrible deprivation that sends children into labor in the first place. That "without also" is crucial for students to understand: Divakaruni may show the unintended consequences of a bill banning goods produced with child labor, but she certainly does not argue *for* child labor. For readers inclined to favor US action on unjust labor practices and similar issues of human rights around the world, Divakaruni's paragraph 5 presents a warning not to evaluate others' situations from a strictly American perspective. In the end, the author suggests the kinds of measures Americans would need to take if they really want to help child laborers.

We have previously included Divakaruni's essay in the argument chapter, and it could still be taught as an argument. It provides an excellent chance to discuss emotional appeals. Ask students to mark places in the essay where Divakaruni works to touch the emotions of readers, and then in class spend some time at the board noting the relevant passages. Small groups of students could each analyze one of the passages: What beliefs and values does Divakaruni appeal to? How accurate is she in gauging her readers' sympathies? Do the appeals work to strengthen her argument? (If you would like students to write on Divakaruni's emotional appeals, see the fourth writing suggestion.)

QUESTIONS ON MEANING

1. Divakaruni wants to make her readers think with greater complexity about the solutions available—or not available—for the problem of child labor in developing countries. The title alerts the readers that the author's perspective is perhaps unusual. The brief paragraph 2 makes it clear that she disagrees with the House's solution. Then in paragraph 4 she begins to explain why.
2. Divakaruni's thesis is stated in paragraph 8: "A bill like the one we've just passed is of no use unless it goes hand in hand with programs that will offer a new life to these newly released children."
3. Third World countries are the developing nations of Asia, Africa, and Latin America. The term comes from the Cold War: The First and Second Worlds were the non-Communist and Communist industrialized nations.
4. Divakaruni means that most Americans have already met their survival needs (for "bread," as she puts it) and thus can afford the relative luxury of seeking freedom and other needs at the top of the pyramid.

5. The children lack "food and clothing and medication," there are no schools for them, their governments can't provide these things, and ultimately no one takes responsibility for them.

QUESTIONS ON WRITING STRATEGY

1. The rhetorical questions expand on the opening (thesis) sentence. They push readers to think hard about the negative effects the legislation could have on child laborers and to consider their willingness to "shoulder the responsibility" for the children when they are jobless.
2. Divakaruni explains in this paragraph how child labor affects children. The first words ("It is true that child labor is a terrible thing") establish the idea of the paragraph, and the remainder concisely itemizes the effects.
3. In telling the detailed story of one child, Divakaruni grounds her essay in a specific case. She establishes her authority as an observer of child labor abroad, and an open-eyed and sympathetic observer at that. Though Nimai had a life that was "hardly a desirable existence for a child," he still was better off, Divakaruni contends, than the nonworking children in his village.

QUESTIONS ON LANGUAGE

1. The survival of the families is so borderline that caring for their own children could ruin them.
2. The words show compassion—"ribs sticking out," "hunger was too much to bear," "ate whatever they could find," "knew they'd be beaten for it."
3. *Blithe* has roots in Old Saxon, Middle Dutch, Old High German, and Old Norse. It earlier referred to the outward expression of a kindly feeling but has come to mean "heedless or careless, unaware of the full implications of an act."

CHITRA DIVAKARUNI ON WRITING

For Divakaruni, social activism broadens and sensitizes her and is thus a boon to her writing. Our questions prompt students to consider just what a writer gains from having her or his "preconceptions" challenged and from understanding the lives of others. The questions could open up a discussion of critical thinking, not just about others' ideas but about one's own as well.

MARIE JAVDANI

Plata o Plomo: Silver or Lead

Paired with the previous essay—Chitra Divakaruni's look at child labor in developing countries—this essay focuses on another problem that affects children in the Third World: drug production and trafficking. In a good ex-

ample of student research writing, Marie Javdani explores the plight of Colombian peasants caught between rebels who finance their cause through
drug trafficking and government-condoned forces who battle the rebels. Extensive financial aid to the Colombian government from the United States has
done little to stem the production and flow of drugs from the country, largely
because of government corruption. Javdani argues that US money would be
better spent drastically reducing US demand for drugs, which would, in turn,
significantly decrease the profitability of the drug trade and thus improve the
situation in places like Colombia.

Students may be surprised by the connection Javdani makes between
young Americans' use of illegal drugs and the death of a young Colombian.
Class discussion might focus on this connection, which brings the abstractions of globalization down to concrete cases. Do students accept the connection? Do they accept Javdani's conclusion that Americans have a responsibility to change their own behavior in order to help improve conditions in
developing countries?

QUESTIONS ON MEANING

1. Javdani states her thesis at the end of paragraph 3, forecasting the organization of the essay. In paragraphs 4–7 she describes "what's happening in drug-source countries," in paragraphs 8–9 she covers "how the
   United States can and cannot help there," and in paragraphs 10–11 she
   makes a case for "what, instead, can be done at home."
2. Many peasants fear the government more than the rebels, in part because the rebels can provide protection from the government, whereas
   the government provides little protection from the rebels. Also, the
   peasants evidently receive money from the rebel drug lords to farm
   coca.
3. As Javdani writes in paragraph 8, money used to eradicate coca fields
   has "alienated peasants" and "escalated violence," and money intended
   to "help peasants establish alternative crops" and further legitimate police efforts has wound up helping arm paramilitary forces or simply dis-
   appearing. Javdani argues that greater efforts must be made to reduce
   the US market for drugs.

QUESTIONS ON WRITING STRATEGY

1. Students may have different thoughts about Javdani's intended audience, but in her final paragraph she clearly appeals to people her own
   age to recognize the extent to which their use of and tolerance for drug
   use in this country has harmful effects elsewhere. Javdani wrote the
   essay in a freshman writing class, so she may have had in mind an audience of her classmates.
2. Javdani's sympathies seem to lie with the Colombian peasants. For evidence, students might point to her opening description of Miguel and
   her discussion throughout of the Colombians' plight and the atrocities
   they face.
3. Javdani's extensive use of sources backs up her claims and gives her
   writing authority. The source citations are particularly effective in the
   detailed descriptions of the situation in Colombia.
4. The contrast Javdani sets up in her opening paragraphs is between a
   suburban teenager scoring drugs in the United States and a peasant boy
   facing execution because of his family's resistance to drug trafficking in

Colombia. She creates a connection between the two that she returns to in her conclusion: It is the demand for drugs in the United States, typified by Eric, that endangers peasants in Colombia, typified by Miguel.

QUESTIONS ON LANGUAGE

1. The phrase "between a rock and a hard place" means being stuck between two equally bad choices with no alternative. The peasants can either work with the government and face torture and execution by the rebel drug lords or work with the drug lords and face the same fate from government-condoned paramilitary forces.
2. Javdani writes that Eric lives in a "suburban paradise" and yet still faces the "stress of homework and ex-girlfriends"; obviously, she intends readers to see his life as not terribly stressful at all and certainly not an excuse to use drugs. Students should see immediately that Javdani has no sympathy for Eric.
3. The peasants are "traitors" to one side or the other no matter what their choice, so they are not literally traitors, and the "cooperation" the peasants are accused of is not voluntary but forced, so it is not literally cooperation.
4. *Guerilla* comes from the Spanish word for war, *guerra*, with the diminutive ending *-illa*; it might be translated literally as "small war." The word was coined in the early nineteenth century to describe the Spanish resistance movement against the French regime established by Napoleon Bonaparte. The Spanish word for "guerilla fighter" is *guerillero*, but in English *guerilla* has long referred to those who participate in guerilla warfare, as well as to the warfare itself.

MARIE JAVDANI ON WRITING

Javdani offers much useful advice for other student writers. We emphasize her counsel to care about one's topic because inexperienced writers, especially reluctant ones, often don't make the effort to find their own angle on a subject. We also like Javdani's warning that interest doesn't justify the speechifying of a soapbox orator: Moderation is the key.

DAN ARIELY
Why We Lie

In this accessible and compelling overview of his own scholarly research, renowned behavioral economist Dan Ariely challenges accepted models of human decision making and proposes a new understanding of both why people lie and how they might be persuaded to be more honest. A glance through the comments on the *Wall Street Journal's* Web site reveals that readers can easily misinterpret Ariely's ideas if they don't read carefully. Students, too, might be surprised by Ariely's apparent acceptance that most people lie, if only "just by a little." You might wish, then, to begin discussion with the question of Ariely's purpose (the first question on meaning). Far from justifying or condoning such behavior, as some might think, Ariely seeks to put a stop to it.

When assigning Ariely's essay, you could also conduct an exercise to make his point concrete for students. Set a timer, and ask them to solve the puzzle on page 442. How long does it take them? Do they think they could solve four such puzzles in five minutes? Can they understand why most test participants cheated?

Some longer works on Ariely's topic are *Lying: Moral Choice in Public and Private Life,* by Sissela Bok (1978); the title essay in *On Lies, Secrets, and Silence,* by Adrienne Rich (1979); and of course Ariely's *The (Honest) Truth about Dishonesty: How We Lie to Everyone—Especially Ourselves* (2012), from which this piece is adapted. Students who enjoy Ariely's voice and would like to hear his suggestions for overcoming procrastination when facing a writing assignment or similar task could be directed to his video comments on the subject at *bigthink.com/users/danariely.*

QUESTIONS ON MEANING

1. Ariely is writing mainly to examine the implications of his research and to use them to propose a better way to prevent dishonesty.
2. As Ariely explains in paragraphs 4–5, cost-benefit analysis is the mental practice of weighing potential benefits of an action against the potential risks. Although it is "the traditional, rational model of human behavior" (5) that most people assume drives decision making, Ariely stresses that his research has shown the model is wrong. Efforts to prevent cheating by raising the potential costs (fines, punishments, shame, and so forth) are therefore doomed to fail.
3. By testing multiple variables with the "matrix task" (par. 5), Ariely and his colleagues discovered several factors that increase the likelihood of dishonesty: "making the prospect of a monetary payoff more 'distant,' in psychological terms" (11), witnessing another person cheating (12), a weak sense of ethics (13), mental depletion (13), and a belief that the dishonesty will benefit others (13). The infographic on p. 445 lists additional factors: "ability to rationalize, conflicts of interest, creativity, previous immoral acts, being depleted, others benefiting from our dishonesty, watching others behave dishonestly, culture that gives examples of dishonesty." A reduced "probability of getting caught" (9), surprisingly, is not a factor.
4. Ariely suggests that reminding people of morality before they may be tempted to lie is the best way to prevent dishonesty, and he is guardedly optimistic that "[s]uch tricks" (par. 22) could have wide-ranging effects. Although he acknowledges that his suggested tactic won't prevent "flagrant misbehaviors" (25), he insists that it would, indeed, prevent most people from cheating "just by a little" (22) when the opportunity arises.
5. Ariely hints at his thesis early in the essay, with "it is this kind of small-scale mass cheating, not the high-profile cases, that is most corrosive to society" (par. 4). He previews his solution in the middle, when he first says "simply being reminded of moral codes has a significant effect on how we view our own behavior" (17). He then continues building to his thesis, which he states in his conclusion: "All of this means that, although it is obviously important to pay attention to flagrant

misbehaviors, it is probably even more important to discourage the small and more ubiquitous forms of dishonesty—the misbehavior that affects all of us, as both perpetrators and victims" (25).

QUESTIONS ON WRITING STRATEGY

1. Ariely's mix of academic and colloquial diction, along with his examples from business, sports, culture, and politics, reveal that he is writing for a general audience of educated readers who are interested in the psychology of human behavior. Presumably he counts researchers, insurance administrators, bankers, the IRS, and his study participants among the "perpetrators and victims" of "the misbehavior that affects all of us" (par. 25).

2. Paragraphs 4–9 report the results of Ariely's matrix experiments to establish that most people cheat on a small scale, 10–14 examine the causes of that cheating, and 15–21 explore an idea for making people more honest. Ariely gives the essay unity by ensuring that each section is clearly introduced with a transitional topic sentence (or question) that establishes its relation to his thesis. And the repetition of certain key words and phrases (see question 3 on language)—such as *dishonesty*, *cheat*, *lie*, and, most notably, *just by a little*—adds to the essay's coherence.

3. The joke previews the moral of Ariely's story, so to speak, and offers a nice transition to his proposed solution. As he explains, the joke "suggests . . . that simply being reminded of moral codes has a significant effect on how we view our own behavior" (par. 17). Repeating it also lets the author inject some humor into his essay.

4. The matrix presents an example of the puzzle Ariely challenged his research subjects to solve and helps readers visualize what might otherwise be an abstract concept. The infographic summarizes in clear visual form both the causes of dishonesty and the proposed solution that Ariely outlines in his essay.

5 The anecdote encapsulates Ariely's main point, or, as he puts it, "captures rather nicely our society's misguided efforts to deal with dishonesty" (par. 1). The idea that we lock our doors to keep honest people honest offers a nice metaphor for Ariely's moral-reminder solution, and so he circles back to it in his conclusion.

QUESTIONS ON LANGUAGE

1. Examples of colloquial language include "just by a little" and "just by a bit" (pars. 4, 7, 9, 10, 23, 24), "a simple little experiment" (5), "something funny happens" (7), "putting more money on the line" (8), "mini-Madoff" (12), and "the 'What the hell' effect" (13). Among Ariely's figures of speech are the understatement "Unable to get the IRS to give our theory a go in the real world" (20) and the metaphors (verging on clichés) "a few bad apples spoil the bunch" (3), "in a nutshell" (4), "waltz away with a wad of cash" (12), "balancing act" (13), "game the system" (24), and "grease the psychological skids" (25). Such language lends authenticity to Ariely's voice and makes his ideas more accessible, although some readers may find it inconsistent with an academic subject and purpose.

2. *Integrity*, from the Latin *integer*, "whole" or "complete," can refer to a state of being complete or undivided (as in the integrity of a geometric form) or to a condition that is sound or unimpaired (as in the integrity

of a mechanical system). Ariely uses it in its more common sense of "adherence to a code of moral or ethical values."

3. *Cheat* and *lie* are harsh synonyms for *dishonesty*; they connote judgment. *Just by a little,* on the other hand, implies self-delusive rationalization. Repeating the terms as much as he does lets Ariely underscore his main idea: that the accumulation of minor transgressions among the bulk of the population poses a greater problem than the major frauds that usually capture people's attention.

CHRISTOPHER BEAM

Blood Loss

Prompted to write by the lackluster media response to a serial killer's conviction and sentencing, Christopher Beam comes up with an interesting theory to explain a decline in serial killings over the past few decades. Drawing on examples of sensational crimes throughout the twentieth century (and the early twenty-first), he concludes that we are most caught up with those misdoings that tap into generalized anxieties. Ignored by the media because more pressing concerns have moved to the forefront of the national consciousness, serial killers have less incentive to do what they do. And in their place, it seems, we have an epidemic of mass murders.

Students may have a hard time accepting Beam's suggestion that media coverage contributes to the incidence of some types of crime. The author is, after all, a crime reporter. You may want to begin discussion by asking the class to recall examples of recent "media frenzies" over sensational crimes. What elements do the big stories have in common? Did the perpetrators, in fact, seem to want the notoriety their actions brought them? Could they have been motivated by a desire for fame? If so, what responsibility do the media bear for their actions?

QUESTIONS ON MEANING

1. As the structure of the essay suggests, Beam has a dual purpose: to report that serial killings have declined significantly since their peak in the 1980s, and to propose a theory explaining why. In the first four paragraphs he establishes the fact of the trend, showing that the number of serial murders has dropped dramatically, and with it the public's fascination with serial killers. The next two paragraphs examine possible explanations for the drop but dismiss them, and the remainder of the essay develops the idea, introduced in paragraph 7, that media coverage of serial killers "tapped into the obsessions and fears of the time."
2. Beam assumes an audience of true-crime buffs, it seems. At the very least, he expects that readers will have a passing knowledge of the events and cases he cites, whether recent or historic. Even if they don't, however, Beam's interest is not in the individual crimes but in their accumulation and their cultural symbolisms. The details are not necessary to get his point across.

3. Yes, he does. Beam suggests a correlation between sensational crimes
    and media coverage, claiming that the "short path to celebrity" offered
    by the "media's growing obsession with serial killers in the 1970s and
    '80s" (par. 5) helped to fuel such killings. He adds, in paragraph 7, that
    one serial killer (David Berkowitz) went as far as to contact the news
    media directly. His point seems to be that by sensationalizing certain
    kinds of crimes, the media give criminals an added incentive to commit
    them.

4. Beam's thesis is that the crimes that attract the most media attention
    are those that resonate with or somehow symbolize prevailing cultural
    fears—such as kidnappings and "societal decay during the Depression"
    (par. 9), serial murders by "sex-addled psychopaths" (7) in the 1970s
    and 1980s, and terrorism today. Serial killings don't capture our atten-
    tion anymore because we're worried about "instant mass annihilation"
    (11). He comes closest to stating his general idea in paragraph 9: "Infa-
    mous crimes almost always needle the anxieties of their periods."

QUESTIONS ON WRITING STRATEGY

1. The gruesome details in Beam's story about an archetypal serial killer
    grab readers' interest. That the "crossbow cannibal" was more or less
    ignored by the media starts the essay on an ironic note and sets up
    Beam's claim that serial killers murder partly for the media attention.

2. Beam uses the word *structural* in its sense of "related to or concerned
    with systematic structure in a particular field of study" (*The American
    Heritage Dictionary*). His point in paragraph 5 is that serial killings
    didn't necessarily increase in the 1970s and 1980s: It's possible, he ac-
    knowledges, that they were simply better documented. But as he goes
    on to say in paragraph 6, that questionable cause-and-effect relation-
    ship is not relevant to his inquiry. Regardless of whether or not there
    was an actual rise in serial killings four decades ago, the number has
    declined since then.

3. In paragraph 6 Beam considers the possibility that police work and
    longer jail terms for captured killers might have contributed to the de-
    cline in serial killings. But he has a different explanation: He suggests
    that serial killings have dropped off the radar because the public isn't
    as fascinated by them as it once was, giving "psychopaths" (par. 7) less
    reason to kill.

4. The statistics support Beam's claim that "serial murders peaked in the
    1980s and have been declining ever since" (par. 4). Readers may rea-
    sonably question their reliability: The data were gathered by a single
    scholar and represent cases reported in popular sources. But there is
    little other data available, according to Beam.

5. Beam cites James Alan Fox's definition in paragraph 4: "a string of four
    or more homicides committed by one or a few perpetrators that spans
    a period of days, weeks, months, or even years." He also identifies the
    first recorded instance of "serial murderer" (as cited in *The Oxford En-
    glish Dictionary*) and the source of the synonym "serial killer" (it was
    coined by an FBI agent in 1981) in paragraph 8.

QUESTIONS ON LANGUAGE

1. Beam uses complex, formal words and phrases—such as *incarcera-
    tion* and *caveat* (par. 6), *conversely* (10), "structural explanations for

the rise of reported serial murders" (5), and "As the raw numbers have declined" (7)—alongside colloquial expressions, including "just aren't the sensation they used to be" (1), "hard to come by" (4), and "returned the favor" (8). The informal language helps him connect with readers and build a casual tone; the formal language emphasizes that he has studied his subject thoroughly and takes his argument seriously.

2. "Golden boy" carries with it a sense of resentment for somebody who appears to be perfect; it also implies that such a person is an insincere sycophant. Applied to Ted Bundy, a wealthy political supporter, the term also hints at Americans' distrust of the greedy and powerful in the 1980s.

3. Beam uses *needle* as a transitive verb ("needle the anxieties of their periods"), whereas students may know it only as a noun (a sewing implement). The informal use creates a compelling image, implying both a prick of conscience and the lethal injection of a death sentence.

CHRIS ANDERSON
The Rise and Fall of the Hit

Chris Anderson's essay explains a major change in the way consumers relate to the popular culture of movies, television, and especially music. The blockbuster, Anderson claims, is virtually a thing of the past because the Internet and other technological innovations make it possible for businesses to respond to our individual interests and that kind of response is, in turn, what we now demand.

To good effect, we think, Anderson delays fully stating his thesis until near the end of the essay. He first establishes that change has occurred by providing sales figures and other statistics for the music business (pars. 1–4), and he offers explanations for the change, from file-sharing networks to failed marketing (5–10). Then he traces the rise of popular culture from the Industrial Revolution to the 1990s (11–20). Only in his final two paragraphs does he tie together "the rise and fall of the hit" by pointing to the Internet as the primary cause.

Undoubtedly, at least some of your students will have firsthand experience with the revolution Anderson describes. If they're old enough to remember when popular music was dominated by a few radio stations and record stores, ask them to discuss the differences between then and now. (Some of the writing suggestions after the essay could help get this conversation going.)

QUESTIONS ON MEANING

1. Anderson suggests his thesis in paragraph 5: "[T]he traditional model of marketing and selling music no longer works. . . . We are witnessing the end of an era." But he states the thesis fully only in the first few sentences of paragraph 21. Restated briefly, the thesis might read: The Internet has inverted the former top-down dissemination of popular

culture so that people's individual interests, rather than corporations, determine what gets seen and heard.

2. Anderson is making the point that popular culture, as it was defined beginning in the late nineteenth century and until around the year 2000, resulted from technological advances that began in the Industrial Revolution: railroads, printing, photography, the phonograph, movies, and so on. The latest technological innovations—computers and the Internet—both intensify the consumption of popular culture and, almost paradoxically, return us to niches—now based on interests rather than on geography.

3. The "water-cooler effect" refers to workers gathering at the office water cooler to discuss "a shared cultural event." The "virtual" water cooler is of course online. Instead of bringing people together to discuss what the TV networks decided they should watch, it brings together people who share interests.

4. Anderson seems to want readers to recognize and also to feel excited and empowered by their ability to escape from "the tyranny of the top" (par. 21). As he writes in paragraph 5, "There has never been a better time to be an artist or a fan." In his final sentence he transfers the power to decide "who will win" from those "big players in the distribution system" to his readers ("You do"). His purpose is both to inform readers of their options and to encourage them to take advantage of them.

QUESTIONS ON WRITING STRATEGY

1. Anderson wants to make the point in his opening that pop-music packaging and marketing reached an apotheosis with the huge sales of this 2000 release. As he goes on to show, the album's performance has not been equaled and may never be. NSync's success marked "the end of an era" (par. 5).

2. Anderson explains some causes for the decline in record sales in paragraphs 6–8: file-sharing networks, CD burning and trading, and the ability to purchase single tracks online. Paragraphs 9 and 10 offer causes for the decline in rock radio ratings: market fragmentation and competition, homogeneity, and cell phones and iPods. Paragraphs 11–22 discuss technological developments that led to the expansion of mass popular culture—greater mobility, improved commercial printing technology, the invention of photography, the phonograph, and movies. Finally, paragraphs 21 and 22 show how the Internet is changing the way culture is transmitted.

3. This question relates to the fourth question on meaning about Anderson's purpose: Anderson sees his audience as active participants in the changes he writes about.

4. Students should note Anderson's use of examples in paragraphs 1, 3, 6–8, 14–16, 18, and 19. In each case the examples help clarify how and why the blockbuster increased or declined.

QUESTIONS ON LANGUAGE

1. Examples of words used to describe mass marketing: "all about looks and scripted personalities" and "The music itself . . . hardly mattered" (par. 1); "manufactured pop" (4); "a packaged act" (7); "cookie-cutter playlists" (9); "tyranny of the top" (21); and "monopoly" (22). The

language suggests that Anderson sees such marketing as stifling, uncreative, and undemocratic.

2. The italics for *free* emphasize just how unbelievable (or "mind-blowing," as Anderson puts it) it was that the earliest broadcast media cost consumers nothing.

3. Some uses of *culture* or a variation: "limited the mixing of cultures" (par. 11); "vehicles for carrying common culture" (12); "hives of commerce," "powerful engine of new culture," and "mass media" (13); "the first great wave of pop culture" (14); "potent carriers of culture" (15); "gregarious" and "celebrity age" (16); "broadcast media" and "vehicle for stardom" (17); "television took over" (18); "a shared cultural event" (19); "the great American unifier" and "mainstream" (20). This language adds cohesion to Anderson's discussion, keeping clearly in the reader's mind the change he is describing.

4. On an à-la-carte restaurant menu (from French for "by the bill of fare"), each item is priced separately. Anderson uses *à la carte* figuratively to refer to the purchase of individual songs.

CHRIS ANDERSON ON WRITING

Anderson's thoughts on the diminished roles of "traditional gatekeepers" like himself are remarkable for not being self-protective: Evidently, he welcomes the upending of culture even at the risk of losing his own job. We hope students will find encouragement in Anderson's words and take advantage of the Internet's openness for their own self-expression.

BONNIE BERKOWITZ AND LAURA STANTON
Roller Coasters: Feeling Loopy

As print journalism struggles to survive in the early twenty-first century, online editions of newspapers have become almost mandatory. Bonnie Berkowitz and Laura Stanton worked together to create "Roller Coasters: Feeling Loopy" for the Web version of the *Washington Post*, one of the most respected and enduring newspapers in the United States (perhaps tellingly, it was purchased by *Amazon* founder and CEO Jeff Bezos in 2013). The benefits of online technology are evident in their interactive graphic, which relies on the viewer to click the play button in the center of a roller coaster to virtually travel through the ride and get information about popular features and their effects along the way.

Berkowitz and Stanton are not, of course, physicists, doctors, or roller-coaster experts: They rely on data and information from others. You might want to spend some time in class evaluating the credibility of the sources they list below the graphic. Given the emphasis that roller coasters are safer than they seem, what kinds of expertise seem most reliable? Do students detect any potential bias from the authors' sources? Does such bias detract from the effectiveness of the graphic's central point? Why, or why not?

QUESTIONS ON MEANING AND STRATEGY

1. The graphic's primary purpose is informative, with an objective focus on the most popular features built into modern roller coasters and the physical effects they have on riders. (The section below the coaster provides additional information for readers interested in coaster innovations.) Students might note that the authors use simple language and graphics to make the information presented easy to understand. "Roller Coasters: Feeling Loopy" also makes a subtle argument that roller coasters are safe despite what riders may experience or what readers may assume; the persuasive element is reinforced by the use of expert sources for evidence (particularly the early quotation from coaster designer Rob Decker) as well as the playful, even childlike, tone used to impart the information.

2. Individual causes and effects are explained in each of the seven stages depicted in the interactive graphic: (1) rapid acceleration ("linear G-force") pushes riders' cheeks and bodies backward; (2) steep drops intensify the effects of gravity ("positive G-force"), pushing blood toward riders' feet and creating a sense of heaviness; (3) the effect of circling through loops ("centripetal force") keeps riders in their seats even though they're upside-down; (4) the initial descent after a hill counteracts gravity ("negative G-force"), temporarily causing internal organs to shift position and blood to rush upward; (5) deceptive visual cues induce "fear and adrenaline," increasing riders' heart rates; (6) sharp turns ("lateral G-force") push riders to the outside of a car and may cause injury if not tempered by banking of the track; and (7) the cumulative effect of multiple unfamiliar motions sometimes causes a stomach valve to release, making a rider nauseous.

3. Berkowitz and Stanton use a combination of division or analysis and process analysis to organize the causes and effects of the imagined coaster ride, with their principle of analysis being the physics behind common design features and what they do to the human body. While there is a clear beginning, middle, and end to their interactive graphic, the parts in the middle are not chronological because the design features appear in varying order on actual roller coasters: Drops, banks, loops, crests, and so forth do not necessarily occur in the order described by the graphic.

4. Terms such as *positive G-force*, *lateral G-force*, *negative G-force*, and *centripetal force* may be unfamiliar to a general audience, but Berkowitz and Stanton use simple language and clever illustration to ensure that the scientific terms are adequately defined for their purposes (see the answer to question 2, above). Interested readers should have no trouble grasping the basic concepts and how they apply to the experience of a typical roller-coaster ride. Notice in particular the authors' animated definition for stage 3, in which the path of a bird in flight clearly shows the difference between a circular loop and a clothoid loop. If any students complain that the concepts are unclear, you might ask them to examine the stages in question more closely or to consider what might have been lost if the graphic didn't include the technical language.

12
DEFINITION
Tracing Boundaries

"When they come to definition," said the late Richard Beal, an author of textbooks, a director of composition, and our sage adviser, "most authors of rhetorically organized readers seem not to know what it is nor what to do about it."

Definition, he suggested, is not in itself a distinct and separate expository method, but a catchall name for a kind of explaining that involves whatever method or methods it can use. It would break with tradition, Beal said, to place definition last among methods of exposition. Then the instructor might use it to review all the rest.

We hope that this ordering of the book's contents proves useful to you. You will also find the book carefully distinguishing a short definition (the kind found in a dictionary), a stipulative definition (the kind that pins down an essential term in a paragraph or two), and extended definition (the kind found in whole essays).

All the essays in this chapter trace the shape of a definite territory and attempt to set forth its nature. In the paired selections, Gloria Naylor and Christine Leong demonstrate how words change meanings in different contexts: Each explores the alterations in a derogatory word for her race depending on who uses it. (As a bonus, Leong, a student, responds directly to Naylor—thus modeling a common writing assignment.) Meghan Daum takes issue with popular usage of *narcissist*, insisting on the value of the psychological term's clinical meaning. Barbara Kingsolver defines what *rural* means to people like her, who live far from urban centers. Augusten Burroughs strives to help victims of domestic abuse learn to love themselves. And in the e-Pages, graphic artist Schroeder Jones offers a useful explanation of a misunderstood minority.

GLORIA NAYLOR
The Meanings of a Word

Focusing on the highly charged word *nigger*, Naylor maintains that context determines interpretation. Many students will disagree with this assertion, arguing that language carries its own meaning, so it might be useful to open up this issue right away. Students will certainly agree that saying something like "It was all my fault" carries a completely different meaning depending on whether it is uttered with sincerity or with sarcasm. Can students think of other instances when they have relied on inflection to convey meaning? Have they manipulated language — through exaggerations or half-truths, for example — for their own benefit? William Lutz's "The World of Doublespeak" (p. 389) provides another perspective on how we can (and often do) twist language to suit ourselves.

Part of Naylor's point, too, is that speech can be more precise (or more nuanced) than writing. How do writers overcome (or try to overcome) the limitations of written language? Students can explore the connections among tone, context, and meaning. Give groups fifteen or twenty minutes to look over essays they have already read this semester, in search of sentences, ideas, or passages that might be easily misinterpreted if read out of context. (It will be helpful if you read aloud a few examples as models. Promising examples appear in Anna Quindlen's "Homeless," Chap. 6, and Jessica Mitford's "Behind the Formaldehyde Curtain," Chap. 8.) Have students identify different interpretations for an isolated excerpt as well as interpretations for the excerpt when considered in the context of the entire selection. After each group explains its examples, the class will be better prepared for a discussion of writing strategies and/or Naylor's sense of the multiple meanings of language.

QUESTIONS ON MEANING

1. Written language, with less inflection and immediacy, doesn't offer the variety and richness of spoken language.
2. This was the first time it sounded offensive, so it was the first time she was shocked enough to really notice — "hear" — it.
3. They took a derogatory term and redefined it, gaining power from using it as a form both of praise and of informed condemnation rather than simply as a term of prejudice.
4. She wants to show how the meanings of a word change with the context in which it is used. (See the next question.)

QUESTIONS ON WRITING STRATEGY

1. Naylor holds that spoken language is richer and more powerful than written language and that the power of words derives from their context. The rest of the essay presents examples of these assertions in uses of *nigger*. To us, the opening is a bit flat and perhaps unnecessary: The assertions are well made through the examples. But some students may appreciate the initial overview.

2. Paragraphs 3, 14, and 15 discuss racist uses of the term: They sandwich nonracist uses, as the African American experience is sandwiched by racism. At the same time, the discussion of nonracist uses is longer, emphasizing the positive. The two definitions come together in paragraphs 14–15, in which Naylor sums up the nonracist uses and distinguishes them from the racist uses.
3. These last sentences make clear that despite the empowering use of the word within her family and community, her mother knows Naylor will face more uses of the word in a racist context. It also suggests a protective bond between Naylor and her mother.
4. They suggest how the word might be used in a sentence, so that the audience can get a sense of different inflections. Through them Naylor tries to add a spoken component to written language.

QUESTIONS ON LANGUAGE

1. The old question is "Which came first, the chicken or the egg?" This debate helps Naylor show the circular ways that language and reality influence one another.
2. They identify, respectively, a sex-crazed woman and a person sexually interested in corpses. Both connote perversion, twistedness. Naylor uses the words to emphasize the unfamiliarity of *nigger*, but she implies with them just how venomous was the little boy's insult.
3. The religious connotations of *mecca* suggest a sense of reverence for a place that offers a retreat from daily strife. The word can be understood both in a religious sense (a spiritual center in Islam) and in a secular sense (a center for people who share a common interest). Describing the grandmother's house as a *mecca* identifies it as a safe and spiritual gathering place.

GLORIA NAYLOR ON WRITING

Naylor's remarks could fuel a discussion about the literary canon—what's included, what's excluded, who decides. Naylor turned a perceived disadvantage, a dearth of "approved" African American literature, into an advantage by deciding to help right the wrong herself. When she says she attempts to "articulate experiences that want articulating," she evokes many silenced forebears.

CHRISTINE LEONG

Being a Chink

Leong's essay is clearly modeled on Gloria Naylor's "The Meanings of a Word." Like Naylor, Leong explores the power to be gained from refusing to allow words, especially those originally intended as demeaning or offensive, to have fixed meanings. For students who resist the idea that language is flexible and that context often determines meaning, you might wish to consider some of the suggestions and questions we pose in the introduction to Naylor's essay.

Deborah Tannen's "But What Do You Mean?" (p. 379) is another interesting counterpart to this essay; both discuss ways that communication relies on mutual assumptions about the meanings of words. In clusters of three or four, students could brainstorm a list of groups that have "private" language. (Students may need to be reminded that groups may be defined not just by race, ethnicity, or gender, but also by age, occupation, marital status, education, hobby, and so on.) How does knowing the private language create a position of power for a speaker or a listener?

QUESTIONS ON MEANING

1. Leong explains *chink* in paragraph 10: a label that describes specific external characteristics but not internal ones.
2. For this group of friends the word has become a way to comfort each other by acknowledging the way they have all had to deal with racism (par. 11).
3. Her purpose is the last one listed: Although her essay does both of the other things to some degree, Leong wants to show the reader how the flexible nature of language allows for power through redefining racist terms. You know this from the conjunction of her first and last paragraphs.

QUESTIONS ON WRITING STRATEGY

1. Both essays have an introduction on language and meaning, a story that starts "I remember the first time . . . ," and a conclusion that explains the power in co-opting racist terms. Leong places her experiences in the context of racist issues generally and of Naylor's reading of them specifically.
2. Leong builds suspense as she sifts through the trash. Ending with the envelope accomplishes several things: The envelope is both grouped with other forgotten rubbish and set apart by its racist inscription.
3. This example sets up the parallel between Naylor's family's redefinition of *nigger* and Leong's redefinition of *chink*, enhancing Leong's explanation of the way she and her friends dealt with the label and their reasons for doing so.
4. To make clear that they are consciously subverting the original meaning of *chink* and not misunderstanding it.
5. She assumes the slur is directed at her father, and she is outraged on his behalf.

QUESTIONS ON LANGUAGE

1. Words like "imposed," "small," "weak," "insignificant," "paralyze," and "belittle" all suggest that racist language is debilitating.
2. This characterization of their use of *chink* suggests affection, gentleness, and mutual understanding, almost like a nickname—all of which are in contrast to racist uses.
3. Students should notice how careful Leong is with the language of labels: In terms of both race and gender, she is very politic, using "Cau-

casian" instead of "white," and "human" or "person" instead of "man." You might ask students how this care contributes to her essay's message.

CHRISTINE LEONG ON WRITING

Leong's insistence on the writer's personal involvement in writing is refreshing, especially coming from a student. Your students may be surprised by Leong's assertion that inspiration counts more than grammar and sense in reaching readers. With "Being a Chink" and her comments on writing—both not only correct but sensible—Leong makes a strong case for clarity informed by passion.

MEGHAN DAUM

Narcissist—Give It a Rest

In Greek mythology Narcissus was a handsome Greek youth who, as punishment for ignoring the advances of the nymph Echo, was made to fall in love with his own image. He then pined away, changing into the flower that bears his name. *Narcissism* has come to mean excessive self-love, and Daum has a problem with that. In this column abridged from the *Los Angeles Times*, she examines popular usage of the word, explains why such usage is inappropriate, and begs people to stop.

Students may not catch the significance of this essay's timing and context, although Daum hints at it in paragraph 5. She published "Narcissist—Give It a Rest" about a month after the American Psychiatric Association announced the controversial decision to drop narcissistic personality disorder from the latest edition of the *Diagnostic and Statistical Manual of Mental Disorders*, or DSM-V, psychologists' official catalog of mental illness. We point that out in the writing suggestion labeled "Critical Writing" and encourage students to learn why the decision sparked debate.

QUESTIONS ON MEANING

1. Daum asserts that the misuse of the word began in the 1970s and by the 1990s became so overused as to become meaningless, apparently dropping out of popular use in the first decade of the twenty-first century. As she sees it, however, people have just recently begun flinging it around again as an insult, giving "the impression that they just discovered it" (par. 3) when in fact it's been around for decades.
2. Daum's essay goes beyond defining *narcissist*. She is writing to explain how others use the word inappropriately, to complain vocally about the misuse, and to implore people to stop.
3. Daum divides her thesis between paragraphs 5 and 7: "The term has been misused and overused so flagrantly that it's now all but meaningless when it comes to labeling truly destructive tendencies. . . . So

perhaps it's time to declare a moratorium on the indiscriminate use of this particular n-word."

QUESTIONS ON WRITING STRATEGY

1. The "[p]rofessional pundits . . . , bloggers, politicians, religious leaders, celebrity shrinks, cultural critics, Internet commenters and blowhards at parties" (par. 3) whom Daum criticizes would likely take umbrage at her accusations and her tone. Actual narcissists probably would not care what she thinks, one way or the other.
2. While popular usage of *narcissist* treats the word as a synonym for "any behavior you don't like" (par. 4), Daum argues for the American Psychiatric Association's clinical definition as it appeared in the *Diagnostic and Statistical Manual of Mental Disorders* for more than four decades — a serious disorder that causes "self-destructive" (pars. 1, 5) behavior.
3. Daum opens with her complaint that "a whole lot of people" (par. 1) are using the word *narcissist* as a general insult. In paragraph 2 she establishes the history of the popular usage. Paragraphs 3 and 4 rattle off examples of people who use the word and people to whom it's applied. In paragraph 5 Daum explains her objection to the usage. Her conclusion (6–7) offers her alternate characterization of Americans' behavior. Each paragraph relates directly to Daum's thesis, includes a topic sentence, and is developed with details.
4. Daum gives examples of "narcissistic" people in paragraph 4: "Democrats, Republicans, red state folks, blue state folks, baby boomers, Gen Xers, millenials . . . , [p]arents, nonparents, vegans, meat eaters, city dwellers, rural dwellers, people who travel a lot, people who refuse to travel, writers who use the first person. . . ." By setting up most of her examples as diametrically opposed pairs (implicitly comparing and contrasting the two groups) in a breathless string, she emphasizes her point that *everybody* can be accused of narcissism, usually by someone whose tendencies are different.

QUESTIONS ON LANGUAGE

1. The writer is clearly annoyed.
2. A *vector*, from the Latin *vehere*, "to carry," is an organism that transmits disease. Given that Daum is arguing to preserve the clinical meaning of *narcissist*, readers should appreciate her implication that people casually refer to the disorder as though it's contagious, even though it's not.
3. Both phrases connote shame and taboo (especially the latter); Daum is taking her own advice and refusing to use the word.

MEGHAN DAUM ON WRITING

Daum's comments on a reader's responsibilities reinforce our own advice about reading actively and critically, as well as about writing being a transaction between writer and reader. The questions for discussion encourage students to explore in more detail what a reader brings to that transaction.

BARBARA KINGSOLVER
Rural Delivery

With Michael Pollan's *The Omnivore's Dilemma* (2006), Barbara King-solver's *Animal, Vegetable, Miracle* has been credited with galvanizing the local-food movement, exposing the dangers of commercial agriculture, and inspiring thousands to pay more attention to what they eat and where it comes from. Our food, both writers have argued, has physical, cultural, eco-nomic, and political consequences. In this excerpt from her book, Kingsolver draws attention to a few of the political implications by asking readers to reconsider what the word *rural* (and by extension, *farmer*) means to them.

You may want to point out that Kingsolver defines largely by negation, explaining what rural people are not—"hick, redneck, hayseed, bumpkin" (par. 3) and so forth—to show them instead as she sees them. For King-solver, rural communities are not only sophisticated, cultured, and diverse but also essential to everybody else's survival, so we'd all better start show-ing more respect, both culturally and politically.

The vast majority (83%) of people in the United States live in urban or suburban areas, and many more relocate to densely populated areas every day. To engage your class in the topic before getting into the essay itself, you might begin discussion by focusing on students' own assumptions about rural living. What, if anything, do they know about it, and what have they heard? Would they ever willingly live "*so far from everything*" (par. 6)? Why, or why not?

QUESTIONS ON MEANING

1. Here is a possible summary: Rural communities are sparsely populated areas where farming dominates the landscape and the economy. They are characterized by a proud insularity, unacknowledged sophistica-tion, a strong sense of community, cultural and political diversity, and a history of being exploited by urban dwellers—who would starve without them.
2. Yes and no. Kingsolver was not raised on a farm, but because her family did not live in town, others classified them as "farm" people (par. 1). As an adult, however, Kingsolver strongly identifies with farmers and does seem to count herself among them, even if she does not make a living from working the land. (She currently cultivates a small plot to feed her family, something we mention in the introduction to the essay, but which Kingsolver does not discuss in it.)
3. Paragraphs 9–11 expand Kingsolver's definition to the landscape and politics of the nation as a whole, highlighting the significance of her subject for readers in rural and urban areas alike.
4. Kingsolver's purpose goes well beyond defining *rural*. The essay is a tribute to the lives and cultures of rural Americans, farmers in particu-lar. Kingsolver wants to share her vision with readers from all back-grounds and counter negative assumptions about rural life and politics. Most important, she wants readers to understand that the nation liter-ally cannot survive without the contributions of its rural communities.

QUESTIONS ON WRITING STRATEGY

1. Opening with a depiction of a nonsensical "caste" system imposed by classmates draws readers in and shares an experience to which most can relate. Kingsolver's point is that distinctions between rural and urban are as arbitrary—and as relative—as were the distinctions between "farm" and "town" where she grew up.
2. Kingsolver covers quite a bit of ground in "Rural Delivery"; she maintains unity by ensuring that each paragraph includes a clear topic sentence related to the thesis. Kingsolver is also careful to mark transitions among her paragraphs and to repeat key words such as *farm*, *rural*, and *urban*.
3. Stipulative definitions in the essay include those of "farmer" (par. 1), "everything" (6), "Interior" (6), "Conservative" (7), and "insider" and "outsider" (8). With each definition Kingsolver emphasizes that common assumptions about rural America are wrong.
4. During the 2000 presidential campaign political commentators and newscasters began categorizing states as either Democratic (blue) or Republican (red), based on predicted election results. The labels have stuck in the popular consciousness and are still used to characterize whole regions by their supposed political leanings—even though, as Kingsolver asserts, such labels are grossly oversimplified and misleading. She considers the political divide at length because it has come to signify a country polarized by difference and because it parallels the urban/rural "antipathy" that so concerns her. Ultimately, she hopes to bridge the gulf by questioning its existence.

QUESTIONS ON LANGUAGE

1. Berry is a well-known and respected writer who also happens to be a practicing farmer, so he lends authority to Kingsolver's arguments on two levels. The first quotation helps her to establish the importance of recognizing the politics of food; the second, which closes the essay, raises a dire warning of what will happen if the politics of food is not recognized and dealt with.
2. Kingsolver uses complex, formal words—such as *numinous* (par. 1), *bourgeoisie* (2), *symptomatic* (6), and *extractive* (9)—alongside colloquial expressions, including "Maybe you see where I'm going with this" (3) and "Okay, I'm exaggerating a little" (6). The informal language helps her connect with readers and build an earnest tone; the formal language expressly counters assumptions that rural people like Kingsolver are uneducated or unsophisticated.
3. Some readers will detect Marxist connotations in *bourgeoisie*, French for "middle class." By using that word in the same introductory paragraphs with *castes* (a reference to India) and *apartheid* (a reference to South Africa), Kingsolver strongly hints that her essay will emphasize political and class issues.

AUGUSTEN BURROUGHS

How to Identify Love by Knowing What It's Not

Augusten Burroughs's essay imploring abuse victims to recognize their problem and leave their abusers is likely to strike a painful chord for at least a few people in your class. According to the National Coalition Against Domestic Violence, one in five college students is currently in an abusive relationship, and more than a third were abused in previous relationships. We include "How to Identify Love by Knowing What It's Not" not to make students uncomfortable, but to help them recognize the scope of the problem of domestic violence: If they see themselves or someone they care for in Burroughs's descriptions, we hope his essay will prompt the affected students to get the help they need. Accordingly, we encourage you to be prepared to refer students to counseling services if your school offers them; it's possible one or two will identify themselves as abuse victims in response to the journal prompt or bring up the issue during office hours.

In preparation for discussing the essay, students could collaboratively devise a portrait of the ideal romantic relationship in America today. What qualities do we find most valuable or important in men? in women? Is gender relevant? What do your students expect of romantic partners? What do they offer in return? Are there different sets of standards? Who decides them? Who might be said to represent the perfect couple? In groups of four or five, students should be able to generate a list of the behaviors and attitudes that offer the best hope of a happy relationship.

Augusten Burroughs presents an unusual character as a writer. Students might enjoy his comments on writing, offered in video format at *bigthink.com/ideas/867*. No doubt they'll be surprised by both his appearance and voice. But hearing Burroughs speak may give them a better appreciation of the tone and urgency of his writing.

QUESTIONS ON MEANING

1. Although the title suggests that Burroughs will define *love* in the essay, his true subject is abusive relationships.
2. The thesis first appears in paragraph 16: "You can be in [an abusive] relationship and not even know it." Burroughs includes variations of this statement in paragraphs 22, 39, 46, 49, 53, and 57: "I knew of somebody . . . who was many years into an abusive relationship but did not know it"; "But probably the number-one reason [for people not leaving abusive relationships] is simply not knowing they're in one"; "Domestic violence is extremely difficult to detect when it is happening to you"; "You could be in an abusive relationship and be unaware that you are, unable to see the abuse for what it is"; "you're more likely to be blind to abuse if it is there"; "What's difficult to see is when you're with somebody who is a full-strength abuser." The relentless repetition lends emphasis and urgency to Burroughs's idea; it also gives the essay unity and coherence.

3. Burroughs presents his definition of love in the introductory paragraphs (1–12) and comes back to it in his conclusion (60–62). His negative examples imply that love is a combination of selfless caring, support, acceptance, and patience. And as he suggests in the paradox of his closing sentence, it starts with self-love.

4. Clearly, Burroughs wants readers to feel empathy for victims of domestic abuse, especially those who stay with their abusers; but even more so, he wants readers to examine their own relationships carefully and honestly and, if they realize they're being abused, to get out. (He expects no response from abusers because they "do not change," par. 29.) Students' own responses, of course, will vary.

QUESTIONS ON WRITING STRATEGY

1. The very short paragraphs give the essay a clipped, urgent feel and emphasize the importance of Burroughs's major points. The single-sentence paragraphs in the introduction also create the feel of a homily, specifically invoking Corinthians 13:4–8, which is commonly recited at weddings: "Love is patient and kind; love is not jealous or boastful; it is not arrogant or rude. Love does not insist on its own way; it is not irritable or resentful; it does not rejoice at wrong, but rejoices in the right. Love bears all things, believes all things, hopes all things, endures all things. Love never ends. . . ." That sense that Burroughs is offering a sermon carries through the rest of the essay.

2. Stipulative definitions in the essay include those of "Love" (pars. 1–12), "patience" (12–15), "physical violence" (16–17), and "emotional violence" (17–28). With each definition, Burroughs emphasizes that abuse comes in many forms and can be difficult to recognize.

3. Burroughs begins with a stipulative definition of "Love" (pars. 1–12), then moves on to definitions of "patience," "physical violence," and "emotional violence" (see the previous question). Once he's established his meanings, Burroughs describes the mentality of abusers, arguing that they won't change (29–37), then moves on to consideration of why victims don't leave (38–40). Because the main reason they stay is not knowing they're abused, Burroughs goes on to characterize the symptoms of abuse, citing evidence from the National Domestic Violence Hotline and elaborating on one symptom, preventing the partner from working (41–45). Finally, he acknowledges (again) that victims often don't recognize abuse and outlines the process by which they may come to see it for themselves, imploring readers to leave if they discover they're being victimized (46–62). The structure allows Burroughs to carry readers through the process he describes toward the end: understanding, recognizing, acknowledging, and then doing something about abuse.

4. Citing an authoritative source lends authority to Burroughs's claims. Perhaps more important, he provides the information as a service to victims of domestic violence. Burroughs is quite sincere in his desire to help, and including the checklist and phone number is a concrete way for him to do that.

5. In paragraphs 22–28 Burroughs relates the experience of a friend who suffered emotional abuse. The anecdote not only illustrates what the author means by emotional abuse with concrete details, but also works as evidence to support his claim. At the same time, his friend's success in leaving the relationship offers inspiration and hope for readers who may be thinking about leaving an abuser.

QUESTIONS ON LANGUAGE

1. Burroughs clearly assumes that many (if not most) of his readers are victims of domestic abuse, whether physical or emotional, and that they do not recognize it.
2. The essay is riddled with inappropriate use of *they* and *their*, but the choice seems deliberate. Burroughs takes great pains to stress that abusers and their victims come in all genders and sexualities; he doesn't want to stereotype with masculine or feminine pronouns or be accused of using sexist language. All the same, the resulting poor grammar will be jarring for many readers. We suggest you take the opportunity to discuss the effects of faulty agreement with your class, asking how they might edit the essay for better readability.
3. In a usage note for the verb *roil*, the editors of *The American Heritage Dictionary* write, the word "means literally 'to make muddy or cloudy by stirring up sediment,' and this meaning has given rise to a number of figurative uses. *Roil* can also mean 'to be or cause to be agitated.'" Given that the turbulence in Burroughs's example's mind caused agitation for both himself and his wife, clouding and fouling the relationship in the process, we find the unusual word choice here especially effective.
4. The tone might best be described as *empathetic*. Throughout the essay Burroughs hints that he, too, has been the victim of abuse (which, as we point out in the author's headnote, is in fact the case) and that he is pulling examples from his own experience. The hint is especially strong when he writes about victims who, like himself, "possess talent" but are prevented from pursuing their "crafts" (pars. 20, 42–45).

SCHROEDER JONES

Dr. Carmella's Guide to Understanding the Introverted

Although he has illustrated two books and self-published dozens of cartoons on *DeviantART*, Schroeder Jones is largely unknown as an artist. If the immediate popularity of "Dr. Carmella's Guide to Understanding the Introverted" is any indication, we suspect obscurity will soon be behind him. Already, Jones has translated the cartoon into multiple languages (German, Chinese, Polish, and Czech) and created a pamphlet version to satisfy demand; he's also expanding the viral hit into book form. In a short space and an accessible format, he has managed to define a complex psychological concept in a way that both introverts and extroverts can appreciate and apply to their own interactions with others.

Students interested in reading more about introversion might be referred to Jonathan Rauch's enduringly popular essay "Caring for Your Introvert" (*theatlantic.com/magazine/archive/2003/03/caring-for-your-introvert/302696*). For a longer, more recent consideration on the subject, see Susan Cain's *Quiet: The Power of Introverts in a World That Can't Stop Talking* (2012). Students may enjoy taking Cain's introvert/extrovert quiz, offered at the Web site for her book (*thepowerofintroverts.com*). Some may be surprised (even relieved) to discover where their own social preferences land them on the spectrum.

QUESTIONS ON MEANING AND STRATEGY

1. Here is a possible summary: An introvert is a person who is drained by socializing with other people, *not* somebody who is withdrawn, lonely, or unfriendly.
2. Jones's definition is clarified with an analogy, an extended metaphor that uses something immediate and familiar (a hamster ball) to provide insight into something that is difficult to envision (personal space). This visual device, which encourages readers to apply their knowledge of the concrete subject to the artist's definition of the abstract, allows Jones to explain something complex with a minimum of words.
3. Upon close inspection of the cartoon, students may notice missing periods, comma splices, run-on sentences, sentence fragments, vague and implied pronoun references, and an unnecessary exclamation point in addition to the pronoun-antecedent mismatches. Although sticklers may well be distracted by these apparent errors and deem Jones's cartoon weakened by them, others might respond that the standards of written grammar and punctuation are looser for visual works—much as they are for spoken conversation.
4. Jones's purpose is to help extroverts understand introverts and thus get along with them better (implied throughout the cartoon is the assumption that extroverts find introverts withdrawn or hostile, when really what they are is quiet sometimes). The process analysis is essential to show nonintroverts how to use the artist's definition in their own lives.

13
ARGUMENT AND PERSUASION
Stating Opinions and Proposals

Argument and persuasion are often difficult for students to master, so the introduction to this chapter is more detailed than the others. We spell out the elements of argument, integrating the Rogerian and Toulmin methods and the more traditional inductive and deductive reasoning. Then we cover the most common fallacies and (in the section headed "The Process") discuss possible structures for arguments. We also give emphasis to anticipating likely objections when conceiving and writing an argument.

This chapter's selections start with one piece that flies solo: Linda Chavez's "Supporting Family Values," a liberal argument by a conservative writer. Then we present four casebooks:

- Katha Pollitt and Charles Colson on gay marriage
- Nicholas Carr, Jim Harper, and Lori Andrews on Internet tracking, the practice of mining personal data and analyzing the information to customize Web users' experience
- Bill McKibben, Derrick Jensen, and Margaret Lundberg (a student), on the effects of individual actions on the environment
- Anne-Marie Slaughter's controversial and widely read article from *The Atlantic Monthly* on the challenges of balancing work and family life is accompanied in the e-Pages by a sampling of responses collected by the editors of *Reader's Digest* and one blogger's reflections on the debate Slaughter revived.

LINDA CHAVEZ
Supporting Family Values

Chavez, a politically conservative writer who hails from a Spanish-speaking background, insists in this essay that Hispanic immigrants are both willing and able to adapt to American life and culture. Even more, Chavez suggests, that same group of immigrants so often vilified as lazy, uneducated, or criminal are in fact exemplars of virtue and should be honored, even rewarded, for their moral contributions to American society.

This essay is notable for using conservative ideals (family values) to argue for liberal policy (amnesty for illegal immigrants). Students may have some difficulty reconciling two points of view that would seem almost mutually exclusive, but we find it quite clever of Chavez to intertwine them in such a way that neither position can be easily refuted: As Chavez presents her argument, readers on either side of the conservative-liberal divide have little choice but to accept at least part of their opponents' way of thinking.

QUESTIONS ON MEANING

1. Chavez opens her essay by noting it was prompted by a "new report out this week from the Pew Hispanic Center" (par. 1), but perceptive readers will notice from her remarks in the final two paragraphs that her argument was inspired as well by the ongoing conflict between efforts to aggressively identify and deport illegal immigrants and proposals to offer amnesty to illegal immigrants who meet certain criteria.
2. Although she mentions slight differences in family structure, education level, and income among illegal and legal immigrants, the only real distinction Chavez makes between the two groups is their legal status. Especially because so many immigrant families consist of both illegal and legal residents, Chavez suggests, the distinctions are practically meaningless.
3. Chavez's comparison of attitudes toward current Mexican and "other Latin American" immigrants with attitudes toward European immigrants of a century ago is a commonly used argument in favor of relaxed immigration controls. Her point is that a century of experience has shown that immigrants do assimilate into the larger culture over time and that fears of unfamiliar ethnic groups are unfounded. At the same time, because most of her readers are presumably of European heritage, Chavez subtly chides them for perpetuating the same hostilities that were once directed at their own ancestors—and reassures them that Spanish-speaking immigrants will, indeed, become an integral part of American culture if given the opportunity.
4. Chavez's purpose is revealed in the last two paragraphs: She is writing to argue in favor of "granting amnesty" to a qualified category of illegal immigrants. Her thesis might best be expressed in the penultimate sentence: "A better approach [to deportation] would allow those who have made their lives here, established families, bought homes, worked continuously and paid taxes to remain after paying fines, demonstrating English fluency, and proving they have no criminal record." By withholding her thesis and purpose until the end, Chavez acknowledges that her position will be difficult for readers to accept; she therefore fully makes her case before letting them in on what she wants them to believe.

QUESTIONS ON WRITING STRATEGY

1. Chavez characterizes opponents as unreasonable to the point of hysteria, referring to "hard-line immigration restrictionists," "alarm" (par. 2); "fear" (5); "worries [that] are no more rational today—or born out of actual evidence—than they were a hundred years ago" (6); and "popular but uninformed opinion" (8). In doing so, Chavez suggests that some readers may hold these views, yet she forces them to reexamine their beliefs

by portraying them as irrational. She seems to trust that most of her readers—"the rest of us" (2)—are reasonable people who can be persuaded to change their minds if presented with sufficient information.

2. Chavez states her main assumption in paragraph 2: "One of the chief social problems afflicting this country is the breakdown in the traditional family." Many readers, especially those of a conservative medium like *townhall.com*, will presumably share the writer's concern about family values; others will reject it outright. In either case readers are likely to find Chavez's approach creative at the very least.

3. Chavez appeals to both reason and emotion. She is careful to base her argument on statistical evidence from a published report in paragraphs 1, 3, 6, 7, and 8, using the numbers to draw inferences about the character, values, and potential for success of undocumented Spanish-speaking immigrants, especially as they compare to legal immigrants and native-born families. But she appeals to emotion throughout, citing both family values and fears of cultural disintegration as she makes her case.

4. Chavez names three categories of American "households" in paragraph 3: native, legal, and illegal. As she explains, native families are the least likely to be "made up of two parents living with their own children," while a third of legal immigrant households and nearly half of all illegal immigrant households consist of traditional nuclear families. The point is central to her argument that immigrant families represent a positive influence on the rest of the country and should therefore be supported and encouraged, not broken apart by deportation or harassment.

QUESTIONS ON LANGUAGE

1. *Amnesty* is a political term for a government's pardon of illegal activities; in Chavez's essay, it refers explicitly to ongoing proposals to grant legal status to illegal residents who have nonetheless established themselves successfully. The word comes from the same Latin and Greek roots as *amnesia*, or forgetting.

2. By "native" Chavez means those born in the United States and thus automatically granted citizenship. There are at least two layers of irony in her use of the term: First is the subtle reference to Native Americans, the peoples who were displaced with the first wave of European settlement in the fifteenth century; but Chavez also points out that nearly three-quarters of the children of illegal immigrants are "American-born" (par. 1) and thus citizens—a fact that complicates the issue of deportation, especially for readers with a strong interest in family values.

3. Most students will likely find Chavez's tone reasonable and levelheaded, even appealing. The diction is for the most part plain; Chavez avoids sarcasm and hectoring, and in her conclusion she becomes somewhat informal, saying her evidence "should give pause to those who'd like to see all illegal immigrants rounded up and deported or their lives made so miserable they leave on their own" (par. 9).

LINDA CHAVEZ ON WRITING

Chavez's nostalgia for the old days of sentence diagramming might prompt students to reflect on their own grammatical education. How were they taught the rules? You might point out that understanding the rules is different from following them. Plenty of writers occasionally write "incorrect" sentences, but they do so on purpose and for a particular effect. Readers can tell the difference between intentional rule breaking and error.

KATHA POLLITT
What's Wrong with Gay Marriage?

Pollitt's essay is the first of a pair on marriage between homosexuals. She takes the "pro" position. Charles Colson, in the next essay, takes the "con." Though not directly, Pollitt in essence addresses Colson's main objections to same-sex marriage. In paragraphs 1, 2, 3, and 6 she presents opposing arguments and then refutes them. Even students who do not agree with her position should be able to learn a great deal from her model.

Students may have difficulty grasping Pollitt's conclusion about the separation of church and state. For all its religious trappings, she argues, marriage is ultimately a civil union—conferred by the government—and thus a civil right. If any man and woman can be married in the eyes of the government—no matter how ill suited—then, she asks, why should this status be denied to same-sex couples? Religious objections are irrelevant to Pollitt because religion does not figure in the civil relationship between marrying couples and the government.

One way to begin discussion might be to ask students to consider Pollitt's point in paragraph 6 that "people can live with civil unions but draw the line at marriage." What is it that makes marriage such a hot-button issue?

QUESTIONS ON MEANING

1. Pollitt first presents the argument that the fundamental purpose of marriage is procreation; this she attempts to refute by noting the fact that heterosexuals with no intention of having children are allowed to marry. Then she deals with George Gilder's claim that marriage must be a union of a man and a woman because marriage is "the way women domesticate men." She questions Gilder's premise but then says that allowing same-sex marriage would in no way change the relationship between men and women in a heterosexual union. Finally, she presents the "argument from history"—"marriage has been around forever"—which she claims is false because marriage as currently defined does not have a particularly long history. Pollitt's implicit point here is that the concept of marriage has evolved and there is no reason it should not continue to do so.
2. Pollitt says that marriage "as we understand it" is "voluntary, monogamous, legally egalitarian, based on love, involving adults only" (par. 3); it is "love, commitment, stability" (4). Pollitt herself is not a proponent of marriage, believing that it reinforces unfairness in society and in relations between men and women.
3. Pollitt argues that the basic objection to same-sex marriage is really "religious prejudice" (par. 6)—that those who believe homosexuality to be a sin believe that same-sex marriage rewards sinful behavior.

4. Pollitt's thesis is stated at the end of paragraph 6: "People may think *marriage* is a word wholly owned by religion, but actually it's wholly owned by the state. . . . [T]wo men or two women should be able to marry, even if religions oppose it and it makes some heterosexuals, raised in those religions, uncomfortable."

QUESTIONS ON WRITING STRATEGY

1. The opening question brings to the essay a very human, somewhat grumbling voice, and it immediately establishes Pollitt's topic and viewpoint. The questions in paragraphs 2 and 5 ask readers to see that there is no affirmative answer—or that to answer affirmatively is to answer unreasonably.
2. The concessions make Pollitt sound reasonable. Still, once she makes each concession, she goes on to argue that the point conceded is not really significant.
3. The transitions make it clear where Pollitt is in her argument: Each one refers in some way to the preceding paragraph or paragraphs. (The one in paragraph 3 does so by asking a question that echoes paragraph 2's "How about: Marriage is the way women domesticate men.")
4. Some students may think that Pollitt includes the paragraph because it personalizes the essay or because it reduces the importance of marriage. Others may think that it weakens the argument because it shows that Pollitt doesn't value marriage anyway, so she wouldn't care about undermining it.
5. Pollitt identifies what she sees as the elements of the opposition to gay marriage—the subarguments to the main argument that it threatens traditional marriage.

QUESTIONS ON LANGUAGE

1. Examples of humorous language in paragraph 2 include the "husbandly failings" in various domestic crimes, "barbarian-adoption program," women "haven't been too successful at it anyway," "male-improvement project," and "heterosexual pothead with plans for murder and suicide." The language suggests that Pollitt doesn't take Gilder's argument seriously and underscores her rejection of it.
2. With the phrase "live in sin" Pollitt is adopting the language of social conservatives for rhetorical purposes. She obviously would not agree with the characterization.
3. Putting "sacred" and "gay lifestyle" in quotation marks distances Pollitt from them: These are terms conservatives would use, but she would not.
4. The parallelism and repetition stress the contrast between the view of marriage as a solely religious institution and the reality of marriage as a government institution.
5. *Monogamous* comes from the Greek for "one" and "marriage." It originally meant being married to one person for life, but it now means being married to only one person at a time.

CHARLES COLSON
Gay "Marriage": Societal Suicide

Colson's essay and the preceding one by Katha Pollitt form a pair on the issue of marriage between homosexuals. The arguments in the two essays cover opposing sides of similar points, so you'll probably want students to read and discuss the essays together.

In dealing with Colson's essay, students may have difficulty considering the effectiveness of the argument, particularly those who are opposed to same-sex marriage. Colson stresses his moral grounds for opposing gay marriage only in paragraph 8. For the most part he makes a sociological argument, linking gay marriage to an increasing "decoupling of marriage and procreation" that "would pull them completely apart, leading to an explosive increase in family collapse, out-of-wedlock births—and crime" (par. 4). His reasoning is deductive, and he offers statistics and expert opinion to back it up. In evaluating the argument, students will have to judge first whether the deduction holds up (see the first question on writing strategy). Do they agree that legalizing homosexual marriage would lead more heterosexuals to view marriage as no longer a requirement for having children and thus would increase single-parent households and societal problems?

QUESTIONS ON MEANING

1. Colson states his thesis in the final sentence of paragraph 4 and rephrases it in his concluding sentence.
2. Colson uses the example of Norway—where a rise in rates of out-of-wedlock births followed the legalization of same-sex marriage—to support the first assertion (par. 6). He offers his own experience in prison ministry and the results of "[d]ozens of studies" to support the second (par. 5). We find the evidence for the first assertion shaky: It could illustrate the *post hoc* fallacy as much as a cause-and-effect relationship, and Norway is of course quite different from the United States. In paragraph 5 Colson might have bolstered his statistics by referring to their sources, but perhaps he did not see the need because, as he says at the start of paragraph 6, "Critics agree with this."
3. In paragraph 8 Colson makes a moral argument based on "[h]istory and tradition" that "[t]he family, led by a married mother and father, is the best available structure for both child rearing and cultural health." He also asserts in the final paragraph that marriage is "not a private institution designed solely for the individual gratification of its participants," though he doesn't really make a case for this point. You might ask students to consider the extent to which they can support this assertion.

QUESTIONS ON WRITING STRATEGY

1. Colson's claim is that gay marriage will cause family breakdown and societal problems. His assumption is that any form of marriage besides the traditional one will undermine the traditional one. His syllogism

runs something like this: Any form of marriage besides the traditional one will lead to family breakdown and societal problems; gay marriage is not traditional; therefore, gay marriage will lead to family breakdown and societal problems.

2. With the quotation marks Colson shows that he does not accept the word *marriage* when it is applied to same-sex couples.

3. The question provides an arresting opening, suggesting the worst-case scenario should same-sex unions become legal.

4. Paragraph 7 concedes an argument made by proponents of same-sex marriage: that heterosexuals themselves—including Christian heterosexuals—have weakened marriage. The concession supports Colson's reasonableness: He sees validity in the opponents' side. He then goes on to argue that the issue is not people's behavior but the institution of marriage.

5. The argument is based on cause and effect: Same-sex marriage will lead to a rise in single-parent households, which, in turn, will lead to an increasing number of children who pose a threat to themselves and society.

QUESTIONS ON LANGUAGE

1. "Lawlessness," "gleefully mocking," "egged them on," and "chaos" all have very negative connotations.

2. The words imply that same-sex marriage was forced on the people of Norway against their will. It is not clear if indeed it was.

3. Although *unorthodox* has come to be a fairly neutral word for action or belief that is not commonly accepted but not necessarily wrong, etymologically its meaning is more like "not right or proper" (from the Greek *ortho*, "correct, right," and *doxa*, "opinion").

NICHOLAS CARR
Tracking Is an Assault on Liberty

Nicholas Carr's is the first essay in a three-selection casebook focusing on the problem of Internet tracking. This essay pairs specifically with the following one by Jim Harper: The two were published together as a debate in the *Wall Street Journal*. The essay following Harper's, by Lori Andrews, extends the debate with a third perspective.

Students may be surprised to learn how much information is gathered about them on the Web and what can be done with that information; although having grown up online as they have, many may not see why they should care. Carr tries to make readers care about the issue by revealing surprising facts to support his argument and by suggesting that by failing to safeguard their privacy, Americans risk losing civil liberties.

You might want to start discussion by asking students about their personal experiences with targeted online advertising. How open are they about sharing personal information online? Have they noticed any ads on their

computers or mobile devices that seemed eerily connected to something
they had posted or researched? Do they find such customized marketing
helpful or creepy, and why?

QUESTIONS ON MEANING

1. The problem, for Carr, is the "surreptitious collection of personal information" (par. 1) online by companies and government agencies, a practice that he believes not only poses practical dangers to individual Web
   users (13, 15–16, and 18) but also threatens their liberties and "pursuit of happiness" (19). He suggests two mostly undeveloped solutions:
   Individual Web users should be more cautious about sharing information (14), and "software makers and site operators" should offer more
   control and transparency to users who wish to safeguard their information (17). Implied, but not stated outright, is that regulations should
   require such controls and transparency of technology providers.
2. Information might be disclosed voluntarily by individual users (par. 2)
   and through shopping hubs (4, 6, 11), social-networking sites (11), and
   "location-tracking services like *Foursquare*" (11), often with the false
   assumption that such sharing is anonymous or in forgetfulness of how
   public such services are (4). Perhaps more worrisome to Carr are the
   growth of data-tracking software (5) and the ease with which researchers can analyze disparate bits of supposedly anonymous cookies and
   data, not only to identify individual users (6–10) but also to anticipate
   and manipulate their behaviors (15–16).
3. Carr lists three distinct dangers. The first is practical: Criminals can access and analyze data as easily as anybody else can, creating a risk that
   Web users will be subjected to cons, theft, stalking, and the like (par. 13).
   The second is the problem of "manipulation" (15), Carr's concern that
   personalized marketing will influence people's knowledge and behaviors in ways they don't necessarily recognize (15–16). The final danger
   is more theoretical: Carr worries that as privacy continues to be lost,
   society will cease to value it, leading individuals to feel constantly mon-
   itored and forever on guard, and therefore less free (18).
4. Carr's purpose is to sound an alarm, to warn readers that their privacy
   is at risk and to persuade them to care about it. He is careful to establish the existence of a problem and to examine its scope, but he has
   little to say in the way of proposing a solution.

QUESTIONS ON WRITING STRATEGY

1. By acknowledging data tracking's practical benefits before raising concerns about its personal and political dangers, Carr simultaneously addresses an opposing viewpoint and enhances his ethical appeal by establishing himself as a reasonable observer.
2. Carr's argument appeals to both reason and emotion. The closest reasoning appears in paragraphs 5–12, where the author draws on published research and expert opinion to forge a connection between new
   technologies and loss of privacy. He appeals to emotion throughout,
   but especially when discussing the dangers of exposure (13–16) and the
   potential tragic effects on "life and liberty" (18–19).
3. Carr seems to imagine that the more advertisers (and presumably, governments) know about individual consumers, the more they'll be able

to direct those individuals' choices through subliminal mind control, subtly altering messages and available information to influence people's thoughts and behaviors. Many readers, fully confident in their own free will, will likely dismiss his concerns as overblown, maybe even a little ridiculous. Others more skilled at critical media consumption may find that his concerns ring true.

4. Carr warns that Americans' ability to protect their rights is threatened by the devaluation of privacy in an online culture that assumes "privacy is . . . just a screen we hide behind when we do something naughty or embarrassing" (par. 18). Privacy is more than that, he insists: It is a "boundary" (19) between ourselves and others, and it provides a sense of individuality that is "intrinsic to the concept of liberty" (18). The less privacy we have as individuals, he argues, the more we resign ourselves to the possibility of corporate and government manipulation. The definition allows him to state his conviction that privacy is a foundational American right and to explain how it protects civil liberties.

QUESTIONS ON LANGUAGE

1. Carr accepts that some loss of privacy online is inevitable and even desirable (par. 2), but he worries that Internet exposure is moving beyond individual users' control, creating "real dangers" for them and for society in general (12). His tone, while balanced, is one of deep concern and mild alarm; some readers might even characterize it as paranoid.

2. Earl Warren was Chief Justice of the US Supreme Court from 1953 to 1969; Tom Owad is a computer consultant and experimental researcher; Scott McNealy is the former chief executive of Sun Microsystems, an information technology company; Eric Schmidt heads *Google*; and Bruce Schneier is a computer-security expert. By quoting and paraphrasing expert opinion on both sides of the issue, Carr enhances his credibility while offering reliable evidence to support his ideas.

3. Jim Harper, in the next essay, takes issue with Carr's use of *surreptitious*, meaning secret or stealthy, to describe the "collection of personal information" online. Anybody who doesn't know about such data collection, says Harper, "hasn't been paying attention" (par. 7).

NICHOLAS CARR ON WRITING

Carr addresses an issue that many writing teachers face: how to get students to write thoughtfully and carefully when they're used to dashing off text messages with little attention to critical thinking, rhetorical craft, or, for that matter, grammar, spelling, and mechanics. Carr's insistence that texting is the first stage of a "debased form" of writing provides an occasion to discuss with students "our old linear form of reading and writing" and how it may differ between, say, text messaging and academic writing.

JIM HARPER

Web Users Get as Much as They Give

In a pointed response to Nicholas Carr's argument for safeguarding privacy online, Jim Harper shifts the focus of the debate to business and commerce. In today's "information economy" (par. 1), he insists, personal information is a commodity that has monetary value for businesses and consumers alike. Whether your students agree with him or not will be a matter of both their personal perspectives and their evaluation of his argumentative technique. For some readers, the essay will smack of pro-business bias; others will surely find it very persuasive.

You might want to start a discussion by asking students about their positions on recent calls for privacy legislation such as those made by Nicholas Carr, in "Tracking Is an Assault on Liberty" (p. 538), and by Lori Andrews, in "*Facebook* Is Using You" (p. 551). Do they favor tighter restrictions on data tracking, do they think that individual Web users are responsible for protecting their own privacy, do they think that information should be freely shared, or do they view privacy as a nonissue? Why?

QUESTIONS ON MEANING

1. Harper's thesis is best summed up in his title: "Web Users Get as Much as They Give." The trade in personal data drives Internet commerce (advertising especially) and makes it possible for sites to produce and distribute free content; if Web users restrict access to their personal information, businesses will have less incentive, and fewer resources, to give anything in return.
2. *Cookies* are small files downloaded to Web users' computers by the sites they visit. Those files then send information from the users' computers back to the sites, as well as to third parties, enabling site producers to "customize a visitor's experience" (par. 5). Most sites share aggregate data with advertising networks, which use demographics and individual visitors' interests and habits to personalize marketing messages. As far as Harper is concerned, this data mining and sharing is a good thing, because it increases profitability for businesses and enables them to provide free services and content to consumers.
3. He places the blame on the average American for failing to use the privacy tools that are available, and for failing to understand how the "information economy" (par. 1) works. His solution is to use those tools to control the spread of personal information, as well as to be willing to give up a certain amount of privacy in exchange for the services and materials provided online.
4. Harper's purpose is twofold: He wants to educate readers about the workings of the "information economy" (par. 1); he also wants to persuade them to allow their own data to be tracked because such tracking, as he sees it, is for their benefit. Whether he succeeds in persuading readers will depend on their individual perspectives and concerns about business and privacy.

QUESTIONS ON WRITING STRATEGY

1. Harper previews the organization of his argument with the series of questions he asks in paragraph 2: "Who is gathering this information? What are they doing with it? How might this harm me? How do I stop it?" A rough outline:
   a. Web sites and advertising networks gather Internet users' information (par. 5).
   b. They use this information to personalize Web content and target advertising to individual interests, not to discriminate against people or harm them in any way (5).
   c. Cookies and tracking in general have been in use for a long time; expressing concern about them is disingenuous and beside the point (6–7).
   d. Trying to stop data tracking would harm both businesses and consumers (8–10).
   e. It is not the government's job to protect privacy (11).

   All but point e counter points Carr makes, although Harper's emphasis is decidedly different: While Carr's focus is on individual liberties, Harper's focus is on business and commerce. He does not directly address Carr's arguments about manipulation and potential loss of personal freedoms. Harper concentrates on issues of free trade.

2. The *Wall Street Journal* is a business newspaper with a conservative slant; Harper assumes that his readers are affluent, influential professionals whose primary interest is making money. As businesspeople, Harper's readers may have a vested interest in Web commerce especially, and so are likely to be biased in favor of his claims. Harper also assumes that his readers—business professionals or not—are consumers who enjoy the free content and services provided online and expect unfettered access to such products. Students will likely fit the latter assumption, if not the former.

3. Harper is attempting to establish ethical appeal by disclosing that he is one of those Web producers who relies on data tracking to generate advertising revenue and produce new content for viewers; in other words, he attempts to show readers that he knows what he's talking about. At the same time, by mentioning that his site monitors the government, he implies that the government can't be trusted to protect privacy. Although some readers might feel that Harper's admission increases his credibility, others might find that it reveals a conflict of interest.

4. Harper offers two examples: the Federal Trade Commission's failed bid more than a decade ago "for power to regulate the Internet for privacy's sake" (pars. 10–11), and Microsoft engineers' more recent attempt to tighten the privacy settings on Internet Explorer (12). In both cases Harper argues that had the efforts succeeded, businesses would have been harmed and consumers would have been given less "access to free content" (12): *Google,* he claims, would not have grown to the powerhouse it is today (10), and Microsoft would have been accused of damaging "interactivity and the advertising business model" (12). The implication is that any efforts to protect privacy are ultimately counterproductive.

5. Harper believes strongly that tighter privacy regulations would hurt business and consumers. "If Web users supply less information to the Web," he claims, "the Web will supply less information to them" (par. 9). Businesses would have less opportunity to grow and innovate (10), and

consumers' interests would be both misinterpreted and thwarted (11), limiting their access to "free content, custom Web experiences, convenience and so on" (13).

QUESTIONS ON LANGUAGE

1. The mixed metaphors of Harper's first paragraph (surfing, gleaning, gears, and fuel, all at once) might make students' heads spin, but in general Harper uses figures of speech, especially personifications of businesses and technologies, to establish a friendly and reassuring (if sometimes condescending) tone. Other examples include the simile "[c]ookies are a surreptitious threat to privacy the way smoking is a surreptitious threat to health" (par. 7); the metaphors "eyeballs" (5), "hold businesses' feet to the fire" (11), "fade from view" (11), "passion play" (12); and the personifications throughout, such as "[a] network . . . will recognize a browser" (5), "enabling the ad network to get a sense of that person's interests" (5), "if the engineers' plan had won the day" (12), and "[t]his is not to say that businesses don't want personal information—they do" (13).
2. The Latin phrase *status quo* means literally "state in which." It has come to mean "the way things are."
3. The allusion seems meant to imply that even if government regulators succeed in passing privacy protections, thereby destroying a successful business model, companies will find a way to resurrect the practices of tracking and data mining, or put something similar in their place. Some readers will surely find the reference to Christian tradition unsettling, if not offensive.

LORI ANDREWS
Facebook Is Using You

Lori Andrews is both a renowned legal scholar and an engaging storyteller. In "*Facebook* Is Using You," her narrative skill enlivens and helps support her argument that in systematically violating Web users' privacy, large corporations and government agencies can and do inflict real harm on individual American citizens.

With the previous two essays by Nicholas Carr and Jim Harper, this essay rounds out an argumentative trio on the pros and cons of Internet tracking and data mining. In teaching the three arguments together, you may want to help students see how different each author's argumentative strategies are on the surface: Andrews writes personally and appeals to readers' emotions with examples of data-mining practices and their consequences for real people; whereas Carr and Harper take a more distanced, impersonal, and logical approach. And while Carr's argument is largely theoretical, Harper's and Andrews's essays focus more on practical realities. You might ask students to consider why the subject of privacy lends itself to both emotional and rational appeals on both sides of the issue.

QUESTIONS ON MEANING

1. Andrews introduces her thesis in paragraph 4: "Ads that pop up on your screen might seem useful, or at worst, a nuisance. But they are much more than that. The bits and bytes about your life can easily be used against you." She states the implications of her thesis, her proposal, in the conclusion of her argument: "We need a do-not-track law, similar to the do-not-call one" (12).

2. Data aggregators are for-profit companies, such as LexisNexis, Spokeo, and NebuAd, that gather personal information about Web users and sell it to interested parties such as law enforcement agencies, the IRS, and insurance companies. Unlike advertisers, who gather or purchase the data to customize messages that "might seem useful, or at worst, a nuisance" (par. 4), data aggregators have a vested interest in using data against individuals and can cause people real harm.

3. Aggregators analyze data from hundreds of thousands of users to predict individual behaviors, relying on broad patterns to make assumptions that are often incorrect. Many people, she asserts, have been treated unfairly as a result, and many more will be.

4. The writer's purpose is to expose a problem and to offer a solution. Andrews calls for new laws that "give people the right to know what data companies have about them" (par. 2) and that allow Web users to prevent companies from tracking them (12).

QUESTIONS ON WRITING STRATEGY

1. By setting her argument in the context of *Facebook*'s initial public offering, Andrews emphasizes the relevance of her subject (data aggregation in general) while grounding it in a concrete example and establishing the size of the stakes at hand. *Facebook* and other companies such as *Google*, Andrews points out, gather "stunning" (par. 2) amounts of personal information and stand to make enormous profits from it. Web users, by implication, are at risk of being exploited.

2. Andrews appeals primarily to emotion. Although she offers statistics and examples to support her claims, her emphasis is on readers' desires for privacy, distrust of large corporations, and fear of personal harm. The focus on "stereotyping" (pars. 6–11) and the reference to racial discrimination (9) in particular seem designed to stoke indignation and concern.

3. The sources Andrews cites, *Consumer Reports* and Princeton Survey Research Associates, will seem reliable or authoritative to most readers. Some, however, might feel that in citing the opinions of three thousand survey respondents relative to the hundreds of millions *Facebook* subscribers and *Google* users, Andrews makes a big inductive leap.

4. Andrews writes about herself at three points: She notes that her own personal data are included in "*Facebook*'s inventory" (par. 1); she describes the kinds of potentially damaging Web searches she has conducted and why (7); and she concludes with an image of herself being "interrupted by a telemarketer" at dinner contrasted with "whether my dreams will be dashed by the collection of bits and bytes over which I have no control" (12). Injecting herself shows that Andrews is not a disinterested bystander, but is affected directly by the practices she argues against.

5. Andrews's evidence is almost entirely anecdotal, consisting of examples of companies and government agencies that track personal information and sell it, as well as of people who have experienced or could experience the negative consequences of such tracking.

QUESTIONS ON LANGUAGE

1. A lawyer, Andrews relies primarily on formal, academic language through most of her essay. But being a mystery writer as well, she frequently slips into everyday speech that any reader could understand. A few examples: "big-ticket corporations" (par. 1); "widgets or gadgets" (1); "small potatoes" (3); "bits and bytes" (4); "'Is He Cheating on You?'" (5); "alive and well" (6); "Googled" (7); "make their own rules" (7); "whether my dreams will be dashed" (12); and the direct appeal to readers as "you" throughout. The colloquialisms inject a dose of light-heartedness into what might otherwise become an overly academic or theoretical argument; they also humanize the author and help readers follow her ideas.

2. A *doppelgänger*, as *The American Heritage Dictionary* tells us, is a "ghostly double of a living person, especially one that haunts its fleshly counterpart." The word is also used colloquially to describe an uncanny likeness between two distinct people, usually strangers. Andrews is saying that digital selves are not identical to their real-world counterparts, and also that those digital selves can haunt us in unpleasant ways.

3. *Weblining* is the virtual equivalent of redlining, the discriminatory practice — now outlawed — of mapping out neighborhoods to deny financial services to predefined classes (and races).

4. *Scrutinize* comes from the Latin *scrutinum*, "close search," which came from the Latin *scruta*, "old clothes." Thus, *to scrutinize* is to perform a minute search, such as a used-clothing vendor might conduct in a pile of old clothes.

LORI ANDREWS ON WRITING

Andrews's difficulty with fiction writing, it would seem, was an academic tendency toward abstraction. Her need to "learn the way to describe things" in a physical context offers two useful reminders to students: First, that concrete and specific language, along with plenty of examples, brings specificity to a writer's work and anchors ideas to reality; and second, that all writers can improve.

BILL McKIBBEN
Waste Not, Want Not

"Waste Not, Want Not" is the first of three essays focused on issues related to climate change. Like Derrick Jensen and Margaret Lundberg following him, Bill McKibben considers the effects of individual lifestyle choices on the environment.

McKibben uses an arsenal of persuasive strategies in this essay, including ethical appeals, emotional appeals, and rational appeals (such as statistics and examples), and a clear problem-solution organization. The first two questions on writing strategy will help students see that McKibben takes great care to bond with his audience, perhaps because his proposal may not be easy for even the most environmentally conscious readers to act on.

To introduce the essay, you might have the class as a whole compile a list of objections to reducing personal consumption for environmental reasons. After reading the essay, students can discuss whether—and how effectively—McKibben counters each objection. Then, when they've read Derrick Jensen's rebuttal of McKibben's proposal, they can compare the two essays for their strategies and effectiveness. You could apply the same strategy when introducing Margaret Lundberg's argument for a vegetarian lifestyle. See the discussions of Jensen's and Lundberg's essays on pp. 145 and 147 of this manual.

QUESTIONS ON MEANING

1. Paragraphs 4–5 and 9–10 center on environment, paragraphs 7 and 11–13 center on economy, and paragraphs 6, 8, and 14–15 touch on both at the same time. According to McKibben, adopting a simpler lifestyle would improve the world in two ways: by protecting the planet from the devastation caused by waste, and by allowing people more time and money to pursue relationships, cultural enlightenment, and the common good.

2. McKibben blames the consumer economy, especially the actions of manufacturers and advertisers, but also individuals' desire for money and things. Among the examples of waste he cites are disposable water bottles (par. 3), manufacturing that favors cost-savings over efficiencies (4–5, 8), junk mail (6), automotive torque (7), personal trash (9–10), education (11), military spending (13), soil (14), talent (14), executive excess (15), and large houses (17).

3. McKibben's proposed solution is to reduce personal consumption: "The economic mess now transfixing us will mean some kind of change. We can try to hang onto the status quo—living a Wal-Mart life so we can buy cheaply enough to keep the stream of stuff coming. Or we can say uncle" (par. 18). He asks readers to embrace a lifestyle of thrift, returning to a time of "Yankee frugality" when "we couldn't imagine wasting money on ourselves, made do or did without" (16).

QUESTIONS ON WRITING STRATEGY

1. McKibben seems to expect that many if not most readers will agree with his assessment of the problem but not necessarily his solution—a reasonable expectation, given that he's writing for *Mother Jones*, with its mostly liberal and environmentally aware audience. In opening with a personal tale of the satisfaction of recycling, McKibben presents himself as someone who holds the same values his readers do, but then attempts to jar them into deeper consciousness by stressing the quantity of "unnecessary" waste (3). Throughout his examples of shameful behavior in the rest of the essay, he addresses the perpetrators as *you* and *we*—implicating his readers in the wastefulness and unacceptable behavior he describes. By the time he reaches his proposal, the resulting

sense of shared responsibility for the problem should, he seems to hope, soften readers' resistance to change and sacrifice.

2. Examples of *emotional appeals*: the mention of trees and time wasted by junk mail (par. 6); the suggestion that fast acceleration "makes you look like an idiot, or a teenager" (7); the concern for workers and children (12); the examples of profligate CEOs (15). Examples of *ethical appeals*: McKibben's presentation of his community recycling experience (1–3); his admiration for learning (11); his use of *we* (throughout). Examples of *rational appeals*: statistical evidence (e.g., 7, 9); the structure of the argument, dealing with opponents' arguments (see question 4, below). Students' judgments of these appeals will of course vary widely depending on their knowledge and beliefs.

3. The syllogism:

Major premise:	All waste hurts the economy and the environment.
Minor premise:	Personal consumption produces waste.
Conclusion:	Personal consumption hurts the economy and the environment.

Some students might point out, like Derrick Jensen does in "Forget Shorter Showers" (p. 564), that not all consumption is personal; others might reject the premise that waste is harmful: Either complication could render the conclusion invalid.

4. McKibben addresses opposing viewpoints somewhat obliquely, usually making an attempt at common ground then following it with his own assertion. He acknowledges the effectiveness of the Clean Air and Clean Water Acts in paragraph 4, for instance, and accepts that clean-burning engines reduce carbon emissions before asserting that such emissions still contribute to global warming (5). He accepts that some efforts are "maybe perhaps vaguely useful" before suggesting that other efforts could be "actually useful instead" (8). The closest he seems to come to a direct counterargument is in paragraph 9, where he establishes the volumes of waste produced by a large population before refuting the idea that "population is at the root of our troubles." Some students might feel that the author's attempts at counterargument are unfair or at the very least grudging; others may not be able to identify them at all; still others might report that they enjoyed them.

5. McKibben identifies nine categories of waste in paragraphs 4–14: "old-fashioned waste, the dangerous, sooty kind" (4); "waste that comes from everything operating as it should, only too much so" (5); waste that comes from doing something that manifestly doesn't need doing" (6–7); "waste that comes with doing something maybe perhaps vaguely useful when you could be doing something actually useful instead" (8); solid waste (9–10); wasted education (11); waste of human capital (12); government waste (13); and waste of natural resources (14). In each case he offers examples of the kinds of waste he means and establishes their effects. The distinctions establish the scope of the problem and suggest that personal waste is not only significant but the only kind that readers have the power to reduce: "Our wasteful habits wouldn't matter much if there were just a few of us," McKibben says (9).

QUESTIONS ON LANGUAGE

1. McKibben counts himself among the people overwhelmed by waste. By peppering the essay with colloquialisms and attempts at humor, he

lightens the mood and establishes a bond with readers. The tone also allows him to express frustration at the situation.

2. "Stuffporn" is jargon for advertising; "throughput" is jargon for production or output. Other examples of language borrowed from business and economics include "multiply it by proximity" (par. 9), "inefficiencies" (12), "margin" (14), "open sourcing" (18), "stimulus" (19), and "hyperconsumerism" (19). McKibben uses most of these words ironically, highlighting the absurdity of business philosophies and practices.

3. Literally a decorative cord braided by a child as busywork and typically worn with a uniform (such as those for the Boy Scouts), a *boondoggle* is also a colloquial word for a wasteful or unnecessary task.

DERRICK JENSEN
Forget Shorter Showers

Both Derrick Jensen and Bill McKibben are regular contributors to *Orion* magazine. Although McKibben's essay (p. 557) was published in *Mother Jones,* Jensen's essay, published a month later in *Orion,* seems a direct response to his colleague. Read together, these essays should help students recognize that ideas need not be dual opposites or rigid pro/con debates to merit argument. Jensen's strong reaction to McKibben's proposal (and others like it) also shows students how an intelligent and knowledgeable reader like Jensen can counter what may have seemed airtight arguments. Following Jensen's example, students may in turn question some of his arguments, evidence, or assumptions (the first writing suggestion offers a specific approach).

The essay following Jensen's, "Eating Green" by Margaret Lundberg, adds another perspective on personal choices and their potential for effecting environmental change.

QUESTIONS ON MEANING

1. Jensen's thesis, stated in the first and last sentences of paragraph 8, is that simple living "is ineffective at causing the sorts of changes necessary to stop this culture from killing the planet." What Jensen wants, instead, is to "destroy the industrial economy that is destroying the real, physical world"—a revolution. His purpose is to refute claims that cutting back on personal consumption will help the environment.

2. Jensen agrees with McKibben on many points: Both believe the environment is in trouble, both place a great deal of the blame on consumer economy and inadequate government, and both see a desperate need for change. They disagree, however, on one key point: whether consuming less as individuals will do any good. McKibben sees personal choice as the primary driver of consumer economy; therefore, reducing consumption will reduce the damage caused by industry. Jensen, on the other hand, sees industrial culture as the driver; therefore that culture must be rejected and replaced with a different system of values.

3. A *double bind* is an either-or situation in which both choices lead to bad results. Jensen believes that we've become trapped into seeing only two options: continue consuming and harming the planet at our current pace, or reduce consumption and harm the planet more slowly. Both have the end result of "killing the planet" (par. 7). Jensen proposes a third option: dismantling the consumer economy altogether. (Although note that he doesn't specify what system he proposes in its stead.)

4. By stating that he is a practitioner of simple living himself, Jensen attempts to build common ground with his opponents. He applauds the practice but wants readers to accept that they need to do more.

QUESTIONS ON WRITING STRATEGY

1. *Rational appeals*: Jensen uses statistics and other evidence to support his argument (e.g., pars 2, 3, 5), and he walks readers through his deductive reasoning (e.g., 7–11). *Ethical appeals*: as an environmental activist, Jensen portrays himself as someone who cares deeply about the environment; he also concedes that he practices simple living (6). *Emotional appeals*: questioning the sanity of simple living proponents (1), depictions of death and dying (3, 7–8, 11), multiple repetitions of the phrase "killing the planet" (7–8), the suggestion that humans can help the earth as well as harm it (8, 10, 12), absolving readers from blame (9), the assertion that simple living is an act of "suicide" (11).

2. The examples are shocking and grab readers' attention from the start. But Jensen has a stronger reason for invoking them: He sees the environmental crisis as being on a par with the political crises he uses to frame the essay. Much as activists refused to work within the systems of Nazi Germany, antebellum America, Tsarist Russia, and gender and racial oppression—and instead revolted against them—Jensen believes that environmental activists today must reject the status quo and take decisive political action for radical change.

3. Jensen seems to address environmental activists (*Orion* magazine states that its mission is "to inform, inspire, and engage individuals and grassroots organizations in becoming a significant cultural force for healing nature and community"). He apparently hopes to jolt readers out of what he views as dangerous complacency and persuade them to take, or at least support, strong political action. Students' responses will depend on their openness to his arguments.

4. Jensen suggests from the beginning that simple-living advocates ignore the question and fail to see the real issue at hand. He accuses them of oversimplification in paragraphs 2–5 especially, portrays them as falling victim to either-or thinking in paragraph 7, and questions their deductions by claiming that simple living is "predicated on the flawed notion that humans inevitably harm the planet" (8) and asserting that "the logic behind simple living as a political act is suicide" (11).

Some students might see an element of ad hominem attack in Jensen's portrayal of simple living advocates "dancing naked around a fire" (1). Those unconvinced of global warming or climate change might accuse Jensen of begging the question: Because the planet is dying, we must do something radical to save it. Those who do worry about the environment, on the other hand, might consider Jensen's conclusion—the planet is in trouble, so we must abolish capitalism—a non sequitur, although he takes great pains to explain the connection.

5. The main point—that the current global economic system is destroying the planet—has more punch because Jensen enumerates specific effects of consumer culture.

QUESTIONS ON LANGUAGE

1. *Agribusiness* was coined in the mid-1950s in response to economic and cultural shifts: family-run farms to large corporate interests, individual labor to mass production, local consumption to national distribution.
2. Of the given adjectives, *frustrated* and *militant* seem to be the most appropriate to describe Jensen's tone. At times the author sounds exasperated and condescending, as in "well, no" (paragraph 3) and "Uh, I've got some bad news" (5). At other times he seems cautiously optimistic, especially when he reminds readers that there are positive actions they can take to help the planet (8, 10, 12). Overall, he takes a strong militant tone urging readers to revolution.
3. "Or lets talk water. . . . Or let's talk energy. . . . Or let's talk waste." Each of these deliberate sentence fragments follows the same grammatical pattern. The fragments and the parallelism together build a sense of urgency.
4. Jensen knows his proposal is radical and will come off as extreme. By quoting a respected environmental writer, he attempts to persuade readers that his ideas are both reasonable and shared by others.

DERRICK JENSEN ON WRITING

We find ourselves hard-pressed to disagree with Jensen's rules for writing. Keeping readers in mind at all times is the key to communicating with them. And communication, of course, is the reason for writing in the first place. Jensen does have other rules that he shares with his students—cited elsewhere in his book, they include provide the right details, be very clear, and aim for realistic dialog—but as far as we can see his rules are all variations of the first: "don't bore the reader."

———————————

MARGARET LUNDBERG

Eating Green

In the last of three essays that examine how personal choices affect the environment, returning student writer Margaret Lundberg makes an unusual case in favor of vegetarianism. If everybody stopped eating meat or at least ate substantially less of it, she claims, global climate change and overpopulation might cease to be problems.

Lundberg's argument is heartfelt, thoroughly researched, and compelling, although other students may take issue with a few of her sources or the organization of her points; we encourage readers to tackle these complexities in the third writing suggestion and the second question on meaning. We think they'll find that despite some minor flaws, their peer has done an admirable job of researching a challenging subject, synthesizing information, and putting her ideas into writing.

As a small-group activity, you could have students investigate the eating habits of students on your campus. Each group should devise a plan for observing places to eat both on and near campus, with members reporting back their individual findings and then the group as a whole drafting a brief report. These group reports could then be compared in class.

QUESTIONS ON MEANING

1. Lundberg sets up her thesis with a question in paragraph 2: "If all of us adopting a vegetarian diet could slow or stop all of these [environmental] ills, shouldn't we consider it?" She then develops her argument through the body of the essay and answers her question with a thesis statement in the concluding paragraph: "A vegetarian diet would enable us to healthfully feed many more people, and make much better use of the resources we have."

2. Focusing on the environmental damage caused by large-scale, industrialized beef production, Lundberg presents several points to support her claim. First, she says, the diets fed to cows raised for commercial slaughter make them ill, causing them to release large amounts of methane and nitrous oxide into the atmosphere, contributing to global warming (pars. 5–6). "Raising and packaging livestock animals" (6) uses far more energy, water, and chemicals than growing plants, depleting natural resources and increasing pollution (7). At the same time, more land is used to grow animal feed than food for human consumption, to the point that rainforests are being cleared to create more farmable land, contributing more greenhouse gases to the atmosphere; and with less land available for tending vegetables and grains to feed a growing human population, food shortages become a real possibility, especially for people in developing countries (7–8, 11).

3. Increasing levels of greenhouse gases are largely responsible for the recent rise in global temperatures. Lundberg's point is that the gases released by cows' bodily functions—especially on a mass scale—are more damaging to the environment than the carbon-dioxide emissions that are usually blamed for climate change.

4. Lundberg assumes that her readers have children or plan to have children, and that they're concerned for their own health, for their family's health, and for the health of the environment. She also assumes that most are not vegetarians but are willing to consider the idea.

5. Not necessarily. Although Lundberg clearly wishes that everybody on the planet could be persuaded to adopt a vegetarian diet if not a vegan one, at the very least she hopes to convince her readers to cut back significantly on their meat consumption. She makes this concession in the middle of her essay: Although "giving up meat seems like an unreasonable thing to ask" (par. 9), Lundberg admits, she stresses that the sheer quantities of meat in the typical American diet are unhealthful and unnecessary. It seems she'd settle for a few billion converts (8).

QUESTIONS ON WRITING STRATEGY

1. The personal details set the context for Lundberg's proposal and help to establish her ethical appeal as a reasonable, caring person rather than a militant proselytizer. She has taken up vegetarianism and veganism only recently, she says, and has seen her own health improve; that experience made her wonder how her diet choices could improve the planet's health. In admitting to liking meat herself, she anticipates objections and establishes common ground with nonvegetarian readers.
2. In paragraph 9 Lundberg concedes that meat is nutritious, and in paragraphs 10 and 11 she concedes that corporations are trying to find ways to reduce the environmental impacts of factory farming. She quickly dismisses each claim. Some readers may wish she addressed the counterarguments in more detail; others may have different objections that she failed to address.
3. Lundberg intends these rhetorical questions, all of which suggest the long-term implications of dietary choices, to get her readers to think seriously about the problem she has been describing. The final question, in particular, lets Lundberg end with a flourish.
4. Answers will vary. We think Lundberg does an adequate job of examining the environmental effects of industrialized beef, given her focus and purpose. Some readers may think she overlooks the animal-rights arguments for vegetarianism, but those don't seem important to her. Other readers may question the validity of some of her statistics, especially those from potentially biased sources like the Vegan Society or from questionable authorities like the author of a cookbook. (We encourage them to examine her sources more carefully in the third writing suggestion.)

QUESTIONS ON LANGUAGE

1. Lundberg uses quotation marks around "went vegan" (par. 2), "just what the doctor ordered" (2), "Where's the beef?" (3), "do their part" (10), "cow pies" (11), and "Corn Belt" (12). The quotation marks acknowledge that Lundberg is aware she's slipping into colloquialisms. Some readers may feel that she could have edited them out, but the casual language helps to humanize the author.
2. Wendy's and McDonald's are both huge corporate entities that rely on industrial beef production while feeding the demand for large-scale factory farming. In focusing on fast-food franchises who advertise heavily and whose food few would consider healthy, Lundberg implies that much of the meat we eat is junk food or at best a guilty pleasure that could be given up without great sacrifice.
3. We enjoy the word play in Lundberg's title. *Green* refers both to the color of many vegetables and to environmentally conscious practices. By eating greens, she suggests, we're eating green.
4. Students may not be aware that *vegetarian* and *vegan* have slightly different meanings. A vegetarian does not eat meat but will consume animal products that don't require slaughter, such as eggs and dairy products; a vegan eschews consumption of *any* product derived from animals, often extending the ban to nonedibles such as leather and wool.

MARGARET LUNDBERG ON WRITING

Margaret Lundberg's thoughts on writing could help students who think they have nothing to write about or who have trouble starting to write. If they work from their own experiences and feelings, they'll have an easier time finding a subject.

ANNE-MARIE SLAUGHTER

Why Women Still Can't Have It All

As we mention in the headnote to "Why Women Still Can't Have It All," Anne-Marie Slaughter's new feminist manifesto created an enormous stir when it was published in June 2012. We accompany her article in the e-Pages with two samplings of reader responses: quotations collected by *Reader's Digest* in "The Essay That *Rocked* the Internet," and one man's befuddled perspective on the hubbub in Andrew Cohen's blog entry, "'Having It All'? How about 'Doing the Best I Can'?"

Your students may or may not be parents yet, but as Slaughter suggests at several points in her article, the issue of work-life balance affects everybody—especially college students aspiring for professional careers and future families. Although she pointedly acknowledges that her essay is addressed to a very narrow and very privileged segment of the population, her argument for family-friendly working conditions struck a chord with readers of all socioeconomic backgrounds. Some embraced her ideas wholeheartedly; others objected vociferously. We have no doubt that students' own reactions will be equally mixed, and just as strong; classroom debate is sure to be lively. If you have a mix of younger and older students, you might ask if their experiences bear out the contention of the sources quoted by Slaughter that college women today dismiss the possibility of "having it all" or deny that women (or men) of the author's generation ever achieved it.

Note, too, that Slaughter's article is very long: At more than twelve thousand words, it would have taken up approximately twenty pages in the print version of *The Bedford Reader.* Be sure to tell your students to allow themselves plenty of time to read it—at least an hour or two—and then even more time to reread it closely.

QUESTIONS ON MEANING AND STRATEGY

1. "Having it all," in the feminist sense, might be described as pursuing a rewarding career while raising a happy family. Or as Slaughter puts it, "to rise up the ladder as fast as men and also have a family and an active home life (and be thin and beautiful to boot)." Slaughter argues that the juggling involved in having both work and children is impossible for women because of the social assumptions underlying the way most professional jobs are structured, *not* because working mothers are insufficiently motivated or committed. Citing limited opportunities

for women to obtain leadership positions, impossibly long hours and travel requirements, work schedules that conflict with school schedules and family activities, deeply felt motherly instincts, and pressure to prioritize career growth, Slaughter insists that women who value their children are left with no choice but to opt out. Men are better able to combine work and family, Slaughter asserts, but only because they have been socialized to sacrifice family; she would like to see that change.

2. Slaughter introduces her thesis in the paragraph that closes her introduction: "The best hope for improving the lot of all women, and for closing . . . a 'new gender gap'—measured by well-being rather than wages—is to close the leadership gap: to elect a woman president and fifty women senators; to ensure that women are equally represented in the ranks of corporate executives and judicial leaders. Only when women wield power in sufficient numbers will we create a society that genuinely works for all women. That will be a society that works for everyone." Short of achieving an all-female legislature, Slaughter's solutions are outlined in the sections titled "Changing the Culture of Face Time," "Revaluing Family Values," "Redefining the Arc of a Successful Career," and "Rediscovering the Pursuit of Happiness." In practical terms her proposals might be summarized thus: encourage flexible working hours and telecommuting; create workplace "defaults" that align business and family schedules; establish corporate policies that prioritize family; teach leaders and coworkers to respect the discipline and time management required of caregivers; shift hiring and promotion assumptions to allow for occasional steps down or away (what Slaughter calls "investment intervals"); and normalize family commitments by openly acknowledging them and the happiness they bring. Businesses that take these steps, she argues in the section labeled "Innovation Nation," can expect to see higher productivity and creativity from all of their employees as a result. In sum, as she stresses in the final section, "Enlisting Men," Slaughter's thesis is that women in the workplace should stop trying to adhere to traditional masculine values and work instead to persuade men to adopt traditional feminine values.

3. Slaughter is clearly targeting readers like herself—"elite" middle-aged professional women who have children and jobs that allow them some control over their schedules, and who publicly lament that younger women seem to have given up the idea of combining career and family. As she states toward the end of her introductory section, "I am writing for my demographic—highly educated, well-off women who are privileged enough to have choices in the first place." Slaughter addresses these peers directly, informing them that "members of the younger generation have stopped listening" to feminist claims and insisting that "it's time to talk." She acknowledges that for the majority of women, the concept of "having it all" is beyond the realm of possibility, and explains that younger readers don't even see it as an option, but the urgency of her essay and the care with which she outlines causes and effects make it clear that she is also targeting the other readers of the *The Atlantic Monthly*—male and female alike.

4. Slaughter is writing to call into question the assumptions propagated by her generation of feminists and to persuade women in leadership positions to push for change. In the section titled "The Half-Truths We Hold Dear," she enumerates "the stories we tell ourselves, the clichés that [we] typically fall back on when younger women ask us how we have managed to 'have it all.'" Those assumptions are (1) that younger

women aren't determined enough to strike a balance between work and family, (2) that women are comfortable relinquishing parenting responsibilities to their partners, and (3) that women can time having children in such a way that they can build careers in their late thirties and early forties. None of them, Slaughter argues, is true. She is pushing for a new wave of feminism that prioritizes family over career.

READER'S DIGEST

The Essay That *Rocked* the Internet

We include "The Essay That *Rocked* the Internet" as a follow-up to Anne-Marie Slaughter's essay for a simple reason. In curating responses to "Why Women Still Can't Have It All" from around the Web, *Reader's Digest* offers a concise and complex overview of real-world critical reading in action. Students will likely see some of their own opinions reflected in the quotations, but they just as likely will be surprised by how differently other readers interpreted aspects of Slaughter's argument—not to mention how many thousands of people voluntarily wrote about something they read outside of school.

We follow this compilation of excerpts with one full and nuanced reader response from Andrew Cohen, "'Having It All'? How about "Doing the Best I Can'?" That blog entry, too, offers students a model of carefully considered reflective writing in response to reading.

QUESTIONS ON MEANING AND STRATEGY

1. Characterizing "Why Women Still Can't Have It All" as a provocative essay that is "[p]art confessional, part sociological analysis, and part call to arms," the *Reader's Digest* editors focus on the parenting and gender aspects of Slaughter's article (the "confessional" and "sociological analysis") and overlook much of her argument (the "call to arms")—especially her proposals for solving the problem of work-life balance for both women and men. The oversimplification is almost unavoidable, given that the editors attempt to condense a 12,000-word essay to one paragraph and five key points—at the same time, the magazine tends to lean conservative in its political outlook. In general, we'd say it offers a serviceable summary that hits at most of the major issues Slaughter addresses, especially those points that sparked the most debate.

2. As a glance at the magazine's audience demographics shows, the average *Reader's Digest* reader is a middle-aged adult with some college education, a household income of around $60,000, and one or more children living at home; fewer than half are homeowners. More women than men read the magazine (60% of the audience is female), and fewer than a quarter of the readers hold professional or managerial positions (17% are unemployed or retired). They are not, in other words, the "elite" women in leadership roles that Slaughter identifies as her target audience, but average working parents. Accordingly, *Reader's Digest* fo-

cuses on those points and responses that would resonate most with its readers, emphasizing middle- and working-class struggles to balance jobs, families, and traditional gender roles.

3. The examples bear out *Reader's Digest*'s assertion that "[w]omen of every age and background (and plenty of men) let Slaughter know what they thought of her and her ideas about women, work, and family." Offering quotations both critical and supportive of Slaughter's points from women and men of varying socioeconomic statuses—single mothers, stay-at-home fathers, professional writers, "pink collar" workers, older and younger readers, conservatives, feminists, and so forth—the magazine attempts to convey that what readers "thought" of her argument was complex, varied, and deeply felt.

ANDREW COHEN

"Having It All"? How about "Doing the Best I Can"?

Andrew Cohen's impassioned blog entry, the last of three contributions to a debate on work-life balance, offers a man's perspective on what the author believes is at heart a women's issue. As a "single father and a work-at-home dad," Cohen is in a strong position to counter Anne-Marie Slaughter's assumption that men are somehow naturally more inclined to let their partners take care of the children while they climb a career ladder. He is also, like Slaughter, in the enviable position of being able to wield some control over his work schedule; but unlike Slaughter, he doesn't believe that the flexibility gives him any particular advantage as a working parent.

Students may note that although Cohen claims that "earnest public conversation on this topic between and among men is impossible to imagine," several men are among those quoted in the selection sandwiched between his and Slaughter's, "The Essay That *Rocked* the Internet" from *Reader's Digest.* A good starting point for discussion could be to expand on the first question on meaning and strategy: Is "having it all" really a women's-only issue, as Cohen insists? If men really have given up any hope of achieving that state, doesn't that make the issue even more relevant? Why, or why not?

QUESTIONS ON MEANING AND STRATEGY

1. Cohen offers his tentative definition of the phrase: an occasional, temporary feeling of "pride and peace" in having successfully contributed to both work and family. Men can't be part of the debate, he claims, because "having it all," at least as conceived as a "pursuit of a lifestyle that is rich, rewarding and successful in all of its many facets," is solely a women's issue. Most men, he claims, have never believed they could commit equally to their careers and their children, and they understand that they must make sacrifices on both fronts. Although he admires women who aspire to reach the pinnacles in both areas of their lives, Cohen believes that the goal is an impossible one.

2. Cohen is writing to analyze and contribute to the debate spurred by
    Slaughter's article, but also to defend himself—and other fathers like
    him—against her claim that men are more comfortable than women
    sacrificing family life for career aspirations. Most emphatically, he in-
    sists that they are not.
3. Cohen gives multiple examples drawn from personal experience and
    cites the experiences and attitudes of other men in his life to demon-
    strate his understanding of the issue and to prove his claim that most
    fathers (and mothers) are deeply committed parents who "live nanny-
    less lives of quiet desperation, just hoping that the choices we make,
    for ourselves and our families, end up being sound ones." At the same
    time, he stresses throughout his blog entry that he respects women
    and applauds their efforts to do better; he also goes out of his way to
    "give Slaughter credit" for those aspects of her argument that he either
    agrees with or finds illuminating. Some readers may feel that he's a
    little too earnest in his self-deprecations or may doubt the sincerity of
    his praises of women, but he certainly makes the effort.
4. Throughout his piece Cohen compares men and women, each time
    concluding that women are stronger, smarter, braver, and so forth. The
    comparisons help him to establish common ground with readers—es-
    pecially women—who may not agree with his position.

PART THREE

MIXING THE METHODS

In this part of the book we provide an anthology, arranged alphabetically by author, of eight works by very well-known writers. The collection has a dual purpose. First, we want to widen the tight focus of the previous ten chapters so that students see the methods as a kit of tools to be used *in combination* as the need arises. All eight selections demonstrate just this flexibility in approach, narrating here, comparing there, analyzing a process for a couple of paragraphs, defining a term when helpful. The headnote to each selection lists the methods the author most relies on, pointing to specific paragraphs. And the introduction to Part Three gives students a list of questions—a kind of crib sheet of the methods—that they can use to explore or focus any subject.

The second goal of this anthology is to give you more leeway in your assignments. You can teach this part as a "mixing the methods" unit, of course, but you can also pluck out individual selections for any number of uses. If you want to show how a particular method works with other methods, you can point to, say, the classification in Judy Brady's "I Want a Wife" or the description in E. B. White's "Once More to the Lake." If you're just seeking another example of a particular method, you can turn to, say, Martin Luther King's "I Have a Dream" for argument and persuasion or George Orwell's "Shooting an Elephant" for narration. If you think students will respond to the thematic pairing of White's "Once More to the Lake" with Brad Manning's "Arm Wrestling with My Father" (in Chap. 5), you can assign them together.

We have highlighted the possible links in several ways. As we mentioned above, the headnote to each essay in this part itemizes the main methods used by the author. Among the writing suggestions for each selection in this part is at least one "Connections" topic that pulls in an essay from Part Two. For more general thematic links among selections, we provide a "Thematic Table of Contents" just after the book's main contents.

SHERMAN ALEXIE
Superman and Me

In this touching essay, Sherman Alexie charts both the plight of American Indians living on reservations and his own escape from that plight through a devotion to reading and sheer willpower. You might begin discussion by asking the class to enumerate the problems that Alexie suggests American Indians face: poverty, malnutrition, addiction, prejudice, an overriding sense of helplessness and failure. Students might then consider the personal qualities they see in the writer that helped him overcome such adverse circumstances. Make sure that students recognize Alexie's deep sense of ambivalence as he tries to cast himself as a saving hero.

Some discussion should certainly focus on Alexie's unorthodox writing style. Students should consider the effect of the very short sentences and relentless repetition. The accumulation of these devices gives the essay much of its power and suggests Alexie's overriding theme of childlike stubbornness and determination to be heard. This aspect of the piece could be the subject of small-group discussion.

Students interested in exploring more of Alexie's prose (he is also a poet) can be referred to his short-story collections *The Lone Ranger and Tonto Fistfight in Heaven* (1993), *The Toughest Indian in the World* (2000), *War Dances* (2009), and *Blasphemy* (2012). In addition, Alexie wrote the screenplays for the independent films *Smoke Signals* and *The Business of Fancydancing*, which are available for download and on DVD; you might consider screening portions of either film to shed light on reservation life. (The oral histories from a Lakota Sioux reservation collected by *National Geographic*, available in the e-Pages could accomplish the same goal.) Alexie also has a Web site at *fallsapart.com*.

QUESTIONS ON MEANING

1. On its surface a literacy narrative, "Superman and Me" is also a plea for better education for American Indians and a statement of why the author writes. Or as Alexie expresses the purpose of all his work so poignantly in his concluding sentence, "I am trying to save our lives."
2. Alexie's childhood on the reservation was painful, except when he was reading—although even then he read "with equal parts joy and desperation" (par. 7). Speaking and writing about himself in the third person in paragraph 5 allows him to distance himself from the past while downplaying his success, especially for "Indians and non-Indians" who distrust intelligent Native Americans (6). Students should note that paragraph 5 is the only place in the essay Alexie uses the third person to speak about himself. The statement is ironic.
3. A "smart Indian," as Alexie suggests, threatens the status quo and is "widely feared and ridiculed by Indians and non-Indians alike" (par. 6) because he (or she) challenges assumptions, battles complacency, aims for improvement, and seeks change for the community. Notice that Alexie explicitly states that he is smart in paragraphs 7 and 8, asserting that he himself is dangerous.

4. Both Superman and Alexie are in the process of "breaking down the door" (par. 4). In each case the door serves as a metaphor for illiteracy and resistance, for the author as a child and for the students he attempts to reach as an adult. By casting Superman as his role model, Alexie implies that he sees himself as something of a reluctant hero. He managed to extract himself from the difficulties of reservation life through education, and he wants the same for others.

QUESTIONS ON WRITING STRATEGY

1. Alexie seems to be writing for a wider audience. He takes pains to describe the conditions of reservation life and the weaknesses of reservation schooling; he also refers to other Indians in the third person, as *they* and *them* (pars. 6, 8).
2. Alexie repeats himself relentlessly throughout the essay. Some examples: "Superman is breaking down the door" / "I am breaking down door" (par. 4); "I pretend to read the words" (4); "an Indian boy living on the reservation" (4); "I was smart. I was arrogant. I was lucky" (7, 8); "I was trying to save my life" (7) / "They are trying to save their lives" (8) / "I am trying to save our lives" (8); "novels, short stories, and poems" (8); and "'Books,' I say" (8). In paragraph 7 the fourteen instances of "I read" stress that the process of learning to read required persistence and ingenuity. Here and elsewhere, the repetitions create a forceful staccato rhythm that is almost hypnotic; they also reinforce the sense of a stubborn child who is determined to learn—and to be heard. And, of course, they give the essay an irresistible coherence.
3. We can infer that Alexie writes serious but accessible fiction and poetry about the struggles of American Indian life, especially on reservations, and that he uses his writing to subvert stereotypes and empower Indian readers.
4. Alexie's sentences in this paragraph (and elsewhere) are a model of parallel structure, both within sentences and among them. Each sentence of comparison shows students performing poorly in school but using the same skills quite well on their own. His point is that these children are much more intelligent than their teachers give them credit for, and that low expectations encourage students to fail.
5. Alexie paints a picture of determination under desperate circumstances. As he portrays it, reservation life is characterized by unemployment and poverty (par. 1), illness and premature death (2), emotional pain (5), illiteracy (6), and fighting (6)—but also celebrations, storytelling, and laughter (6), and perhaps most of all, hope (8).

QUESTIONS ON LANGUAGE

1. The short sentences and simple structure mimic the writing level one would expect of a child in grade school. Alexie writes from the perspective of his childhood self learning to read and write.
2. Paragraphs, Alexie explains, group like things together and help them work "for a common purpose" (par. 4)—in other words, they facilitate unity and coherence. Just as written paragraphs hold together thoughts on a page, Alexie's conceptual paragraphs—communities, families, individual family members—help people stick together and work toward a goal.
3. From the Latin *prōdigium,* or "portent," the word *prodigy* originally referred to an omen of danger; now it is used to describe a person, usually

a child, with exceptional abilities. We enjoy the hints of its obsolete usage in Alexie's emphasis on the dangers of intelligence.

SHERMAN ALEXIE ON WRITING

Alexie speaks and writes freely about his role as an "American Indian
Writer." The quotations we've selected emphasize the mix of humor and pain
evident in "Superman and Me" and his other writing. Most students will be
familiar with "the Earth Mother and Shaman Man thing" that colors much
writing by and about Native Americans. Indeed, it may color students' own
impressions of Indian life, so that Alexie's depiction comes as a surprise.

JUDY BRADY

I Want a Wife

In the late 1980s newspapers and magazines quoted an instantly famous
remark attributed to the actress Joan Collins after her divorce from musician
Peter Holm. Declaring that her bitter public divorce battle had soured her on
remarrying, Collins is also said to have quipped, "I don't need a husband, I
need a wife." But we suspect that the credit for originating this epigram be-
longs to Judy Brady.

Instructors who have taught this essay in earlier editions report that it's
a trusty class-rouser, evoking lively comments and a few intense disputes.
Does Brady overstate her case in "I Want a Wife"? Some students, reading
her essay in the new millennium, may think so. Perhaps their skepticism indicates real advances in the status of women since Brady first wrote in 1972.
Do wives today play roles as humble and exacting as the one Brady details
here? Are men as well as women freer today to depart from prescribed patterns of behavior? Are women still as angry as Brady was? Note that similar
questions are addressed in the third writing suggestion. The trio of arguments about balancing work and family that appear in the e-Pages implicitly
and explicitly counter some of Brady's attitudes toward men and feminism,
so the four selections together create an even stronger basis for discussion
and writing.

Give students some time to consider the above questions by having them
collaboratively update Brady's essay: What are the requirements of a wife
these days? Students can replace "wife" with "husband," "girlfriend," or
"boyfriend" if they prefer. You might ask a few groups to read their responses
aloud to the class as a way to open discussion of Brady's essay.

QUESTIONS ON MEANING

1. The essay lists them all. In general, the duties of a wife seem to entail
    making life easy and comfortable for everyone in the family—except the
    wife herself.

2. What it all boils down to, in Brady's view, is that husbands shoulder whatever responsibilities they want to assume. All others they assign to their wives.
3. The thesis is implied: Wives are not persons but conveniences whose subservient roles have been fashioned by husbands.
4. Answers will vary. Are all men as demanding and insensitive as the composite male chauvinist Brady draws? Are there fewer who resemble him nowadays than there were in 1972, when the essay was first published? The class might like to consider the extent to which traditional roles have changed in the past decade.

QUESTIONS ON WRITING STRATEGY

1. Because the author's name clearly indicates that she is a woman, the title is a surefire attention-getter.
2. The first two paragraphs establish Brady's credentials, position her essay in the real world, and show from the outset that wishing for a wife is not uncommon—among men.
3. Brady's tone is sardonic.
4. Avoiding the pronoun, though a bit awkward here and there, contributes greatly to the irony of "I Want a Wife." It dehumanizes a wife; she is not a woman but a thing to be used.
5. Readers of *Ms.* have feminist leanings. To us, the essay's observations of husbands and wives remain fresh: "Supermom" is, after all, a recent coinage. However, not everyone will agree.
6. The principle of analysis is determined by the thesis: The role of a wife can be divided into jobs that serve others, especially the husband. Other principles of analysis might be the jobs a wife does that require brainpower or the satisfactions of the role of wife—but these, of course, would produce entirely different essays.
7. The groups of duties are nurse-governess (par. 3), maid (4), confidante (5), social planner (6), and sex object (7). Today, "bread winner" might get more play than Brady gives it (par. 3).

QUESTIONS ON LANGUAGE

1. It emphasizes the selfishness and the demanding tone of the words. The words themselves reduce a wife to the level of a possession.
2. You might be able to elicit a definition of *monogamy* by asking your class to list other words they know that contain *mono-* and to list what all the definitions have in common.
3. The essay's diction is appropriate, the words easy for any intelligent reader to understand. The repetition of "I want a wife" and the author's use of short sentences give the essay a staccato beat that underscores the anger behind it.

JUDY BRADY ON WRITING

Brady's essay is a perfect example of writing derived from the rhetorical situation. She went from "complaining" at a meeting of frustrated women to reading her essay in front of a crowd to, later, publishing it. Students should be made aware of their own opportunities to turn their private gripes into coherent and audience-appropriate public arguments, perhaps in the form of an opinion piece for the campus newspaper.

JUDITH ORTIZ COFER

The Cruel Country

Judith Ortiz Cofer's moving essay uses academic theory to navigate complicated emotional terrain—the conflicting senses of grief and liberation upon a loved one's death. Students should be inspired, we hope, to see how effectively writers can adapt ideas from scholarly works to make sense of their own lives and feelings. They might also be inspired to conduct their own analyses of family photographs, a project we suggest in the journal prompt and the first writing suggestion.

It seems likely that Cofer's musings on her mother's life were inspired at least in part by the posthumous publication of Roland Barthes's unfinished *Mourning Diary*, which was curated and translated with much fanfare in 2010. Like Cofer, Barthes examines his deeply conflicted emotions upon the death of his mother after a long illness. Unlike Cofer, he was writing solely for himself. *The New Yorker* published excerpts from the book in its September 13, 2010 issue; you may wish to share some bits of it with your class.

Students who are intrigued by Cofer's Latina perspective may want to read more of her writing, such as the books *Silent Dancing* (1990) and *The Meaning of Consuelo* (2003), or one of the following: *Reclaiming Medusa: Short Stories by Contemporary Puerto Rican Women*, edited by Diana Velez (1988); Julia Alvarez's *How the Garcia Girls Lost Their Accents* (1991); or Laura Esquivel's *Like Water for Chocolate* (1992). A film based on Esquivel's book was released in 1993 and is available for download or on DVD.

QUESTIONS ON MEANING

1. The family moved to New Jersey, Cofer suggests, because her father joined the US Navy and was stationed there. Her mother returned to Puerto Rico as soon as he died: The reason behind her "*exilio*," or exile (par. 6), passed, she was no longer tied to the States and could return home.
2. Cofer is mystified by what Roland Barthes calls the "*punctum*" (par. 3) of the photograph, "the point of intersection between viewer and image, that detail" that draws the viewer in (4). In this case that detail is "the little spray of white flowers adorning her [mother's] hair" (8). It intrigues Cofer because, although her mother would have been in mourning, the flowers suggest celebration or flirtation (8). The photograph suggests to Cofer that her mother felt ambivalent in her grief, possibly even relieved by her husband's death, much as Cofer seems to feel in her grief for her mother. (We encourage students to explore this implication in the third writing suggestion.)
3. Students may need to look up *muse* in a dictionary to understand Cofer's allusion. In Greek mythology, each of the nine Muses—daughters of Zeus and Mnemosyne—presided over one of the arts or sciences. The word has come to mean a guiding spirit, or any source of creative inspiration. What Cofer is saying is that most of her work as a writer has been inspired and guided by a desire to understand her mother.

4. Cofer wants to memorialize her mother and express how the woman in-
    fluenced her career as a writer. At the same time, she seems to want to
    examine her own "struggle" (par. 11) with mixed feelings upon a parent's
    death.

QUESTIONS ON WRITING STRATEGY

1. The line expresses a paradox: Mourning, Barthes suggests, is a mental
    state that is at once painful and liberating. The quotation forecasts a
    theme of grief mixed with a twinge of relief.
2. Cofer assumes an audience familiar with the running themes in her work
    and with the philosophy of Roland Barthes—essentially well-educated
    readers versed in literature and theory. She also assumes some familiar-
    ity with the cultural shifts that accompanied Puerto Ricans' migration
    to the mainland United States in the 1950s and 1960s, a subject she has
    written about extensively. While citing Barthes might seem esoteric to
    most first-year college students, we think Cofer does an effective job of
    giving her readers credit for intelligence while also offering accessible
    examples to help ground both his and her ideas.
3. The conflicting details Cofer provides—bright clothing (par. 1), "shiny"
    hair (7), bared tan arms (7), the spray of flowers (8), and a painting of
    "an idealized seashore scene at dusk" (9), alongside a stiff posture (1),
    a face "neither smiling nor frowning" (1), a "hint of gray" (7), a sense of
    "seriousness that belies the outfit" (7), and a feeling of being "alone in
    a place that had grown strange" (11)—create a dominant impression of
    a confused, struggling woman "caught . . . between emotions" (2).
4. Cofer uses Barthes's concept of the "*punctum*" (par. 3) of a photograph
    as her principle of analysis. Drawing on his theory, she examines that
    one aspect of the photograph that "touches you or triggers a quickening
    of the pulse" (4).

QUESTIONS ON LANGUAGE

1. The title borrows Roland Barthes's metaphor for mourning (see the first
    question on writing strategy) and adds an implication that living in the
    United States, for Cofer's mother anyway, was an unpleasant experience
    of exile.
2. Using formal, academic language and concepts to explore her mother's
    and her own emotions, Cofer's tone might best be described as ambiva-
    lent. She is at once detached from and immersed in her grief.
3. Cofer uses the word *planes* in its geometrical sense of intersecting
    lines, whereas students may know it only as an abbreviation of *air-
    planes*. The word comes from the Latin *plānum*, "flat surface"

MARTIN LUTHER KING, JR.

I Have a Dream

Although King's speech was meant to be heard aloud, it remains impressive on the page, and it supplies a splendid illustration of a proposal that appeals to emotion. You will probably wish to point out, however, that some of its strategies are directed primarily toward listeners: the strong use of repetition, parallelism, and direct references to the audience.

Your students will better appreciate the power of this speech if they see or at least hear it as delivered by King in 1963. (One source for video of the speech: *youtube.com/watch?v=iEMXaTkUFA*.) Have students in small groups discuss the differences between reading and hearing this speech. Alternately, have a group of students listen to the speech and make a presentation to the rest of the class, playing certain brief selections and commenting on the differences in hearing versus reading.

If you do have students listen to the speech, you might encourage them to consider the textual differences in the spoken and printed versions. King revised the original text of his speech, no doubt after he had received many requests for a printable version. (Speakers often make such changes, either because a transcription from spoken delivery might contain elements that would transfer awkwardly to the page or because they want to make improvements.) The printed version of King's speech adds a few passages that were not part of his original delivery, including from "*Now* is the time" through "1963 is not an end, but a beginning" in paragraphs 4 and 5, and paragraphs 8 and 9 in their entirety. In our view, the new passages are wonderful: "to lift our nation from the quicksands of racial injustice to the solid rock of brotherhood" (4) and "You have been the veterans of creative suffering" (8) in particular. We don't believe that in making changes Dr. King lost the power of his spoken discourse; if anything, he strengthened it. Some students, however, may disagree.

QUESTIONS ON MEANING

1. The purpose is to inspire its hearers, despite their setbacks and disappointments, to go on working for civil rights.
2. African American people have yet to receive the freedom and the justice that the nation's founders guaranteed.
3. While King praises the rise of black activism, he believes it can advance its cause by nonviolent means, as he makes clear in this paragraph.
4. King recalls both early American history and the present occasion in his opening paragraph and in paragraphs 3 and 5.

QUESTIONS ON WRITING STRATEGY

1. Besides directly addressing his followers (in pars. 6–8), King employs parallelism in phrases such as "from the dark and desolate valley of segregation to the sunlit path of racial justice" (4). Still more impressively, he builds parallel structures by repeating phrases and clauses,

lending them tremendous emphasis. This strategy informs much of the essay. In paragraph 2 there is a refrain ("One hundred years later"), and in paragraph 4 another (*"Now* is the time"). Most powerful of all are "I have a dream" (11–18) and "Let freedom ring" (20–27) — repeated again and again, at the start of each paragraph.

2. Paragraph 6.
3. Though he begins by recalling the past and its disappointments, he devotes by far the largest part of his speech to the future, in his extended description of his dream (pars. 10–27).
4. King's reasonableness is especially evident in his condemnation of bitterness and violence (par. 6). His personal authority — having been discriminated against and failing, having led demonstrations and achieving victories — combines with his rhetoric to give the speech its power.
5. In paragraph 2 the metaphors strengthen King's connection with the African Americans in his audience by showing his understanding of his race's hobbled, outcast state. In paragraph 4 the extended metaphor of the promissory note gives an argument by analogy, linking African American history to something concrete. The remaining metaphors in this paragraph intensify King's urgent appeal by contrasting what is with what could (and should) be.

QUESTIONS ON LANGUAGE

1. King uses concrete words in much of his imagery: the metaphors of "manacles" and "chains" (par. 2), that of the "check" (4), the visualization of the "governor's lips" (16). But for most of the speech his diction is largely abstract, as seems necessary to encompass two centuries of the past and the whole of the future.
2. King employs many figures, some biblical in connotation. Besides those noted in question 5 on writing strategy and in the preceding question, they include "summer of . . . discontent" (5), an echo from Shakespeare ("Now is the winter of our discontent / Made glorious summer by this sun of York" — the opening lines of *Richard III*); "the palace of justice," "the cup of bitterness" (6); "justice rolls down like waters" and "righteousness like a mighty stream" (7); "storms of persecution" and "winds of police brutality" (8); "valley of despair" (9); the "heat of injustice and oppression" and the "oasis of freedom and justice" (13); the topographical references in paragraph 18; the "mountain of despair" and the "stone of hope" (19); and the "symphony of brotherhood" (19).
3. There seems freshness in King's application of *curvaceous* to California mountain peaks, instead of to (as in the usual cliché) Hollywood film goddesses.

MAXINE HONG KINGSTON
No Name Woman

Students are usually moved by Kingston's evocation of a haunting childhood story. Ask them to describe their own reactions to the tale of Kingston's aunt. Does it seem completely alien, from a world far away, or more immediate? Does it hold students' imaginations?

Kingston's books *The Woman Warrior* and *China Men* are sources of further mystery and understanding about Chinese and American culture. In addition, a number of films have depicted Chinese village life: *Ju Dou, Raise the Red Lantern*, and *To Live* are just a few available on DVD. Students who are interested in the films might consider writing a comparative paper on the role of women, for example, in Kingston's essay and in one of the films. How important is the medium to the message? What do the two media say in common? Another use of the films, given their complicated imagery, is to assign a collaborative paper. Interested students could watch one film together, discuss it, and prepare a comparison between it and Kingston's essay, addressing the questions above.

QUESTIONS ON MEANING

1. Kingston and her mother share the purpose of telling a riveting story. Kingston's purpose is also self-examination and an inquiry into Chinese cultural attitudes; her mother's is also to instill these cultural attitudes in her.
2. Her aunt's husband could not have been the child's father (par. 3). Kingston posits two possible fathers: a man who "commanded [the aunt] to be with him" (15), and a man she herself was drawn to (21).
3. It is meant to warn her against adultery and, by extension, sexuality.
4. Kingston is haunted by her Chinese heritage; she seeks "ancestral help" (par. 22). Her aunt is a powerful representative of that heritage, an example of its grip on women and their emotions. Her life and death are a profound "family secret" that transcends Kingston's own immediate family.

QUESTIONS ON WRITING STRATEGY

1. Kingston's family and other older Chinese would be unlikely to read the essay: Kingston does address Chinese Americans directly (par. 12), and her detailed descriptions of Chinese and Chinese American cultures indicate that she is trying to explain them to other Americans. Older Chinese, and particularly her family, would be shocked that she is breaking the silence about her aunt. Chinese Americans would see themselves and their own "haunting" in her story. Other Americans might be enlightened about the complexity and power the Chinese heritage holds.
2. The story of the aunt is supposed to be kept secret by the mother. The mother's tale is supposed to be kept secret by Kingston but is instead examined minutely in this essay. Kingston's telling the secret of her

aunt's story is an act of rebellion equivalent to her aunt's. Thus, the opening line presages all the themes of the essay (and creates suspense as well).

3. The effect is to intensify the confusion of reality and truth and to show the subjective nature of memory and family history. Kingston creates this effect in passages such as "I want her fear to have lasted just as long as rape lasted" (par. 18), "I hope that the man my aunt loved appreciated a smooth brow" (25), and "She may have gone to the pigsty as a last act of responsibility" (44). You might want to draw students' attention to places where Kingston's different sources are intertwined—for example, "My mother spoke about the raid as if she had seen it, when she and my aunt, a daughter-in-law to a different household, should not have been living together at all" (19).

4. The details in paragraphs 15–18 tell a much bleaker story: "She obeyed him" (par. 16), "No one talked sex, ever" (18). The details in paragraphs 21–28 are those of a more romantic tale: "she often worked at herself in the mirror" (23), "my aunt combed individuality into her bob" (25), "she dreamed of a lover for the fifteen days of New Year's" (28). Kingston seems more caught up in the romantic version of the story, in her aunt's desire and need to rebel.

5. Her aunt might have been "commanded . . . to lie with" the father of her child (par. 15), or she might have "let dreams grow" and "offered us up for a charm that vanished" (21). The raid might have been organized by her rapist (16) or by villagers who were "speeding up the circling of events" (39). She might have killed her child because it was "a foreign growth that sickened her every day" (43) or because "Mothers who love their children take them along" (46). In the end Kingston concludes that her aunt's suicide was caused by her feelings of imprisonment within the conventions of village life.

QUESTIONS ON LANGUAGE

1. Kingston's poetic language shows how deeply she responds to her Chinese heritage and its tales. Some striking phrases include "a protruding melon of a stomach" (par. 3), "the heavy, deep-rooted women were to maintain the past against the flood" (20), "women looked like great sea snails" (27), "violence could open up a black hole, a maelstrom that pulled in the sky" (37).

2. You might want to explain the "commensal" tradition (par. 19), in which food is shared by the generations of an extended family. The idea of food and its allocation is central to societies, like China's, where resources are stretched to their utmost. Kingston underscores this in paragraph 15, when she describes her ancestors as "people who hatch their own chicks and eat the embryos and the heads for delicacies and boil the feet in vinegar for party food, leaving only the gravel, eating even the gizzard lining."

3. Kingston blurs the distinction between history and her interpretation of it.

MAXINE HONG KINGSTON ON WRITING

In this interview Kingston discloses a profound belief in the power of writing to generate writing, even to bring order and meaning to one's life. Some students may have had this experience of writing, and perhaps they can confirm Kingston's words for students who haven't. (Students often don't realize that the turmoil of writing can actually be productive.) Kingston also slips in a small warning: It's fine to let yourself go in drafting, but eventually the "intellectual" (Kingston seems to mean "critical") side must kick in for revision.

GEORGE ORWELL
Shooting an Elephant

Orwell's gripping narrative, told with vivid detail and an appealing self-effacement, tends to stick in the memory of anyone who studies it. Orwell's elegant prose may at first put some students off, but even they will soon enough be caught up in the narrator's tale.

Indelible as it is, the essay may strike students as remote from their concerns because it takes place in a country and a time far from their own. If you find this response, point out that the essay tells of doing what seems necessary, even what's wrong, to save face. Governments and their representatives everywhere, including our own, commit dubious actions for just this reason. The second writing suggestion can help students discover the relation between Orwell's experience and their own: Ask students to scour newspapers, TV news programs, or news blogs for examples of contemporary face-saving among public officials. In small groups each student could present one such example for discussion of the perpetrator's likely motives as well as the effects of such behavior.

QUESTIONS ON MEANING

1. Orwell explains that he took his .44 Winchester with him because "the noise might be useful *in terrorem*" (par. 3). His borrowing the elephant rifle later (4) seems a wise precaution because the elephant had killed a man. As he explains in paragraph 5, the rifle was for self-defense only.
2. The answer is twofold. He had to save face—that was the more important reason. But, as he mentions in paragraph 9, his being a bad shot also influenced his behavior by injecting an element of fear.
3. He expresses the epiphany most clearly and vehemently in paragraph 7: "I perceived in this moment that when the white man turns tyrant it is his own freedom that he destroys." And so on to the end of the paragraph.
4. The coolie's death put the young Orwell "legally in the right." By the time he wrote "Shooting an Elephant," though, Orwell was no longer motivated by any need to save face. He had the courage to tell his story truthfully and unsparingly, awful as it was. It seems clear that the mature Orwell did not share his younger self's view of the coolie's death.
5. Orwell's purpose is clearly to show, through his experience of shooting the elephant, how the need to save face motivates—indeed, compels— the actions of himself and every other imperialist.

QUESTIONS ON WRITING STRATEGY

1. These paragraphs, because they reveal so much about the author's feelings toward his job and toward the Burmese who made it difficult, shed light on the complex motives that resulted in the unnecessary shooting. They also, perhaps, somewhat justify the author's behavior—to himself and to us.

2. He explains the circumstances best in his opening paragraphs. He had come to hate imperialism and all that it stood for. Still, because it was his job, he had to do "the dirty work of Empire." Adding to his misery was the abuse he and his English compatriots had to endure from the Burmese.

3. With hindsight, Orwell has a broader and deeper perspective on the events. At the time, he was bitter, embarrassed, and a little afraid. In retrospect, he can see his foolishness and the tyranny he helped to further.

4. The paragraphs seem to unfold almost in real time, and the details of the wounded elephant are excruciating. We understand, almost too plainly, Orwell's horror at his act.

5. The Burmese are portrayed as both detestable (spitting on European women, yelling "with hideous laughter," "sneering") and pitiable ("wretched prisoners huddling in the stinking cages," "gray, cowed faces," "scarred buttocks"). The contradiction makes Orwell's position "perplexing and upsetting."

QUESTIONS ON LANGUAGE

1. The term refers to the annual period during which a male elephant is most sexually aroused and is often violent.

2. Some examples: "chucked up my job" (par. 2), "had taken the wrong direction" (3), "rubbish van" (3), "had come suddenly upon him round the corner of the hut" (4), "I ought not to shoot him" (6), and various uses of *got*, such as "I had got to do it" (7), "I had got to shoot" (7), and "I had got to act quickly" (8).

3. *Sahib* is a title of respect from the Urdu use of the Arabic *cahib*, meaning "friend."

GEORGE ORWELL ON WRITING

This is a grim account of the writing process! "Writing a book is a horrible, exhausting struggle, like a long bout of some painful illness." But students who have suffered when writing even a brief paper may take heart from Orwell's account of his agonies.

Orwell's remark about the need to efface one's own personality (cited in the second discussion question) echoes similar advice given by T. S. Eliot in his familiar essay "Tradition and the Individual Talent" (1919). Blasting the Romantic poets' notion of writing as self-expression, Eliot finds the poet obligated to do something more interesting than vent personal emotions. He adds: "But, of course, only those who have personality and emotions to express know what it means to want to escape from these things."

Orwell here stresses the importance of writing both to achieve something readable and beautiful and—more important, because it affects the artistry of the finished work—writing to improve society.

JONATHAN SWIFT
A Modest Proposal

That Swift is being ironic in proposing this monstrous solution to the problems of Ireland usually dawns slowly on a few students. It will be a highly entertaining class wherein someone thinks Swift is serious. From Swift's essay a perfectly straightforward argument for Christian charity may be inferred. For a contemporary satiric essay that depends on irony, see Linnea Saukko's "How to Poison the Earth" (p. 309).

The irony of Swift's essay is masterful and inspiring. Students who would like to imitate Swift's tone will benefit from feedback on their attempts. Try assigning the class a single paragraph written in a tone of heavy irony. (You may wish to leave the subject up to students, or integrate this with the first writing suggestion.) Give students time in class to read their paragraphs aloud in small groups (it will help if every student in the group has a copy) and to discuss how they might revise their work to improve the tone and the point(s) they are making.

QUESTIONS ON MEANING

1. Swift is proposing that the Irish poor sell their year-old children to the rich for meat.
2. Swift is calling for charity and compassion. Some specific alternatives for relieving poverty are given in Swift's list of "other expedients," paragraph 29.
3. Swift's essay calls attention to both the plight of the poor in Ireland and the hard-heartedness of their oppressors.
4. Swift's image of the begging mothers and their children immediately arouses readers' sympathy and prepares them to react with horror against the "modest" proposal.
5. Objections should be obvious, unless one regards a human being as an animal to be butchered.

QUESTIONS ON WRITING STRATEGY

1. The author writes as a reasonable, kind, serious do-gooder, impatient with the failure of those in power to do anything about the problem.
2. Swift does this effectively by calling his proposal "modest," by citing authorities and experts to back him up (such as the "very knowing American," par. 9), by carefully listing the advantages of the proposal (21–28), by his concern that the flesh would spoil if exported (31), and by professing at the end that he doesn't stand to make a penny himself.
3. Probably not until paragraph 9.
4. Surely to our feelings. Most of the reasonable arguments are deliberately monstrous, although other convincing points appeal to reason in paragraph 29.
5. The process analysis makes us study the proposal in its every gruesome particular. It forces our noses into the proposal, and thus into the plight

of the Irish poor, in a way mere generalities would not have. The cause-and-effect analysis specifies the ways in which the proposal will achieve its goals, summarized in paragraph 33 as "advancing our trade, providing for infants, relieving the poor, and giving some pleasure to the rich."

QUESTIONS ON LANGUAGE

1. The words from breeding and butchery include "dam" (par. 4); "breed" (10); "carcass" (14); "flay" (15); "dressing them hot" (16); "mares in foal . . . ready to farrow" (26); "barreled beef . . . bacon" (27); and "customers for infants' flesh" (28).
2. Swift's vocabulary is extensive. When they read "A Modest Proposal," students might have to use their dictionaries more than they usually do when reading an essay. The exercise might increase their vocabularies.

E. B. WHITE
Once More to the Lake

Among White's essays, this is one of the most often reprinted. In July 1941 White made a pilgrimage back to the Belgrade Lakes, northwest of Augusta, Maine, together with his young son, Joel. "This place is as American as a drink of Coca Cola," he wrote to his wife, Katharine. "The white collar family having its annual liberty. I must say it seems sort of good" (*Letters of E. B. White*, 1976). After his return to civilization, White produced "Once More to the Lake" for a column he was then contributing to *Harper*'s magazine. Too marvelous to be a reasonable model for most student writers, the essay can encourage them to believe that their own memories are worth recording and can interest others. "Once More to the Lake" exhibits a whole array of rhetorical methods, too: description, narration, exemplification, comparison and contrast, even process analysis.

Of course, it is White's description—of place, people, feelings—that is most inimitable, but students can try their hand in a small way at first. Give them a one-paragraph writing assignment—even with a word limit, if you desire—to describe a place that is highly familiar to them. Working in small groups, students can read aloud their paragraphs and get feedback on how they might revise them to make the images more vivid, the phrasing more precise, the details more developed. (This will work best if students bring copies of their paragraphs for the other members of their group.) Fine-tuning their own writing on this small scale should give students the confidence to undertake larger writing projects (like those in the writing suggestions).

QUESTIONS ON MEANING

1. White senses that nothing essential at the lake has changed; besides, he sustains the illusion that his son is himself as a boy and that he has become his own father (par. 4 and later passages).

2. Once, inboard motors had made a sleepy sound; today, the outboards seem "petulant, irritable." A central detail: "this was the note that jarred, the one thing that would sometimes break the illusion and set the years moving."

3. White's son is engaged by the same attractions: the joy of getting up early and going off by himself in a boat (par. 4), the fun of learning tricks with a motor (10). But the essay sets forth an insight that is White's alone, and the boy is not portrayed in any clear detail until the final paragraph.

4. White's purpose, made explicit in the final paragraph, is to set forth a theme: that although time at the lake seems to have stood still, time for the writer has been passing. He has aged and he will die like his father before him.

QUESTIONS ON WRITING STRATEGY

1. The repetitions help set forth the central theme of the essay. (In the answer to question 4 above we suggest one way of stating it.)

2. Beautifully arranged, this essay doesn't completely unfold its purpose until its final line. By a multitude of details, we have been lulled into accepting the illusion that time stands still. Suddenly, in one unforgettable image, White invokes reality. The feeling of donning an ice-cold bathing suit is a familiar sensation from childhood, but the cold of the suit also suggests the cold of the grave.

3. Young readers, we trust, will understand and appreciate it, too. Ask them. Students might not be greatly excited by White's slowly unfolding account at first, but most do warm to it.

4. The author's tone, sometimes gently humorous, in general is nostalgic, even dreamlike—as if he were viewing the lake and his early adventures there through a gentle haze.

5. White's images appeal to all five senses. They capture the smells of the bedroom and wet woods (par. 2); the sight of a dragonfly, the boat, and its contents (5); the sounds of motors (10); the taste of donuts dipped in sugar (11); and the tactile sense of damp moss in the bait can (5), of the "soggy, icy" bathing trunks (13).

6. The comparison, notably between White's childhood experiences and his son's, contains the essay's theme of time and mortality.

QUESTIONS ON LANGUAGE

1. For the word *cultist* (par. 6), it might be worth pointing out that White apparently means an enthusiast for cleanliness.

2. The diction might sound exaggerated, but "unique" and "holy" describe the way the lake appears to White in memory.

3. White's description of a thunderstorm is only one of the essay's rich array of figurative language. The lake in early morning preserves "the stillness of the cathedral" (par. 2). Waves keep "chucking the rowboat under the chin" (5). In paragraph 10 a one-cylinder engine was like a wild animal "eating out of your hand," and a boat could approach a dock like a charging bull. In paragraph 11 a steamboat used to look like a Ubangi, and a drink of soda pop would backfire like an engine. In paragraph 12 the storm becomes a wild concert, and the generations are linked "in a strong indestructible chain." The essay ends in a splendid metaphor.

E. B. WHITE ON WRITING

For aspiring writers—probably every class has at least one or two—E. B. White's advice must be among the most encouraging in existence. To the discouraged seventeen-year-old who wrote to him, White simply said, "Write." What eager aspirants might fail to notice at first glance is White's confession that he wrote "half a million words" before trying to get any of them into print. This statement comes as a cool, refreshing breeze in a world where too many people try to get published before they are ready.

E. B. White isn't big on market tips, either. His whole point is that if you really care about what you write, if you really work at it until it's as good as it can be, someone will want to read it. Clearly, not every aspiring writer was born with a gift equal to White's. Still, we hope you agree that one of the most helpful things you can impress upon students is that their writing will be better if they care about what they're saying.